D0385778

Battle for Antwerp

TAMPA-HILLSBOROUGH COUNTY LIBRARY SYSTEM

Battle for Antwerp

The Liberation of the City and the Opening of the Scheldt 1944

Major General J. L. Moulton
CB, DSO, OBE

C1

LONDON
IAN ALLAN LTD

Books by the same author:

Haste to the Battle
Defence in a Changing World
The Norwegian Campaign of 1940
The Royal Marines.

First published 1978

ISBN 0 7110 0769 1

All rights reserved. No part of this book may be
reproduced or transmitted in any form or by any
means, electronic or mechanical, including photo-
copying, recording or by any information storage
and retrieval system, without permission from the
Publisher in writing.

© J. L. Moulton 1978

Published by Ian Allan Ltd, Shepperton, Surrey,
and printed in the United Kingdom by
John G Eccles Printers Ltd, Inverness.

Contents

Preface

Of the battles fought by the Allied armies in the autumn and early winter of 1944 on the frontiers of Hitler's Germany, two, Arnhem and the German counter-offensive in the Ardennes that became known as the Battle of the Bulge, caught the public eye at the time and have retained it since. A third, the three month long battle to open the port of Antwerp, has been called by the Canadian official historian a Cinderella battle, undertaken reluctantly and belatedly by the British command and receiving later little attention from historians. Yet it was a battle of prime importance, at least as decisive in determining the date of final victory in the West, with all that implied for the future of Europe, as Arnhem and the Battle of the Bulge.

The consequences for the western Allies of delay in opening Antwerp were serious. Restriction of supplies and transport held back the Allied armies all along the front and prevented the early deployment of the full power of the American divisions streaming to Europe across the Atlantic. Had the delay continued a few more weeks, had Antwerp not been open at the time of the German counter-offensive, and had Allied recovery and return to the attack in consequence been starved of supplies, final victory must have been still further delayed. As General Guy Simonds once put it with the licence permitted an after dinner speaker, if Walcheren had been a defeat, it would have been as famous as Arnhem.

Walcheren, of course, was only a small part of the battle to open Antwerp, in which Poles, French, Belgians, Dutch and Norwegians as well as Canadians, British and Americans fought. Taking into account losses at sea, in the air and in the Second British Army in October, as well as those in the First Canadian Army from September onwards, British casualties must have exceeded those of the Canadians, but the Canadians, and especially the Canadian infantry in the flooded polders, had the hardest ordeal. For a number of reasons, however, I have treated the attack on Walcheren, the final phase of the battle, at greater length than the severity of the fighting alone might seem to justify.

First, the story of the fighting in the polders of the Breskens Pocket and of the South Beveland isthmus tends to be repetitive. 'Great courage was required to do the simplest things,' writes a Canadian regimental historian, but the problem was a constantly recurrent one. It was indeed the essence of the ordeal of the Canadian infantry that the cold, the wet and the losses went on week after week. The attack on Walcheren, technically complex and in some ways unique, was during those weeks being prepared, the many problems it posed being studied and solutions to them decided upon. Then, when the attack went in, it was all over in a week, the batteries taken and the minesweepers at work sweeping the channel to Antwerp. Secondly, although I have had generous help from Canadians, it has been possible for

6

me to approach many more people on this side of the Atlantic. Added to that, while the Canadian operations have been described in masterly fashion and at some length in the Canadian official history, nothing comparable has appeared concerning the British part in the battle. To find out what happened in Antwerp in the early days of September and in the closing scenes in the Scheldt and on its northern shore one has to go to regimental histories, unpublished typescripts, official reports and personal recollections of participants.

Last but not least, until the nettle was grasped, it was the prospect of attacking Walcheren that from the first loomed largest and most ominously in the minds of the Allied higher direction of war. To Churchill and Cunningham in Whitehall, to Ramsay and Eisenhower at Supreme Headquarters, to Simonds and the planners at Headquarters, First Canadian Army, even, I suspect, to Montgomery in his reluctance to turn from Germany to tackle the problem of the Scheldt, it was the inaccessible batteries of Walcheren and the minefields they guarded that seemed to pose the greatest and most daunting obstacle to the exploitation of the chance that had given the Allies the great port of Antwerp almost undamaged.

For those acquainted with the present day topography of the area or who consult modern maps of it, a word of warning. Restoration of war damage, industrial and other development and the Dutch custom of winning land from the sea have made many changes since 1944. In 1944 the Antwerp docks extended downstream only as far as the Kruisschans Lock, and, with the exception of 4 Havendok, the areas north and south of Leopolddok and Hansadok were low-lying scrubland. Austreweel, Wilmarsdonck and Oorderen, whose churches today stand as pathetic relics among the surrounding warehouses, were living villages. Since then, as well as the new docks, the vast new petroleum complex and the warehouses being built, the general level of the land has been raised. A new autoroute system encircles Antwerp and extends from it, an additional tunnel under the Scheldt has been constructed, and the built-up area much extended.

Across the frontier in Holland, the Braakman, in 1944 a six-mile inlet of the Scheldt, is now polder. North Beveland, then an island, is now joined at one end to Walcheren and at the other to South Beveland. Walcheren, then connected only by the causeway to South Beveland, has now been joined to it by the reclamation of the Sloe Channel, a motorway now runs from Walcheren through South Beveland to the mainland, and a second canal is being built across the eastern end of South Beveland. At Flushing the Britannia Hotel has been rebuilt as a multi-storey block and the sea dyke raised. At Westkapelle the sea dyke has been rebuilt on a new alignment leaving a lagoon where the gap was.

My first acknowledgment must be to Colonel C. P. Stacey OBE, CD, PhD of Toronto University, whose official history, *Operations in Europe*, Volume III, *The Victory Campaign*, with its meticulous examination and referencing of official sources is an essential basis for the study of the opening of the Scheldt; with that go my grateful thanks for his kindness in reading in typescript and commenting on those chapters of my book most closely concerned with Canadian formations and units. My warm thanks also to Dr P. A. C. Chaplin, Senior Research Officer, Directorate of History, Headquarters Armed Forces, Ottawa, for his help and hospitality during the short visit I was able to pay and in correspondence. The many other sources, published and unpublished, that I have used are given in detail at the end of each chapter. I am grateful to all who knowingly or unknowingly have contributed to my studies and thank authors and publishers for permission to quote where I have done so.

Monsieur J. Vanwelkenhuyzen, Director of the Centre de Recherches et d'Etudes Historiques de la Seconde Guerre Mondiale, Brussels, has been most kind in advising me on sources on the Belgian Resistance, while Messieurs E. Colson and E. F. Pilaet, as well as sending me lengthy accounts of the Antwerp Resistance and answering my postal enquiries, have most kindly conducted me on a tour of the scenes of the fighting in the city and docks, answering my questions and describing the events of 1944 and the many subsequent topographical changes since then. Kapitän zur See Dr Friedrich Forstmeier and Dr Arenze, both of the Militärgeschichtliches Forschungstamt, Freiburg-im-Breisgau, have been most kind in providing me with information on the German forces involved. Similarly I am grateful to Major General N. W. Duncan CB, CBE, DSO, until lately Curator of the Royal Armoured Corps and Royal Tank Regiment Museum, to Major G. J. B. Egerton, Curator of the Museum of the Royal Regiment of Wales, Mr M. E. Jones Curator of the Regimental Museum of the King's Shropshire Light Infantry, Major Alistair Donald, Archivist and Assistant Curator of the Royal Marines Museum, to the Librarians of the Ministry of Defence and of the Royal United Service Institute, and to Mr T. C. Charman of the Department of Printed Books, Imperial War Museum for their help especially in tracing participants and regimental histories, and to the officials of the Public Record Office.

I am most grateful to the following who have provided me, often at considerable trouble to themselves, with accounts of their own experiences, documents and comments: Major M. M. Aldworth, VRD, Brigadier C. N. Barclay, CBE, DSO, Captain J. M. Barry, MBE, Major General J. B. Churcher, CB, DSO, Lieut. Commander D. Claydon, DSC, RN, Captain P. G. Cowper, RM, Lieut. Colonel R. W. P. Dawson, CBE, DSO, Lieut. P. M. Donnell, DSO, Major J. D. Dunlop, MC, Captain R. D. Franks, DSO, OBE, DSC, RN, Major General Sir Edmund Hakewill Smith, KCVO, CB, CBE, MC, Brigadier M. W. Hope, DSO, Captain H. G. Hopper, DSO, RN, Major J. J. How, MC, Brigadier F. W. Houghton, DSO, MC, Major J. S. Jewers, MBE, Brigadier B. W. Leicester, DSO, Mr R. T. Masterman (son of the late Captain T. N. Masterman, OBE, RN), Lieut. Colonel M. E. Melvill, OBE, Commander Hugh Mullinieux, DSC, RN, de Heer Willem Poppe, Rear Admiral A. F. Pugsley, CB, DSO, Lieut. Colonel I. L. Reeves, DSO, MC, Commander K. A. Sellar, DSO, DSC, RN, Captain C. R. Steven, de Heer J. S. van Soest, Colonel T. M. P. Stevens, CBE, MC, Mons Robert Vekemans, MC, Mons R. Verlinden, Lieut. Colonel N. P. Wood, MC, and Mr K. G. Wright.

8

1

A Pistol Pointed

Great Chatham with his sword undrawn
Stood waiting for Sir Richard Strachan;
Sir Richard, eager to be at 'em,
Kept waiting, too — for whom? Lord Chatham.[1]

Lampooning the dismal failure of the expedition of 1809, the lines have become inextricably associated in British folk memory with the name of Walcheren and to a lesser degree with what were once known as conjunct expeditions and later as combined or amphibious operations.

The history of British political and strategic involvement with Antwerp and the Scheldt began long before 1809 and lasted until, in the early years of the twentieth century, it was absorbed in the larger problem of supporting France against the dominant military power of the Kaiser's Germany. In it there is a recurrent theme, the vulnerability to land as well as to sea power of the seaward approaches to Antwerp. It is a theme of which the allied British and American armies were to be forcibly reminded when in the autumn of 1944 they arrived on the frontiers of the Third Reich, intent on the final drive that would end the war against Hitler.

By the middle of the sixteenth century Antwerp had become the chief port and commercial centre of the Hapsburg Netherlands, controlling the money market of the known world and dominating the trade of northern Europe. In the Eighty Years War which followed the rebellion against Spain, the two coastal provinces, Holland and Zeeland, lying across the mouths of the Rhine and Scheldt, quickly became the hard core of armed resistance.* Antwerp, prominent in the early risings, fell in 1585 to Spain and thereafter was absorbed in the Catholic south. In the years that followed, Antwerp, blockaded by a Calvinist squadron at Flushing, declined

---

*In October 1572 3,000 men of the Duke of Alva's Spanish army marched at ebb tide across the ten-mile wide channel, then separating South Beveland from the mainland, and seized Goes by surprise. 'The water, as they crossed, rose to the breasts and shoulders of the soldiers. But their deeds of horror had filled the minds of the stern Hollanders and Zeelanders with the fierce and indomitable courage of despair; and the long narrow strip of swampy, half-submerged land stretching from the Scheldt to the Helder became the scene of one of the most prolonged and ferocious struggles that the world has ever seen.' In September 1575 in a thunder storm 3,000 picked men of the same army crossed by similar means from Tholen to Phillipsland and thence to Duiveland and Schouwen. This time the water came up to their necks, and the Zeelanders assailed them from boats with harpoons and boathooks as well as with musketry and cannon fire, but enough got across to capture the islands, which were later recovered by the Dutch. G. Edmundson, 'The Revolt in the Netherlands', Chapter VI in *The Cambridge Modern History*, Volume III, 1904, pp. 234 & 242 in the 1934 edition. 370 years later Canadian and Scottish soldiers would perform similar if not quite so desperate feats, now to liberate the Dutch from another cruel invader.

and Amsterdam rose. Holland became the dominant member of the rebellious United Provinces, and when peace was made in 1648 its merchant oligarchs insisted on continuing the closure of the Scheldt, so that Antwerp might not recover and rival Amsterdam.

Under William and Mary and under Anne, England made common cause with the United Provinces against Louis XIV of France, as under Elizabeth she had against Spain. By the time of the French Revolution, however, the Dutch commercial empire was in decline and the people discontented. In the winter of 1794-5, after an earlier repulse, the ragged armies of revolutionary France returned to the attack and, throwing back Austrians, Prussians and a British army under the Duke of York, reached Amsterdam, where they were welcomed by the Republican party. The French, who had already annexed Belgium, now declared the Scheldt opened as of natural right. Natural right or not, it was soon to be closed again by British blockade and the Napoleonic Continental System.

Frustrated in his northern maritime plans by the British blockade of Brest, Napoleon built a naval base at Antwerp. By 1809, when he marched south to deal with a resurgent Austria, he had a fleet of ten ships of the line at Flushing, with ten more and numerous auxiliaries building at Antwerp, presenting with the newly built dockyards and arsenals at Antwerp, Flushing and Terneuzen, a tempting target to Britain, now looking for a success to encourage the neutral German states against Napoleon. A fleet was ready and might perhaps have caught the French ships at Flushing, but by the time an army and transports had been assembled, the French ships had withdrawn upstream to Antwerp. On 28 July, as the news arrived that the Austrians, defeated at Wagram, had signed an armistice, the expedition under Lieutenant General the Earl of Chatham and Rear Admiral Sir Richard Strachan sailed from the Downs, 600 warships and transports with an army of 40,000 embarked, and a few days later arrived off the mouth of the Scheldt.[2]

The main shipping route to Antwerp, then as now, ran south of Walcheren island by the West Scheldt. Although South Beveland had not then been connected to the mainland, shoals blocked the passage from the East Scheldt between it and the mainland. Consequently, while the East Scheldt was largely undefended, the West Scheldt was guarded by batteries at Flushing and at Breskens across the estuary from it. Above these there were other batteries on the south coast of South Beveland; a boom and batteries at Lillo, ten miles below Antwerp; and the defences of Antwerp itself.

Forced by a gale to land on the northern tip of Walcheren, instead of as intended on its southwest coast at Zoutelande, the main body of Chatham's army failed to take Flushing until, after a destructive bombardment from land and sea, it surrendered allowing Chatham to enter on 19 August. Meanwhile a force of 8,000, landing from the East Scheldt, had occupied South Beveland, where it now faced a rapidly growing force of French regulars and local troops on the mainland under Marshal Bernadotte.

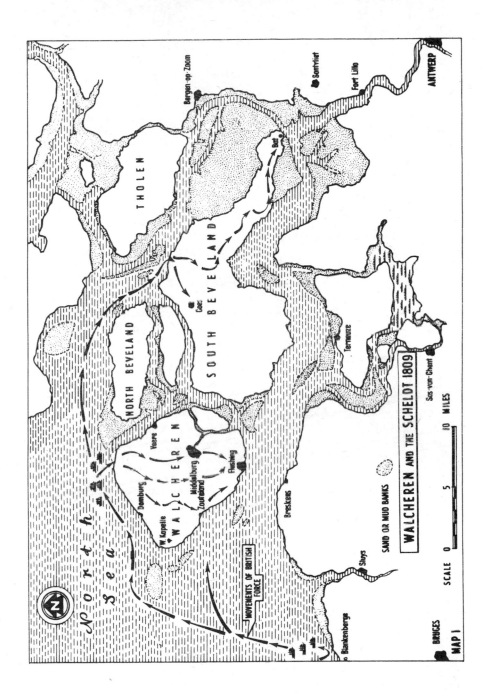

WALCHEREN AND THE SCHELDT 1809

North Sea

THOLEN

NORTH BEVELAND

SOUTH BEVELAND

WALCHEREN

Domburg
Veere
W. Kapelle
Middelburg
Zouteland
Flushing

Breskens

Sluys

o Blankenberge

BRUGES

Bergen-op-Zoom
Santvliet
Fort Lillo
ANTWERP
Bad

Goes
Ternuize
Sas-van-Ghent

SAND OR MUD BANKS

MOVEMENTS OF BRITISH FORCE

SCALE   0   5   10   MILES

MAP I

11

It was a wet summer, and the defenders of Flushing had opened the sluices to flood the surrounding country against the invaders. The floods bred mosquitoes and probably contaminated the drinking water, for, as well as malaria, called by the soldiers 'polder fever', dysentery and typhoid had broken out in Walcheren. The diseases spread to South Beveland, and Chatham's army weakened daily. On 27 August he decided to return to England leaving a garrison of 18,000 in Walcheren. The Walcheren garrison, shaking with fever and dying in the squalor of dysentery, stayed on until December; then it too was withdrawn.

In Kent and Hampshire peaceful towns and villages were shocked by the appearance in their midst of the disease riddled wreckage of Chatham's army, as at the beginning of that year others in Devon had been by the return of Moore's army from Corunna. But, while Moore had dislocated Napoleon's occupation of Spain, all that the Walcheren expedition could show for its calamities was one frigate captured in the Scheldt and the wooden frames of a ship of the line found building at Flushing, dismantled, taken to Woolwich, and eventually completed as the 74-gun *Chatham*.[2]

The French ships were still at Antwerp four years later when Napoleon, defeated at Leipzig, was forced back across the Rhine. The Netherlands rose against the French, calling for British assistance, but the main British army under Wellington was now crossing the Pyrenees, and all that could be scraped together in England was a half-trained army of 6,000 under Sir Thomas Graham, recently invalided from Spain. These landed in the East Scheldt in December 1813, made contact with a Prussian Corps under von Bulow at Breda and in January reached Merxem on the northern outskirts of Antwerp, only to find that their artillery was quite inadequate to destroy the French ships lying half a mile away in the docks. Returning to Merxem again in February after reinforcements and more guns had reached him, Graham bombarded the French ships, but, still lacking his main seige train, could do little against them.

On the night of 8 March Graham made a daring attempt on the French-held fortress of Bergen-on-Zoom, coming within an ace of success. But, after holding the ramparts for six hours, the stormers were driven back with the loss of half their numbers. The Allies were now approaching Paris; on 11 April Napoleon abdicated, and the British were welcomed into Antwerp.[3]

The Congress of Vienna joined Belgium to the Netherlands, but in 1839, after an earlier rising in Antwerp, Holland recognised the independence of Belgium, retaining Zeeland, but opening the Scheldt to the commerce of both countries, Antwerp grew rich again and, defended by three lines of canals, forts and trenches, became the Belgian *Reduit National*.

In August 1914, as the powerful right wing of the German Army swept through Liege and Brussels to attack France, the Belgian field army withdrew to Antwerp. Then, after the Battle of the Marne, the Germans turned their attention to Antwerp, and on 2 October the British cabinet learned with dismay that the field army was about to withdraw from the city. The First Lord of the Admiralty, Winston Churchill, ordering a

Marine brigade at Ostend to Antwerp and two newly-raised brigades of naval reservists from England to join it there, left for Antwerp hoping to inspire the defence. Kitchener placed a regular British division under orders for Antwerp, and the French government ordered two territorial brigades to the city. Encouraged by the prospect of these reinforcements, the Belgian government agreed that the field army should remain in Antwerp for the present.

But Dutch neutrality closed the Scheldt to military traffic, so that any reinforcement, supply or withdrawal from Antwerp would have to pass through the narrow strip of Belgian territory between the Dutch frontier and the upper Scheldt. When on 7 October the Germans crossed the Scheldt near Termonde, the Belgians ordered the withdrawal of the field army, and, in accordance with their instructions, the three British brigades followed it. Antwerp surrendered to the Germans, and the attempt to rescue it with a scratch force came in for bitter criticism, although subsequently the force's success in delaying the German advance on the Channel ports has been recognised.[4]

Between the wars Antwerp regained her prosperity. By 1938 ten square miles of docks were handling some 60,000 tons of freight a day and could berth a thousand ships at a time. There were 26 miles of quays, 625 cranes, marshalling yards, granaries, cold storage plants, coal hoists and oil tankage. Strategically Antwerp remained the *Reduit National*, but its defences were a quarter of a century older in design and concept than in 1914.

In May 1940, as German parachutists dropped on Holland and on the Belgian fort of Eben Emmael, Belgium again called on Britain and France for help. The British Expeditionary Force and the French First Army advanced from Northern France to join the Belgian Army on the line of the Dyle, while the French Seventh Army, crossing the Scheldt by the Antwerp tunnels and the Terneuzen ferry, pushed forward to Breda, South Beveland and Walcheren. The right of the Seventh Army had already been driven back and had lost Bergen-op-Zoom, when on 13 May the army was recalled to France to help stem the German break-through at Sedan. One regiment was overrun on the South Beveland Canal, its remnants escaping by ferry to Breskens; another made a last stand in Flushing, whence it was daringly rescued by French submarine-chasers from Dunkirk. When on 27 May, the Belgians sued for terms as the British Expeditionary Force withdrew towards Dunkirk, Antwerp had already fallen into German hands.[5]

For Operation Sea Lion, the projected German invasion of Britain, it was planned that the German Sixteenth Army should embark at Antwerp and Rotterdam, while other armies embarked at the Channel ports. That was the nearest in three great wars that Antwerp, once described by Lazare Carnot as a pistol pointed at the heart of England, came to threatening her effectively. When in 1944 the turn came for the British and American armies to strike back at Germany, the Dutch coast, beyond the range of fighter cover from British airfields, was ruled out for the Allied landings.

But once the Allied armies had broken out from the Normandy beachhead and were in hot pursuit of the beaten Germans, then Antwerp, if the Scheldt could be opened quickly, might become instead a pistol pointed at the heart of Germany. Surprisingly in view of this history, the opportunity found the British command ill-prepared to deal with the problem of the Scheldt.

References

1 The lines first appeared in the *Morning Chronicle* of February 1810 and are ascribed to Joseph Jekyll, Whig MP for Calne, see Sir Gurney Benham, *Benham's Book of Quotations*, Harrap, 1948.

2 The Hon. J. W. Fortescue, *A History of the British Army*, Macmillan, Vol VII, 1912, pp.56-68; Sir William Laird Clowes, *The Royal Navy, A History*, Sampson Low, Vol V, 1900, pp.271-7.

3 Fortescue, *op cit*, Vol X, 1920, pp.2-52; C. Aspinall-Oglander, *Freshly Remembered: The Life of Thomas Graham, Lord Lynedoch*, Hogarth Press, 1956, pp.266-71; A. Brett-James, *General Graham, Lord Lynedoch*, Macmillan, 1959, pp.290-4.

4 John Gooch, *The Plans of War: The General Staff and British Military Strategy, c. 1900-1916*, Routledge, Kegan Paul, 1974, pp.280-93, examines the switch between 1905 and 1912 from direct support of Belgian neutrality to deployment on the northern flank of the French Army. M. Gilbert, *Winston S. Churchill*, Vol III, *1914-1916*, Heineman, 1971, supersedes earlier accounts of Churchill's intervention. Sir Julian Corbett, *History of the Great War, Naval Operations*, Longman's Green, Vol I, 1920, pp.180-201, for operational detail.

5 Guy Chapman, *Why France Collapsed*, Cassell, 1968, pp.95-8 for the French Seventh Army; Major L. F. Ellis, *The War in France and Flanders 1939-1940*, HMSO, 1953, pp.35-58 and others for the advance of the BEF and French First Army into Belgium.

2

Taurus Pursuant

Two months after the successful assault of 6 June 1944, the Allied armies broke out from the Normandy beachhead and the pursuit began. On Hitler's orders the German Seventh Army, rather than make an orderly withdrawal when it could, had held its positions around the beachhead to the bitter end. At Mortain the Fifth Panzer Army, counter-attacking in a last effort to check the Allied breakout, threw away any chance that remained to make good the German retreat. Caught in the shambles of the Falaise gap, the two German armies suffered shattering losses. Large numbers of men and some thousands of vehicles did indeed escape across the Seine, but Field Marshal Walter Model, who had just taken over the command of Army Group B and Commander-in-Chief West,* reported on 21 August that the Seventh Army had ceased to be an effective fighting force, while the Fifth Panzer Army, by the time it had crossed the Seine on the 29th, was in little better case. To their north, manning the coastal defences of the Pas de Calais, the Fifteenth Army had escaped the fighting, but since the end of July it had been drawn upon to reinforce the Seventh, so that by now only six of its original nineteen divisions remained.[1]

Given the chance to re-organise and refit, these broken armies might still give a good account of themselves, but for the moment there seemed nothing to stop the Allied pursuit. With the main weight of the German armies engaged with the Russians in the east, the Rhine, the Ruhr, even Berlin, were uncovered to the west.

On 1 August the First and Third US Armies had been formed into 12 Army Group under General Omar Bradley, leaving General Sir Bernard Montgomery† at 21 Army Group with the First Canadian and Second British Armies, but still responsible for the operational control and tactical co-ordination of the two army groups. On the 17th Montgomery suggested to Bradley that a force of forty divisions from their two army groups should advance north eastwards to secure the Rhine crossings and envelop the Ruhr, taking appropriate steps to protect their flanks. '21 Army Group, on

*Oberbefehlshaber West (C-in-C West) was used both for the appointment and the command. The command comprised Army Group B in northern France, Army Group G in central France and on the Biscay coast, and 19th Army on the Mediterranean coast. When Field Marshal Erwin Rommel was seriously wounded on 17 July, Field Marshal Gunther von Kluge, who had relieved Field Marshal Gerd von Rundstedt as C-in-C West on 2 July doubled as Commander Army Group B. Relieved of his commands on Hitler's order by Field Marshal Walter Model on 16 August, von Kluge committed suicide.

†Montgomery was promoted Field Marshal on 1 September.

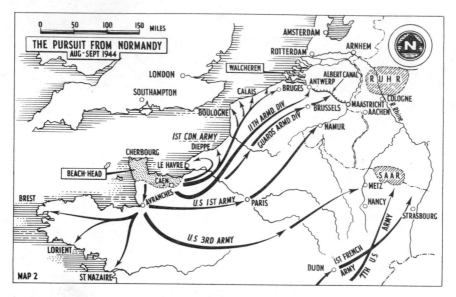

MAP 2

the western flank, to clear the Channel coast, the Pas de Calais, West Flanders and secure Antwerp and West Holland.' Mistakenly, it was to appear, he thought he had obtained Bradley's agreement to the plan.[2]

Lieutenant General George Patton, commanding the Third US Army, for his part urged on Bradley a plan to halt 21 Army Group on the Seine so that all available resources might be concentrated on a thrust south of the Ardennes through Metz for Frankfurt. Bradley supported the proposal, although not to the extent of wanting to halt Montgomery, to whose support he was willing to contribute one corps of Lieutenant General Courtney Hodges' First US Army.

On 20 August General Dwight Eisenhower, Supreme Commander Allied Expeditionary Force, announced that he would take control of the two army groups on 1 September together with Lieutenant General Jacob Dever's 6 Army Group, about to be formed from the Seventh US and First French Armies which five days earlier had landed in the south of France. Montgomery protested that it was impracticable for the Supreme Commander to control the land battle directly in this fashion. On the 23rd, hoping to persuade Eisenhower to give up the idea and to concentrate all available resources on a single massive thrust in the north, Montgomery argued his case alone with him for an hour.

Eisenhower already planned to use the British and American airborne forces available in England to support Montgomery, but, like Bradley, had intended to employ the First US Army with the Third south of the Ardennes. Now at Montgomery's request he agreed that Bradley should direct the First US Army north of the Ardennes in support of the right flank of 21 Army Group and authorised Montgomery to 'effect as necessary operational co-ordination' between 21 Army Group and the left wing of 12

Army Group, that is the First US Army. But, although Patton's Third US Army would have lower priority for supply than Montgomery and Hodges, Eisenhower would not agree to stop the thrust south of the Ardennes. Nor would he agree to alter his decision to assume direct control of the three army groups.[3]

'And so we got ready to cross the Seine and go our different ways', writes Montgomery in his *Memoirs*.[4] Montgomery's way took the armoured spearheads of the Second British Army from the Seine, where they completed their crossings on 29 August, 200 miles in six days to Brussels, into which the Guards Armoured Division in 30 Corps drove through cheering crowds on 3 September; Antwerp, where the 11th Armoured Division also in 30 Corps surprised the German defenders on the 4th; and Ghent, which the 7th Armoured Division in 12 Corps entered on the 5th. On their right the First US Army reached Namur on the 4th. South of the Ardennes, Patton's Third Army, after a brief delay due to shortage of fuel, reached Metz on 5 September.

In June 1944, while the first battles were fought, in Normandy, the Germans had turned their attention to the defence of Antwerp and to preparations for the destruction of the docks, should the danger arise of the port falling into Allied hands. By what must have been a coincidence, Major General Christoph Graf Stolberg-zu-Stolberg arrived from Brittany on 5 June to take command in Antwerp, to be followed a week later by the 136th Divisional Staff. In an emergency Stolberg would take tactical command of all Germans in his sector in the armed forces or in government employment, amounting by September to 15-17,000, but no proper fortress division was available, and the army units under his full command were limited in numbers and for the most part poorly armed and of low fighting value. There was a security battalion, one of stomach invalids, one recruited from Russians, one of Flemish renegades, fort and prisoner of war guards, administrative units and, for emergencies, the staff of the Maria Ten Heide manoeuvre area a few miles to the north. In the docks there were a number of naval servicing and administrative units, and on the airfield Luftwaffe ground crews, transport units, guards and anti-aircraft batteries. There was a serious lack of anti-tank artillery, the last heavy batteries having been withdrawn on 1 September. After that anti-tank gun defence would depend on the 88-mm anti-aircraft batteries of the Luftwaffe and on a couple of immobile 75-mm sited to cover the Scheldt tunnels.[5]

Perimeter defences, amounting in practice to road blocks covered by bunkers or fortified houses at the main road junctions, were established on the line of forts at the outskirts of the city, cutting across the bend in the Scheldt to Fort Ste Marie and Kruisschans village at the far end of the docks. Later a second line was started based on the ancient inner forts and extended to Merxem. In the Central Park three large bunkers surrounded by barbed wire and connected by an underground tunnel to his offices in nearby buildings, housed Stolberg's battle headquarters.

Outside the city fields were obstructed against air landings, and arrangements made to flood low-lying areas. To block entry from the west, the vehicle and pedestrian tunnels under the Scheldt were prepared for demolition, and to the south, where the River Rupel and its tributary, the Nethe form a natural defensive line between the Scheldt and the Albert Canal, the Germans established defended posts at the main road crossings and prepared the bridges for demolition. Meanwhile in the docks preparations went ahead in the usual thorough-going German style for the destruction of all port facilities.

In Belgium, occupied by Germans in 1940 for the second time in a generation, the organisation of resistance in its various forms had been spontaneous. Of the movements for armed resistance, the more important in Greater Antwerp were: *l'Armée Secrete*, composed mainly of regular and reserve officers; *les Milices Patriotiques; les Partisans Armées;* and *le Mouvement National Royaliste* — all four national movements — and *la Brigade Blanche Fidelio* — a local Antwerp movement. Of these, only the Secret Army was in direct touch with the government in exile in London. Critical of King Leopold's actions in 1940, the government refused to recognise the MNR which nevertheless was in close touch with the other Resistance movements.

The first efforts towards co-ordination began in September 1940, and by 1942 there was talk of forming a national committee to co-ordinate resistance throughout the country. Meanwhile *le Comité Clandestin de Coordination de la Résistance d'Anvers* had been formed. Under the presidency of Colonel Norbert Laude it undertook responsibility for civil resistance, support of the maquis, aid to Jews, the Red Cross and the wounded, information, finance and administration, as well as for co-ordination of the armed resistance groups.

In July 1944 the *Comité de Coordination* placed in overall command of the armed groups, which by then numbered some 3,500 men, one of its members, Lieutenant Reniers of the Secret Army, code name *Reaumur*, a regular officer who would one day be a general. Another committee member, M. Edouard Pilaet, code name *François*, was appointed as his assistant for the militia and partisans, and Colonel Scharf as his chief of staff and tactical adviser. Reniers and the committee appointed or confirmed in their commands commanders in the various sectors to take tactical control of the groups. Armed with weapons which had been dropped to them by Allied aircraft, these would interfere with German demolitions, seize key points, hinder the movement of German troops and assist the entrance of the Allies.[6]

In the port area M. Eugene Colson, code name *Harry*, a merchant navy officer and a member of the National Royalist Movement, had already established a resistance organisation among those using and working the port: merchant navy officers and men, river and dock pilots, officials of the harbour master's department, harbour police, dock workers and ship repairers, all of them familiar with the port complex and from the nature of their work able to observe the German preparations for demolition, and a group of young students from the university. Reniers now confirmed Colson in command of the resistance battalion in the port.

To prevent the Germans blowing the quay faces into the water, men in the shipyards sabotaged the concrete liners intended for the borings being made along the wharves, while others delayed the manufacture of the steel containers for the explosives. Fighting groups took under surveillance block ships, floating installations, cranes and machinery, and others prepared to attack key positions. To ensure mobility among the six miles of docks and quays, men guarded lifting bascule bridges at lock entrances, and plans were made to seize tugs for water transport. A group, none of whom were in the event to survive, had the task of taking over the power station in Merxem which supplied the docks.

The safety of the Kruisschans Lock, the western entrance to the docks from the Scheldt six miles below the city, was vital to the port. Not only did the lock play a major part in passing shipping into and out of the dock complex, but, still more important, its gates controlled the water level in that complex. If both outer and inner gates should be destroyed or damaged in the open position, the water level would fall with the tide, and, relieved of the water pressure, the quay faces would fall forward into the docks rendering them unusable. Colson in consequence allocated three groups to the task of seizing the lock, one to move overland from the village of Eekeren north of the docks, one to reach it by water through the docks, and one to be led by Colson himself in an attack from the scrubland between the docks and the Scheldt. Men were detailed to cut the electric cables controlling flame throwers guarding the lock, and others, from the harbour master's office, were infiltrated into *Stutzpunkt Kruisschans*, the German strong point immediately beyond the entrance from the Scheldt.[7]

Then, on the morning of 25 August, the Gestapo struck, arresting Laude and a number of committee members. Happily some escaped, among them Reniers and Pilaet, and under Professor Caemerlinck were able to set up a new committee to carry on the work, but the arrests, as well as dealing what might well have been a crippling blow to the Antwerp Resistance, in taking Laude severed communications with London, which were not re-established until the evening of 3 September.

In the next few days the Antwerp Resistance heard among the BBC personal messages the sentences signifying the preliminary alerts, then, given out twice on 1 September and repeated on the 2nd and 3rd, came the final message to take action, *'Pour Francois la lune est clair'*.* Along the Scheldt waterfront armed groups took post among the wharves ready to harass German troops moving into the city from the west and to prevent demolition of the pedestrian and vehicle tunnels. To their north along the

*The earlier messages were: *Le fermier a mis ses gros sabots*, signifying general alert; and *Les narcisses jaunes sont en fleur*, distribute arms and take post.

Albert Canal others faced the Germans in Merxem. On the roads entering the city from Brussels, groups stood ready to assist the Allied advance. The first German prisoners were picked up and in the docks on the morning of the 4th Colson's groups scored their first success, capturing the German port commandant and his staff, then went on to gain control of the older part of the port area at the southeast corner. Reports from Merxem told of Germans firmly in control there. Now everything depended on the arrival of the Allies in strength.

Pilaet, who had been captured and sentenced to death in 1943 but had escaped, came out of hiding on the alerts and toured the city to check that his men were at their posts and knew their tasks. Then early on the 4th he left for Boom, where the western of the two main roads from Brussels crosses first the Willebroek Canal and then, a couple of hundred yards further north, the Rupel.

The canal, some sixty yards wide, is a considerable water obstacle; the Rupel, deep, a hundred and sixty yards wide, with a built-up quayside waterfront along the southern edge of Boom, is a formidable one in its own right, even more formidable in conjunction with the canal. If the bridges were to be blown, forcing a crossing might be a long and costly business.

There were in all five bridges at Boom: two large modern bridges carrying the main road across the canal and then the river; two modern railway bridges half a mile to their west, and half a mile to the east the Pont van Enschodt, a nineteenth century toll bridge crossing the Rupel by a number of short spans from Boom to the village of Klein Willebroek, whence a cinder track ran southwards along the eastern bank of the canal which here turns south for Brussels. The two main road bridges were known to be guarded and prepared for demolition, and the Pont van Enschodt was thought to be dangerously exposed to fire from the main road, but the *Comité de Coordination* had recently learned that the two railway bridges were only lightly guarded and not prepared for demolition. The committee therefore planned to direct the Allied forces to these latter, and Pilaet carried orders to this effect.[8] He was to be forestalled by the speed of the British advance.

'If there is any one exploit for which the 11th Armoured Division is to be remembered, this will probably be the pursuit to Antwerp and the capture of that city', wrote the anonymous author of the divisional history, *Taurus Pursuant*, in 1945? The division had landed in Normandy on 13 and 14 June under 8 Corps in the early build-up of the beachhead. Like so many other divisions, it had spent the previous four years in the United Kingdom, but a few of its units, among them the 3rd Battalion, Royal Tank Regiment, and the divisional commander, the 37-year-old Major General G. P. H. Roberts, were veterans of the 8th Army's desert campaigns. On 26 June the division led the corps' attack west of Caen, Operation Epsom, the first major British offensive, in which 8 Corps in six days heavy fighting against the main German armour gained some five miles. On 18 July it attacked again, this time east of Caen in Operation Goodwood, in which the British 1 and 8 Corps and 2 Canadian Corps gained seven miles at heavy cost in tanks before being brought to a halt by a skilful combination of German tanks and anti-tank guns. West of Caen again in the bocage country, 8 Corps attacked from 30 July to 6 August at the shoulder of the American breakout. Then on 13 August in preparation for the pursuit, the 11th Armoured was transferred to 30 Corps, now under Lieutenant General Horrocks recently arrived in Normandy after a severe wound in North Africa.

On the 21st, as the German withdrawal began, the 11th Armoured Division led the advance of 30 Corps eastwards, then on the 23rd dropped back as the 43rd Infantry Division came up for the Seine crossing. While it waited, the 11th Armoured re-organised for pursuit and replaced the tracks of its battle-worn vehicles, sending its tank transporters back to the beaches to collect new tracks for them. On the 28th the first units of the 29th Armoured Brigade were called forward to cross. That evening they bivouacked east of the Seine and at first light next morning, in thick mist and heavy rain, started out for the Somme.*

Small parties of Germans with a scattering of tanks and anti-tank guns held them up occasionally at crossroads or in defiles, but by nightfall they had advanced twenty miles and taken a thousand prisoners. On the 30th, passing through villages where church bells rang and crowds along the roads cheered and threw flowers, they reached the vicinity of Beauvais, another twenty miles on. As they cooked their evening meal, the order reached them from Horrocks to go on to Amiens as soon as the moon came up. The expected moonlight night turned out to be one of pouring rain and black darkness, but the pursuit went on. Dawn found the 3rd Bttn RTR and G Company, 8th Battalion, the Rifle Brigade, a few miles south of Amiens. By 6 am they had reached the centre of the city in confused fighting with Germans surprised in the streets, and by 11 o'clock the 29th Armoured Brigade had two unbroken bridges across the Somme in its hands. 'Breakfast tasted wonderful that morning, and, despite our weariness, we felt on top of the world.' Listening to the news bulletin they heard that according to the BBC they were still thirty miles short of Amiens, but going well.[10]

In the evening units of the 50th Infantry Division arrived to take over Amiens. Continuing the pursuit next morning, the leading units of the 11th Armoured reached Arras by nightfall. On 2 September the 29th Armoured Brigade reached Lens and the 159th Infantry Brigade, Vimy Ridge, some miles east of Arras. About this time the order reached them that the plan to drop airborne troops ahead of them around Tournai had been abandoned owing to the weather and that their next objective was Antwerp. The officers of the 3rd Battalion, the Monmouthshire Regiment, left the order

*In 1944 an armoured division had one armoured and one infantry brigade, the former comprising three armoured regiments and one infantry motor battalion, the latter three infantry battalions. West of the Seine the division had, however, operated as two mixed brigade groups. On the 27th it re-organised as separate armoured and infantry brigade groups so that the armour could lead the pursuit.

group that evening with large bundles of maps, over which they pored for most of the night plotting the route for the next day.[11]

By-passing Lille on the 3rd, the 29th Armoured Brigade was held up for several hours by Germans holding Seclin in some strength, then crossed the frontier near Tournai and drove on into Belgium. The 23rd Hussars and H Company, 8th Rifle Brigade, now in the lead, reached Wolvertem, a few miles north of Brussels, at 8 pm. On their left the 3rd RTR and G Company, moving by minor roads and encountering small bodies of Germans in the darkness, reached Termonde some time after midnight. Following the armour, the 159th Infantry Brigade reached a bivouac area around Alost during the night.

For the 4th Roberts ordered the 29th Armoured Brigade to turn north for Antwerp along the two main roads from Brussels, while the 159th Infantry Brigade watched the southern flank and prepared to move into Antwerp as soon as the armoured brigade reported the way open. Starting at first light, the 23rd Hussars and H Company, the Rifle Brigade, drove on to Vilvorde, then turned northwards by the eastern road through Malines. They crossed the Dyle at Malines without difficulty and three miles further on the Nethe, but were then held up for the rest of the day in the southern outskirts of Antwerp by a screen of 88-mm guns.

Meanwhile, after a few hours rest at Termonde, C Squadron, 3rd Bttn RTR and G Company had also started at first light for the western road, to be followed shortly by the main body of the tank battalion. 'Even after our speedy advance into Belgium it seemed most unlikely that we should be unopposed, and, in that country with many water obstacles, the likelihood of being blocked seemed high. But we had plenty of experience of the success that followed a swift side-step and the use of secondary routes', writes Major John Dunlop, the squadron commander.[12] So, unknown to each other, starting almost simultaneously, Dunlop and Pilaet converged on Boom, where the Germans might be expected to blow the bridges on the appearance of hostile armour.

Lieutenant Robert Vekemans, an engineer officer and a repatriated prisoner of war, although not a member of a Resistance movement, had also given some thought to the problem of saving Antwerp and had come to the conclusion that any chance of doing so must depend on the early arrival of Allied Forces. As the German defences to the west would effectively block any approach from that direction, these forces would have to come from the south. On the morning of 3 September, hearing on the BBC news that Allied forces had reached Tournai, Vekemans reconnoitred the southern outskirts of the city and went on to Boom. There he found the two main road bridges guarded by a barbed-wire fence and trenches. A look-out post on the roof of the bridge house gave observation over the country to the south and down the road for rather more than a mile until it disappeared over the railway by a large double viaduct, to the east of which the buildings of an ammonia factory and gasworks blocked the view.

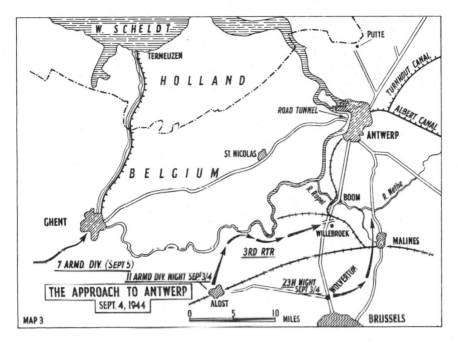

MAP 3

On the map:

W. SCHELDT
PUTTE
TERNEUZEN
HOLLAND
ROAD TUNNEL
TURNHOUT CANAL
ALBERT CANAL
ANTWERP
ST. NICOLAS
BELGIUM
R. Rupel
BOOM
R. Nethe
GHENT
WILLEBROEK
MALINES
7 ARMD. DIV. (SEPT 5)
3RD RTR
11 ARMD DIV. NIGHT SEP 3/4
THE APPROACH TO ANTWERP
23H NIGHT SEPT 3/4
WOLVERTEM
SEPT. 4, 1944
ALOST
0   5   10 MILES
BRUSSELS

Sentries ordered Vekemans away, but a Belgian waterguard told him that demolition charges had been placed in the main spans and piers of both bridges. The Pont van Enschodt, too, he found guarded, but buildings prevented observation southwards, and the firing leads, which could be seen along the guardrail, seemed to indicate that only one of its short spans was prepared for blowing.

To Vekemans it seemed that the Germans would blow the main road bridges as soon as they saw Allied forces appear over the distant viaduct. But it occurred to him that, if he could stop the leading Allied troops short of the viaduct and lead them across the Breendonk crossroads beyond to cross the canal at Willebroek, they would be concealed by buildings for most of the way, and there was a chance that they might reach the Pont van Enschodt before the Germans identified them as hostile. Vekemans spent the night with his parents-in-law who lived nearby, then next morning installed himself at the crossroads cafe at Breendonk, rather less than half a mile from the viaduct.[13]

Half an hour later the first of Dunlop's Shermans reached the crossroads and swung left down the main road towards Boom, ignoring Vekeman's signals to stop. In the next Lieutenant Gibson Stubbs, standing in the turret hatch, exchanged a few words with Vekemans, who spoke good English, and told him that he should speak to the squadron commander who was following. The fourth tank, warned on the radio, stopped. Dunlop listened to what Vekemans had to say, then halted the leading tanks by radio two hundred yards short of the viaduct and, still on the radio, asked permission

23

from his commanding officer, Lieutenant Colonel D. N. H. Silvertop, to follow the route Vekemans suggested. Regarding the side-step as normal armoured practice, the colonel had no hesitation in telling Dunlop to try it. The only question was whether the minor road bridges would take the weight of the tanks, and about that Vekemans as an engineer left Dunlop in no doubt.

Directed by Vekemans, the squadron went on across the crossroads, along the road behind the ammonia works and so to Willebroek, then across the canal to the cinder track. Led by two Shermans and a scout car with Vekemans in it, the tanks turned left down the cinder track and made for the Pont van Enschodt at top speed, their tracks throwing up a cloud of dust. As Vekemans hoped, the Germans were taken by surprise. The two Shermans crossed the bridge, Stubbs leading the way. Vekemans following them stopped the scout car to cut the firing leads, and the rest of the squadron crossed.

Leaving G Company to guard the bridge, the tanks turned left through the narrow waterside streets to reach the town square, then, accompanied by the Resistance, up on to the main road to seize the great bridge from the rear, taking the Germans completely by surprise. Although the main charges were in place in the piers of the lifting spans, they had still to be primed. Lining the approach embankment the German bridge guard of about fifty made a half-hearted attempt to hold off the attackers as engineers rushed to the bridge with primers, detonators and leads, but before they could get very far Dunlop's tanks had them in their sights and they surrendered. Threatening a German NCO with his revolver, Vekemans forced him to show him the firing point then cut the leads. As he did so he heard the canal bridge to the south go up.[14] The divisional sappers would get a Bailey bridge across that night.

Following on Dunlop's heels, Silvertop entered Boom by the Pont van Enschodt with the main body of the tank battalion. Here he met Pilaet who told him of the measures taken by the Resistance in Antwerp and of the assistance he might expect on the way there. Then, leaving the Rupel bridges to be guarded by the Boom Resistance and taking Vekemans and Pilaet on his tank, Silvertop started through cheering crowds down the main road for Antwerp with B Squadron now as vanguard and A Squadron taking the road on the left through Niel, Hemiksem and Hoboken to enter the city along the bank of the Scheldt. There were a number of brushes with Germans along the road, including one, it is said, with troops coming south by tram to reinforce the line of the Rupel. Then beyond the inner ring of forts, about where the memorial tank* is now mounted, B Squadron ran into trouble, the squadron commander was wounded and the advance held up by Germans in prepared positions with machine and anti-tank guns covering a road block and minefields. Dismounting from its half-tracks, G

*The memorial tank in Boomse Steenweg is a Cromwell. The only regiment of the 11th Armoured Division equipped with Cromwells was the 15th/19th Hussars, the divisional reconnaissance regiment, but no Shermans were available at the time the memorial was erected.

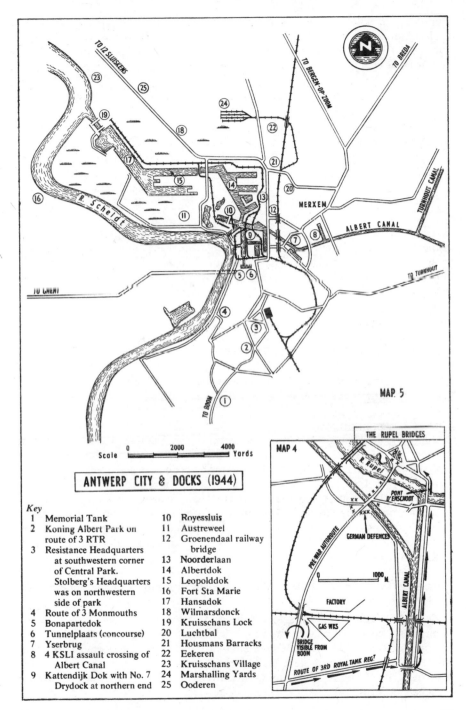

MAP. 5

Scale 0 2000 4000 Yards

ANTWERP CITY & DOCKS (1944)

Key
1 Memorial Tank
2 Koning Albert Park on route of 3 RTR
3 Resistance Headquarters at southwestern corner of Central Park. Stolberg's Headquarters was on northwestern side of park
4 Route of 3 Monmouths
5 Bonapartedok
6 Tunnelplaats (concourse)
7 Yserbrug
8 4 KSLI assault crossing of Albert Canal
9 Kattendijk Dok with No. 7 Drydock at northern end
10 Royessluis
11 Austreweel
12 Groenendaal railway bridge
13 Noorderlaan
14 Albertdok
15 Leopolddok
16 Fort Sta Marie
17 Hansadok
18 Wilmarsdonck
19 Kruisschans Lock
20 Luchtbal
21 Housmans Barracks
22 Eekeren
23 Kruisschans Village
24 Marshalling Yards
25 Ooderen

THE RUPEL BRIDGES

MAP 4

R. Rupel

PONT D'ENSCHODT

GERMAN DEFENCES

PRE-WAR AUTOROUTE

ALBERT CANAL

FACTORY

GAS WKS

BRIDGE VISIBLE FROM BOOM

ROUTE OF 3RD ROYAL TANK REG.T

Company attacked under cover of smoke and supported by the tanks. It took about two hours to dislodge the Germans, but by 3 o'clock they were through. There were a few more brushes with the Germans, then, writes Major Noel Bell of the Rifle Brigade:

> As we dealt swiftly with the scattered and disorganised opposition, we could see ahead of us the main streets of the city densely packed with crowds awaiting us, and this spurred our efforts. Then came the great moment, as we entered the heart of the city to receive a welcome none of us had ever dreamt was possible. Our vehicles were unable to move and were smothered with people; we were overwhelmed with flowers, bottles and kisses. Everyone had gone mad and we allowed ourselves a few moments to take stock of the situation.[15]

Relying on the Resistance to cover flanks and rear and, if necessary, for infantry support against road blocks and anti-tank guns, the armoured column drove into the great city. At Pilaet's suggestion, Silvertop made for the Resistance Headquarters near the Central Park while other columns made their way towards the docks by various routes.

Dunlop led the first tanks to reach the docks. As well as speaking a pretty fair French, he had stayed in Antwerp on a schoolboy cycling tour, and so knew the way to the docks and spoke enough Flemish to make himself understood. Most of the anti-tank guns had by now been dealt with by the Resistance, but as they drove through the streets the tanks were fired upon by Germans at the upper windows of houses. It made, writes Dunlop, the whole thing seem very personal to the tank commander:

> We never closed the lids of our turrets, because we then became so blind and so deaf that we felt too vulnerable. We felt a lot safer with them open . . . But that afternoon I remember seriously considering closing down. However, this sporadic firing from above was confined to the out-skirts of the town and later, rather more intensively, to some parts of the centre. Our biggest problem was with the crowds of excited civilians who thronged the streets and climbed on our tanks. We had no objection to kisses from charming girls, cigars or bottles of champagne. But we kept meeting bursts of small arms fire and an occasional grenade, and there were civilian casualties.[16]

Reaching the docks, Stubbs's troop sank a small steamer in the Scheldt full of Germans.

From Resistance Headquarters, Silvertop at Pilaet's request sent a troop to support the Resistance in the rescue of Laude and his companions from the prison where they lay under sentence of death. Then, directed by Pilaet, Silvertop's column drove past the old city to the docks, taking part on the way in a brisk fight which suddenly broke out as a Resistance group attacked buildings around the tunnel concourse.

The docks stretched six miles along the Scheldt below the city. The whole area was intersected by the long water barriers of the docks with their quays, sheds and long lines of cranes, which in the newer and more extensive western and northwestern part ran through what was in 1944 still low-lying scrubland. The docks could be crossed by lifting, bascule bridges at the locks, and Colson's men had secured most of the important ones in the down position. Understandably, however, Silvertop, without orders from above, was reluctant to commit his tanks to this extensive and unfamiliar terrain, supported as they were only by a single company of infantry and by the Resistance, at that time an unknown quantity to Silvertop. In answer to Colson's plea to push on northwards into the docks, two tanks were sent about half way along Kattendijkdok, in the older south eastern corner, but that was the limit of British advance on the 4th. Leaving C Squadron and G Company to leaguer for the night near Colson's headquarters at Bonapartedok, Silvertop withdrew the main body of the 3rd RTR to an open area off Boomse Steenweg. All through the night Dunlop, in the docks, was woken by Germans coming in to surrender as Colson's patrols completed their clearance of the dock area south of the Albert Canal and Royerssluis, the southern exit from the canal to the Scheldt.

During the early forenoon reports had begun to come in to Stolberg's headquarters of enemy tanks across the Rupel and of the Resistance rising in the city. Sometime about 2 or 3 o'clock that afternoon he reported to Model asking for instructions and, three-quarters of an hour later, was told to withdraw his troops across the Albert Canal to defend that line, or, if that were impossible, to fight his way out to the southeast. Shortly after that his wireless communications failed, first to Model, then to the docks, Merxem and the airfield. Sending the city commandant across the canal to collect stragglers and others who managed to get away, Stolberg issued orders to those troop commanders he could reach to withdraw as soon as it was dark. Then about 5 o'clock his headquarters reported heavy attacks by enemy tanks and armed civilians.

The 159th Infantry Brigade, which had started from Alost at first light had later been directed across the Pont van Enschodt. Some time after midday Roberts sent for the brigade commander, Brigadier J. B. Churcher, and ordered him to clear the city, taking the 2nd Fife and Forfar Yeomanry under command from the 29th Armoured Brigade. As Churcher remarks, there is no military text-book to tell one how to capture and clear a city of two and a half million inhabitants. Looking at the map with Roberts, he decided to make for the Central Park, from which the roads appeared to radiate like the spokes of a wheel. Once that was in his hands, he could push outwards down the roads to clear the rest of the city.

Following on the 2nd and 3rd the same roads that their 1st Battalion had used to reach the Dyle in May 1940, the 4th Battalion, King's Shropshire Light Infantry, reached the southern outskirts of Antwerp at about 2 pm

27

on the 4th. Here they picked up a squadron of the 2nd Fife and Forfar Yeomanry and went on into the city with orders from the brigadier not be stopped or side-tracked by opposition, but to make straight for the Central Park. 'This they did brilliantly and luck was on our side' writes Churcher.[17]

By now they were working on the 1/250,000 map, on which Antwerp was about the size of a thumb-nail, the pursuit having run off the edge of the last of the larger scale maps so far issued. But the main difficulty at this stage was with the crowds, which in their enthusiasm to welcome their liberators made it hard to make plans, to issue orders or even to make oneself heard, wrote Lieutenant Colonel I. L. Reeves, the commanding officer, to his wife,

> 'The difficulties . . . amongst this mass of populace crowding round still cheering, still flag wagging, still thrusting plums at you, still kissing you, asking you to post a letter to America, to give them some petrol, some more arms for the White Brigade, holding baby under your nose to be kissed, trying to give you a drink, inviting you to their house, trying to carry you away, offering information about the enemy etc., had to be seen to be understood.[18]

Unknown to any of the British, three Resistance groups were attacking German-held buildings in the surrounding streets, but in the Central Park itself the Germans were firmly established in concrete and wire, and, without artillery or mortars, which Roberts had forbidden Reeves to use, difficult to shift. Supported by tanks, A Company attacked from the west and C from the east. The Germans resisted strongly, but by 10 o'clock, after two hours fighting, the park and 280 prisoners were in the hands of the KSLI.

D Company, detailed to clear the Banque Hypothecaire occupied by the German town commandant, forced its way through the crowds to reach it. Then, as tanks fired in through the front windows and infantry through the back, one platoon crawled along a parapet to enter. There was a fierce fight with grenades and Sten guns in office rooms, passages and lavatories until, just as it grew dark, an officer appeared with a white flag and seven officers and 85 men surrendered. By then another company had reached the Albert Canal and done great execution against Germans trying to escape across it.

Shortly before midnight Stolberg, who had been captured by the Resistance, was brought to brigade headquarters. 'I was so tired that I took extremely little interest in the poor German,' Churcher writes, but to others he appeared to be indignant that the British should have arrived some days before he was ready for them. Asked by radio telephone by Reeves what he should do with the 2,000 prisoners by then on his hands, Churcher told him to find a large cinema and lock them up for the night. Reeves replied that there was no cinema in that part of the city, but there was a zoo.

'You can't put them in there,' said Churcher, The animals must be half-starved and will eat them.'

'There aren't any animals. The people are half-starved and have eaten them long ago.'

So the zoo it was, and the prisoners were locked up in cages and bear pits for the night. By the morning there were 6,000 of them, and about midday Churcher ordered them to be marched out of the city escorted by the carrier platoons of the three battalions, driving up and down the long column to prevent the furiously hostile populace harming the Germans.*

As soon as the Central Park was taken, Churcher ordered in the 1st Battalion, the Herefordshire Regiment, to start clearing the eastern and south-eastern part of the city at first light. It was a slow process, but they had little trouble and took many prisoners. Meanwhile the KSLI cleared northwards to the Albert Canal.

The 3rd Monmouthshires, having driven through the previous night, had halted as dawn was breaking on the 4th. 'The men were dirty and hungry and the cooks' trucks were welcome as they arrived in the company areas to prepare food.' They heard on the radio that the Guards Armoured Division had entered Brussels, then, as the men were eating, the battalion was ordered on to deal with Germans holding Londerzeel, a village on the western road a few miles south of Breendonk. When they got there the Germans surrendered and were handed over to the Resistance, while the battalion moved on to Antwerp to occupy the docks under command of the 29th Armoured Brigade. Crossing the Rupel at Boom, the battalion entered Antwerp by the main road in the late afternoon, turning off left for the Scheldt and the docks after passing the inner line of forts. Like earlier units it met a tumultuous welcome. With some difficulty officers and NCOs kept their men together, tired and dirty after the long pursuit, as they threaded their way on foot through the crowded streets. Near the river A Company, in the lead, came under fire at a narrow bridge swept by German machine-guns. After several attempts and some losses a few men got across, but it was not until after dark that a firm bridgehead could be established.

Officers and men slept in the streets, and at 6 o'clock next morning D Company passed through A to lead the battalion down the road beside the Scheldt to the dock area,

'Even at this early hour the people of Antwerp thronged into the roadway to greet the advancing troops as they made their way in long files on either side of the road. Fair ladies of Antwerp, showing signs of having been hurriedly disturbed from their slumbers and with curlers still in their hair, pressed bunches of flowers on the soldiers, who, not wishing to appear ungrateful by throwing them into the gutter, continued on their way with bouquets in one hand and their firearms in the other.[19]

*Towards the end of November, Churcher, by then on the Maas, received a highly confidential letter which had passed through diplomatic channels from Germany, by Switzerland, to London and onwards through the descending levels of army command, accusing him of contravening the Geneva Convention by exposing German prisoners to the public gaze in the Antwerp Zoo. This was, of course, quite untrue.

Three hundred yards short of the docks they were fired on by 20-mms and 88s from across the Scheldt, and the troops pushed on alone. By noon they were established in the south-eastern corner of the docks. The docks were still under fire from across the Scheldt, and bodies of the dead, Belgian and German, lay stretched on the roads and in the gutters.

By then the 159th Infantry Brigade had taken over responsibility for the docks as well as for the city, and the Monmouths had reverted to it; now the 3rd RTR and G Company were ordered back to rejoin the 29th Armoured Brigade in the eastern outskirts of the city. They moved out about noon. Dunlop's last memory of Antwerp is of sitting in a comfortable office chair that morning on the top floor of a sky-scraper block with a gunner major bringing down fire on concentrations of enemy they could see across the Scheldt,

'Meanwhile a trim little Anversoise office secretary was bringing in relays of café — cognac and playing us pre-war American blues on the office record player. Now that was the right way to fight a war.'

In the docks during the previous night, Colson's patrols had pushed northwards to reach Number 7 dry dock and Royerssluis. They had secured the bascule bridges at either end of the dry dock in the down position, and that morning Colson's Resistance groups, crossing by them, made a bid to reach Merxem by Groenendaallaan, only to be held up by Germans entrenched at the Norderlaan crossroads. Attempting to reach Merxem immediately east of the docks by the Yserbrug across the Albert Canal, the university platoon, assisted by British troops probably from the Monmouths, found it too swept by accurate fire, and at 1.30 pm the Germans blew the bridge. After that the only way to reach Merxem from the docks was by Groenendaallaan. It was now clear that to do so would call for heavy weapons and armour, but, to the dismay of Reniers and Colson, the British had no orders to mount an attack, which, the Belgians felt sure, would have opened the way to the Dutch frontier. Nor would they listen to Pilaet's plea to secure a bridgehead across the Albert Canal a few miles east of Merxem at Wijnegem, where his Resistance groups had seized the bridge on the night of the 4th.[20]

Failing an attack on Merxem, Colson's groups had to confine their efforts to the port area, where by nightfall on the 5th they had established themselves in Austruweel village and on the roads leading across Albertdok to Wilmarsdonck. At the far corner of the docks, they had seized Kruisschans Lock, but, finding *Stutzpunkt Kruisschans* too strong to attack without heavy weapons, they had occupied trenches covering the lock.

In the city a captain of the Royal Navy called on Churcher to tell him that, if the gates of the lock were damaged, the port would be out of action for at least six months. Churcher ordered the Monmouths to send their Bren carrier platoon with detachments from the mortar, medium machine gun and anti-tank platoons to guard the lock. At six that evening they set off, and at midnight a platoon from D Company was sent to reinforce them.

Although guided by men from the Resistance, it took the platoon a march of nearly two hours to reach the lock.

Reconnoitring the Albert Canal on the 5th, Reeves had found all the city bridges down and Germans on the far bank firing at anyone who tried to examine possible crossing places. Then at about 8 o'clock that evening, as he was settling down for a quiet night, orders came for the KSLI to cross the canal that night by assault boat to secure a bridgehead so that the divisional engineers could build a bridge for armour and anti-tank guns for the advance to be continued to the Dutch frontier. The 159th Brigade carried assault boats in its troop carrying vehicles, but during the pursuit from Normandy all but one of the KSLI's boats had been damaged by bullets or shell splinters, and numbers had to be made up from other units. It was now too late to make a further reconnaissance, and, although a few street maps were available, Reeves had little idea of what to expect on the far side of the canal, which the enemy were said to be holding with little more than snipers and a few machine-gun posts.

An initial attempt to cross by D Company ran into heavy fire and was broken off, but elsewhere A Company succeeded in crossing, and by first light on the 6th Reeves had three companies across, so far without loss. His letter continues:

So far so good. We found ourselves in the most ghastly factory area, one mass of small streets, lanes, passages, walls, walls within walls, piles of iron and waste of every description. In the half light one couldn't see where the hell one was or which was the best way to go first. We soon discovered some machine-gun posts and started to clear them and that started two days and a night's street fighting, the most tiring and trying type of fighting [even] under the best conditions. The Boche found us and soon had five tanks amongst us. We knocked out two and then ran out of all anti-tank ammunition, so they had the time of their lives as they gradually realised the situation, shooting us up with machine guns, armour piercing shot and high explosive, knowing we couldn't touch them, stalking round and round day and night, blasting us out of houses as they discovered us.[21]

There was no food and only water from the factories to drink, and German machine-guns covering the canal made it impossible to get anti-tank guns, infantry anti-tank or other ammunition or supplies across.

By the evening of the 6th officers and men were very tired and in danger of falling asleep at their posts. About 10.30 next morning Reeves was severely wounded in the thigh by a shell splinter and from then onwards was in considerable pain and unable to move any part of his leg. At 1.30 pm he heard that the sappers were going to cross to ferry his three companies back. It seemed impossible, especially when a sudden gale sprang up to add to the difficulties of the crossing, but that evening, the sappers succeeded in withdrawing the companies without further loss.

When early on the 6th Churcher at his command post nearby found that attempts to get a bridge across in darkness had failed, and that without effective support the infantry could not extend the bridgehead, he had asked permission to withdraw the KSLI. It was refused. Next morning, rather than see a good battalion shot to pieces, he asked again. This time his request was granted. Summoning every available gun, he arranged for at least two field and one medium regiment to fire a heavy barrage as soon as it was dark, and under its cover the withdrawal took place. Some 150 officers and men had been lost in the fighting, and most of A Company, which had been cut off, was not seen again.

In the docks at midday on the 6th, the Kruisschans Lock detachment reported Germans crossing the Scheldt below the docks in strength, and in the late afternoon a force estimated at 300 attacked the lock. The Monmouths detachment and the Resistance withdrew to the near side of the entrance channel, whence they were able to keep the far side and the approaches to it under effective fire and prevent the Germans reaching the gates. During the night a company of the 5th Devons relieved the Monmouths at the lock and in the morning counter-attacked with the Resistance. Abandoning *Stutzpunkt Kruisschans*, the Germans withdrew towards Lillo.

Meanwhile Churcher had called upon the main body of the Monmouths to do what they could to relieve the pressure on the KSLI bridgehead. During the afternoon of the 6th, B and C Companies, supported by two troops of the 23rd Hussars, either crossing the Albert Canal by the railway bridge or going around its entrance through the docks, advanced about three hundred yards before being held up by German infantry along Groenendaallaan. At dusk the commanding officer, Lieutenant Colonel H. G. Orr, warned the battalion for a night attack eastward from the docks, and patrols reported later that the Germans had withdrawn from their positions west of Noorderlaan.

At 3 o'clock on the morning of the 7th, in pitch darkness and pouring rain, A and D Companies started from the docks north of Number 7 drydock eastwards towards Merxem, while C Company moved northwards along the railway embankment to join them. In confused hand-to-hand fighting they took the Groenendaallaan bridge under the railway, to which the Germans had withdrawn, and as it grew light Orr ordered B Company to go through and push on to Merxem. Then, as the company approached the embankment, he cancelled the order having heard that the KSLI were being withdrawn and action to relieve the pressure on them was no longer required.

Trapped beyond the embankment and under heavy fire from Merxem, one platoon of D Company took refuge in slit trenches, some of them still occupied by their German defenders. Tanks of the 23rd Hussars made two attempts to rush through the bridge under the railway, but each time were knocked out by two 88s sited in a nearby garden to cover both Groenendaallaan and Yserbrug. The forward companies spent an unpleasant day until they were able to withdraw after dark, and at midnight the 5th

Dorsets from the 50th Infantry Division* took over in the docks and the Monmouths were withdrawn into reserve. During the 6th and 7th the Monmouths had experienced little difficulty in moving north of the Albert Canal by Number 7 dry dock, but this information appears not to have reached brigade and division, where the primary task of the Monmouths was seen as the vital one of guarding the docks.[22]

On 6 September Horrocks gave new orders to his divisional commanders. The Guards Armoured Division was to advance from Louvain to Nijmegen and Arnhem with airborne forces securing the bridges ahead of them. The 11th Armoured Division, giving up the attempt to cross the Albert Canal in Antwerp, was to move southwards and eastwards behind the Guards to re-enter the battle under 8 Corps on the right flank of 30 Corps. Saying goodbye to the grateful and hospitable folk of Antwerp, the division handed over the defence of the city and port to the 53rd (Welsh) Division and on the 8th and 9th drove off for south-eastern Holland.

Although he had on the 6th sent a reconnaissance patrol to Wilmarsdonck, Colson had on that day and for most of the 7th been engaged in Kruisschans area, hoping to secure 12-Sluiskens, the downstream sluices controlling the water level in the low-lying ground north of the docks. On the 8th he sent a patrol from the north-eastern corner of the docks across Noorderlaan into the Housman Barracks, and on the 9th his patrols reached the Luchtbal district in the northwestern part of Merxem. For the next few days his patrols were engaged in trying to reach the marshalling yards across the Leopolddok between Wilmarsdonck and Merxem.

The 4th Canadian Infantry Brigade, taking over from the 70th Infantry Brigade in the city along the Albert Canal and in the docks in mid-September, found the Resistance active and co-operative. Patrols from the Resistance and from the Canadians, reaching Oorderen and Wilmarsdonck, clashed with German patrols on several occasions. On the 20th Colson's groups supported by Canadian artillery established themselves in the two villages, and on the 22nd the Royal Hamilton Light Infantry moved two companies forward to hold them. Shortly afterwards Colson's patrols reached 12-Sluiskens. Now the tidal water could be drained from the low-lying ground, and the way west of Merxem to the Dutch frontier was clear. On 2 October, as the main advance of the 2nd Canadian Infantry Division passed east of Merxem, the 4th Canadian Infantry Brigade and two Resistance battalions, one of them Colson's, attacked Merxem from the west and south and in two days fighting cleared the suburb.[23]

In this and other fighting from 4 September onwards, the Antwerp Resistance lost 87 killed and 114 wounded, to which must be added 198 executed, missing or died in captivity during the occupation.[24] It is not easy for regular troops, newly arrived in a strange locality, to grasp the methods

*The 50th Infantry Division, at this time in 30 Corps, had been called upon to send one brigade, the 151st, to Brussels and another, the 231st, to Antwerp, while the third, the 69th secured the open left flank of the corps.

and potential of their Resistance allies, and few localities are more confusing to newcomers than a great city and its port. If there was a lack of co-ordination between Resistance and British and a consequent failure to seize the chance to advance from the docks or from Wijnegem to the South Beveland isthmus, then against it must be set the greater achievement of securing the port of Antwerp virtually undamaged.

References

1   Milton Shulman, *The German Defeat in the West*, Secker & Warburg, 1947, p.179. Shulman was an intelligence officer with the First Canadian Army.

2   Field Marshal Viscount Montgomery of Alamein, *Memoirs*, Collins, 1958, p.267.

3   General Omar N. Bradley, *A Soldiers Story*, Eyre & Spottiswoode, 1951, pp.396-8; Montgomery *op cit*, p.269; Major L. F. Ellis, *History of the Second World War: Victory in the West*, HMSO Vol 1, 1962, pp.459-64

4   Montgomery *op cit*, p.269.

5   General Christoph Graf von Stolberg-zu-Stolberg. *Verteidigung Antwerpen*, typescript written as prisoner of war. Camp 222613, Ostend, April 1946.

6   Mons E. F. Pilaet, letters in answer to author's questionnaire, January & February 1976.

7   Mons Eugene Colson, MS of lecture delivered on occasion of visit of Danish Resistance, 26 April 1975, pp.12-22, correspondence and discussion during a tour of the docks.

8   Pilaet as above.

9   Anon, *Taurus Pursuant: The History of the 11th Armoured Division*, privately published in Germany, 1945, p.57.

10   Noel Bell, *From the Beaches to the Baltic: G Company 8th Battalion, The Rifle Brigade during the Campaign in North-West Europe 1944-45*, Gale & Polde, Aldershot, 1947, p.53; Ellis *op cit*, Vol I, pp.469-70; Churcher, see below, for fitting of new tracks.

11   Major J. J. How, *History of the South Wales Borderers and the Monmouthshire Regiment*, Part IV, *The 3rd Battalion. The Monmouthshire Regiment 1939-1947*, The Griffin Press, Pontypool, 1954, p.62.

12   Major J. D. Dunlop, MS narrative kindly written for the author.

13   Mons R. Verlinden (Chef de Resistance in Boom) discussion and typescript in English; Mons Robert Vekemans, correspondence; A. Baldewyns & A. Herman-Lemoine, *Les Batteries de Walcheren*, Rossel, Brussels, 1974, pp.14-18.

14   Vekemans, Verlinden and Dunlop as above; Baldwyns & Herman-Lemoine, *op cit*, pp.18,19.

15   Bell, *op cit*, p.53; Vekemans and Pilaet, as above. Accounts, including War Diaries, vary as to times throughout, but Vekemans has a photograph taken at the conclusion of this attack with a clock in the background showing 3.10.

16   Dunlop MS.

17   Typescript kindly written for author by Major-General J. B. Churcher and correspondence; Pilaet for attack by Resistance.

18   Lieutenant Colonel I. L. Reeves, letters written to his wife and father 1943-45, privately printed, pp.14,15; Anon, *The History of the Corps of King's Shropshire Light Infantry*, bound typescript in the Imperial War Museum, vol III, *1881-1968*, pp.258-9.

19   How, *op cit*, pp.65-70.

20   Colson, *op cit*, pp.27-34; Pilaet discussion in Antwerp.

21   Reeves, *op cit*, pp.15-17; KSLI history Vol III, pp.258-260; Churcher as above.

22   How, *op cit*, pp. 68-70 and correspondence with Major How in which he kindly supplied a sketch map showing the positions reached by companies north of the junction of the Albert Canal and the docks and confirmed that on the 7th the Monmouths had little difficulty in movement north of the canal within the dock area. Colson, *op cit*, confirms the account of the attack on Kruisschans Lock.

23   Colson, *op cit*, pp.34-66; War Diaries of Headquarters 4th Canadian Infantry Brigade, the Essex Scottish Regiment and Royal Hamilton Light Infantry.

24   Colson, correspondence with the author.

3

Tantalising Picture

The sudden appearance of the 11th Armoured Division in Antwerp took the German command at all levels by surprise. In Antwerp Stolberg told his captors that he had not expected them for several days. At Army Group B, Model had on 30 August asked Armed Forces Command, Netherlands, to send him the static, coast defence 719th Infantry Division from Dordrecht for the defence of Antwerp and ordered that elements of the 347th Infantry Division, withdrawing by rail from Normandy, should come under its command as they reached the city. But the 719th had been slow off the mark and had not reached Antwerp by the 4th, so the trains with the 347th had rolled on to Capellen, seven miles north of the city.[1]

To Hitler's headquarters in East Prussia, the news of the fall of Antwerp brought consternation. It was bad enough that the port, if the Allies could open it, would solve the supply problems which Hitler was counting upon in the longer term to halt the advance of Eisenhower's armies. But a much more immediate danger was the 70-mile gap which now yawned along the Albert Canal from Antwerp to Hasselt and Maastricht, where the right wing of the battered Seventh Army would take over on the Siegfried Line. The door to northwest Germany stood open. With the Fifteenth Army now cut off beyond the West Scheldt, there was little available to close it but replacement and rear unit troops in Holland and Germany.

On the 4th Hitler recalled von Rundstedt to take over again as *Oberbefehlshaber West*, leaving Model with Army Group B. To fill the gap, Hitler gave them the First Parachute Army, until then a training and administrative command, under Colonel General Kurt Student, the paratroop general who had commanded the airborne forces in Crete in 1941. In captivity after the war, Student described his problem to Liddell Hart,

At that moment we had no disposable reserves worth mentioning either on the western front or within our own country. I took over command of the right wing of the western front on the Albert Canal on September 4th. At that moment I had only recruit and convalescent units and one coast defence unit from Holland. They were reinforced by a panzer detachment — of merely twenty-five tanks and self-propelled guns.'[2]

In war, it has been said, no situation is ever as good or as bad as it appears to be on first reports, and the German resources, although desperately strained, were rather greater than Student indicates.

Training or refitting in the First Parachute Army there were Lieutenant Colonel von der Heydte's 6th Parachute Regiment, a formation with a great fighting record now reconstituted at a strength considerably greater than that of a normal regiment; one battalion of the 2nd Parachute Regiment; five new parachute regiments; a new parachute anti-tank battalion, and about 5,000 service troops. In the Netherlands Command there were the 719th Infantry Division, now on the Albert Canal; the 176th Infantry Division, another static division; the reinforcement depots of the Hermann Goering Regiment and of the Waffen SS; and a miscellany of lines of communication and security units, Navy and Luftwaffe. To fill the depleted ranks of the divisions coming back from Normandy, Goering transferred to the Army 20,000 men of the Luftwaffe from air and ground crews made superfluous by lack of fuel, and thirty heavy and ten light anti-aircraft batteries, which could be used in the field as well as in the anti-aircraft role. Holding Walcheren Island at the mouth of the Scheldt were the 70th Infantry Division and the powerful coastal and anti-aircraft batteries of the Navy and Luftwaffe, under whose cover it might be possible to get the Fifteenth Army, its six divisions now joined by the remnants of five others, back across the Scheldt.

Meanwhile, along canal lines and in isolated pockets, resolute officers were forming battle groups from broken divisions, press-ganging stragglers, if necessary at pistol point, to fill their depleted ranks. By mid-September the worst of the immediate crisis was over. Although the centre of the First Parachute Army had been forced back from the Albert to the Meuse-Escaut Canal, Student had five divisions or divisional battle groups strung across the gap and had linked up with the Seventh Army holding the Siegfried Line. From west to east the line ran: the 719th Division, Battle Group Chill* and Battlegroup Walther. all under General Hans Reinhardt and Headquarters 88 Corps borrowed from the Fifteenth Army; Parachute Training Division Erdmanm and 176th Division, both directly under the First Parachute Army. The 59th and 245th Infantry Divisions from the Fifteenth Army had crossed the Scheldt, the former in fairly good shape, and were to come temporarily under Student's command. A panzer brigade was on its way from Germany, and, at Arnhem close to Student's command post at Vught, 2 SS Panzer Corps with two panzer divisions was assembling and refitting under OB West. [3]

* Battle Group Chill was based on Lieutenant General Kurt Chill's 85th Infantry Division. Battle Group Walther originally comprised the 6th Parachute ,Regiment, the battalion of the 2nd Parachute Regiment and one of the newly constituted parachute regiments all under the command of Colonel Walther. Later the 6th Parachute Regiment and the battalion of the 2nd were transferred to Battle Group Chill and other units attached to Battle Group Walther. Parachute Training Division Erdmann comprised three of the new parachute regiments under Student's chief of staff, Lieutenant General Wolfgang Erdmann. The 1st Polish and the 4th Canadian Armoured Divisions were in contact with elements of the 245th Division west of the Scheldt between 7 and 13 September (see pp.50, 51 below).

Back in England at Southwick Park, the invasion headquarters, Admiral Sir Bertram Ramsay, Eisenhower's naval commander-in-chief, sent a signal on 4 September to Supreme Allied Headquarters (SHAEF) repeating it to 21 Army Group, the Admiralty and Commander-in-Chief, Nore:

> It is essential if Antwerp and Rotterdam are to be opened quickly enemy must be prevented from:
> 1 (a) Carrying out demolitions and blocking ports.
> (b) Mining and blocking Scheldt and new waterway between Rotterdam and the Hook.
> 2 Both Antwerp and Rotterdam are highly vulnerable to mining and blocking. If the enemy succeeds in these operations the time it will take to open the ports cannot be estimated.
> 3 It will be necessary for coastal batteries to be captured before approach channels to the river routes can be established.

Next day Ramsay wrote in his diary 'Antwerp is useless unless the Scheldt estuary is cleared of the enemy.'[4]

According to Eisenhower, his principal reason for supporting Montgomery's northern thrust with the whole of the First US Army, instead of with the single corps which Bradley had suggested, was to ensure the early use of Antwerp for the supply of both army groups. That the northern thrust would also clear the area from which V1 flying bombs were being launched against Britain and secure valuable airfields from which short-range fighters could escort bombers over Germany were important but subsidiary advantages.[5]

On 17 August Montgomery had discussed the proposals he was about to make to Eisenhower with Major General Sir John Kennedy, the Director of Military Operations at the War Office, who was visiting his headquarters, and at his suggestion had given him next morning an outline for transmission to the Chief of the Imperial General Staff, Field Marshal Sir Alan Brooke, at the time accompanying Churchill on a visit to the Italian front. Describing his proposal for a single massive advance under one command on the northern flank, Montgomery had written:

> 21st Army Group should be on the Western Flank and should clear the Channel coast and the Pas de Calais and West Flanders and secure Antwerp. The American armies should move with right flank on Ardennes directed on Brussels, Aachen and Cologne.

and had given as the initial objects of the movement the destruction of the German forces on the coast, the establishment of a powerful Allied air force in Belgium, and the removal of the enemy from V-1 range of England. On the 22nd, in the absence of Brooke, his Vice-Chief, Lieutenant-General Sir Archibald Nye, flew over to France to discuss the plan further with Montgomery.[6]

Meanwhile Montgomery had asked Sir Anthony Eden, who was visiting

Eisenhower, to come and see him and had described to him his plan. He had asked Sir Anthony about relations with the Belgian government and what help could be expected in the Belgian ports and from the civil population generally. The Channel ports had not the capacity he needed, he told Eden, and, if the battle unrolled as he expected, he must have the use of Antwerp.[7]

On the 23rd, as we have seen, Montgomery met Eisenhower and tried to persuade him to accept his plan. Writing next day to confirm the outcome of the meeting, Eisenhower gave to 21 Army Group objectives similar to those suggested by Montgomery but added to them 'to secure Antwerp as a base,' and later repeated this in a more formal directive which reached Montgomery and Bradley on the 29th. Meanwhile in a directive of the 26th to his army commanders for the pursuit from the Seine, Montgomery had referred to the need to secure Antwerp as a base and in the vital intention* paragraph had written 'to destroy all enemy forces in the Pas de Calais and Flanders, and to capture Antwerp.'[8]

It would be ridiculous to suggest that Montgomery, Nye and Eisenhower and their staffs at 21 Army Group, the War Office and SHAEF were ignorant of the geography of the West Scheldt and the history of its influence on Antwerp, but the lack of emphasis on the port of Antwerp in these exchanges and the references to that city, sometimes as a base, sometimes merely to indicate a geographical area, must be judged in the light of subsequent events as ambiguous and lacking the forceful expression of intention needed to inspire armies to pursuit after hard fighting.

On 29 August, indeed, emphasis on Antwerp suffered a further decline, for at Bradley's suggestion the boundary between 12 and 21 Army Groups was adjusted southwards to include Brussels in the objectives of 21 Army Group, so that now that group might have an exit eastwards around the West Scheldt.[9] Thereafter Brussels rather than Antwerp seems to have occupied first place in the minds of the British command.

Then in the first days of September, Montgomery deliberately altered his intention. Allied Intelligence reported the gap opening between the remnants of the Seventh Army making for the Siegfried Line and the Fifteenth Army withdrawing along the Channel coast. Into this gap Montgomery decided to thrust the Second British Army, leaving the First Canadian Army to take the Channel ports and, when that was done, to open Antwerp. 'The speed of our advance through the Pas de Calais and into Belgium', said Montgomery a year later,

> convinced me that, if the Allies could concentrate and maintain sufficient strength for the task, one powerful and full-blooded thrust

---

*In British staff doctrine great importance was attached to the 'Intention' paragraph of an operation order or instruction, which was kept short and usually drafted personally by the commander issuing the order. Such rules were not necessarily binding at the top levels of command, but it is improbable that a general brought up in this doctrine would have failed to pay particular attention to a paragraph headed 'Intention'.

deep into Germany would overwhelm the enemy and carry with it decisive results . . . In view of the time factor it was agreed that 21 Army Group should launch its thrust to the Rhine before completing the clearance of the Scheldt estuary.[10]

Administrative risks as well as tactical risks have to be taken in war, he continued, and he would rely on the Channel ports, particularly Dieppe, being open before stocks were exhausted.

On 3 September he issued a new directive. The Second British Army in what was to be called Operation Comet was to drive for the Rhine between Wesel and Arnhem as quickly as possible, threaten the Ruhr frontally, bounce a crossing further north, then by-pass the Ruhr and drive on into Germany. Airborne forces would be used to capture the main bridges ahead of the army.* Meanwhile the First Canadian Army was 'to clear the coastal belt' then remain in the area of Bruges and Calais until the maintenance situation permitted its employment further forward.[11]

Eisenhower, too, was optimistic. In a directive issued on 4 September, he said that the weak and partly disorganised German forces facing Montgomery and Bradley amounted to the equivalent of only twenty divisions and it was doubtful if reinforcements could be brought forward from Germany and other fronts in time to man the Siegfried Line. 'Our best opportunity of defeating the enemy in the west is to strike at the Ruhr and the Saar . . . the mission of the Northern Group of Armies (21 Army Group) with that part of the Central Group of Armies (12 Army Group) which is operating north-west of the Ardennes is to secure Antwerp, breach the Siegfried Line covering the Ruhr and seize the Ruhr.'[12] Again there was no direct reference to the port of Antwerp or to the problem of the Scheldt — although it is difficult to imagine why Antwerp should be mentioned if the use of the port were not required — and beyond the order of the words priorities were not given.

When he issued his directive on the 3rd, Montgomery could not know that in the next two days Antwerp and its docks would fall into his hands undamaged, but, when they did, what he saw as the main obstacle to their use remained. On 6 September he signalled General H. D. G. Crerar, commanding the First Canadian Army,

> It looks as if the port of Antwerp may be unusable for some time as the Germans are holding islands at the mouth of the Scheldt. Immediate opening of some port north of Dieppe essential for rapid development of my plan and I want Boulogne badly. What do you think the chances are of getting it soon.[13]

Next morning part of a message from Eisenhower reached Montgomery, which, if incomplete and not without its own ambiguities, might have

---

*On 24 August Eisenhower had provisionally allotted the First Allied Airborne Army to the support of the Northern Group of Armies (Ellis I p.463). His directive of 4 September allotted it to the Northern Group, up to and including the crossing of the Rhine.

warned a co-operative subordinate commander that these proposals outlined to Crerar would not meet the requirements of the Supreme Commander responsible, as he was, for the maintenance of two other army groups besides Montgomery's and their supporting air forces.

The message came in reply to a protest, sent by Montgomery on the 4th, that the First US Army was not getting priority for supply over Patton's Third — Bradley was in fact giving the two armies equal priority — in which Montgomery urged Eisenhower to choose one or other of the two thrusts for full support. Not unnaturally, he recommended the northern.[14]

The pursuit had carried Montgomery's command post forward to the vicinity of Brussels, while Eisenhower, who had strained a knee in a forced landing of his aircraft on the 2nd, was for two days confined to his bed at Granville 300 miles away. The distance suddenly opened between headquarters by the pursuit had strained signal resources, and Eisenhower's reply in consequence did not reach Montgomery until the 7th, when its second part arrived to be followed two days later by the first.

'3. While we are advancing,' began the second part, 'we will open the ports of Havre and Antwerp which are still essential to sustain a powerful thrust into Germany. No re-allocation of our present resources would be adequate to sustain a thrust to Berlin.
4. Accordingly my intention is to occupy the Saar and the Ruhr and by the time we have done this Havre and Antwerp should be available to maintain one or both the thrusts you mention.'

Priority would continue to be given to the northern thrust, the message continued, then ended by asking Montgomery to let Eisenhower know his maintenance requirements for the advance.[15]

Montgomery replied the same day saying that his maintenance was stretched to the limit. Based as he was for supplies on Bayeux, he could not capture the Ruhr. When he had a Pas de Calais port working he would need additional road, rail and air transport to get to the Ruhr and finally Berlin. Would it be possible, he asked, for Eisenhower to come and see him?[16]

By the 9th Montgomery had reached the conclusion that with one good Pas de Calais port, 1,000 tons a day airlift and additional road transport he could reach Munster at the western end of the North German Plain, and that with Dieppe, Boulogne, Calais and Dunkirk plus 3,000 tons a day from Le Havre he could reach Berlin.[17]

Meanwhile Operation Comet had begun. On 6 September, as in Antwerp the 4th KSLI beat off the first German attacks on its ill-fated Schijnpoort bridgehead and at higher levels the orders which would switch the 11th Armoured Division from the left to the right flank of the Second British Army were issued, further east, armoured cars of the Guards Armoured Division searched along the Albert Canal from Beeringen to Herentals for crossing places. They found the bridge near Oostham blown, but another at

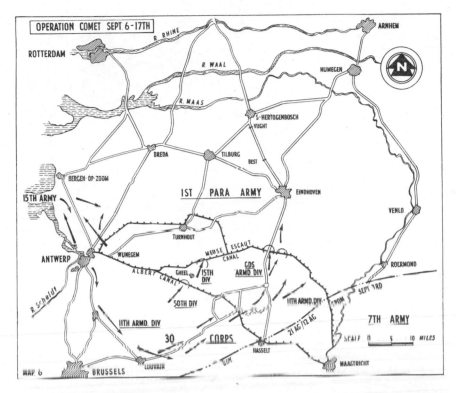

Map showing Operation Comet Sept. 6-17th with locations including Rotterdam, Arnhem, Nijmegen, Antwerp, Brussels, Eindhoven and military unit positions.

Beeringen still passable to infantry. On the appearance of the Welsh Guards, Germans on the opposite bank withdrew, and by first light on the 7th the sappers had a Bailey bridge across. That day the Welsh Guards took the Helchteren cross-roads, but Hechtel, halfway to the Meuse-Escaut Canal, was strongly held and did not fall until the 12th. By-passing it, tanks of the Irish Guards and infantry of the Grenadiers captured intact on the 10th the de Groot bridge on the Eindhoven road near Neerpelt.

On the 7th Horrocks ordered the 50th Infantry Division supported by the 8th Armoured Brigade to secure another bridgehead across the Albert Canal, at Gheel, ten miles west of Beeringen. Only one brigade of the 50th Division was immediately available, the 69th. Early on the 8th it seized the bridgehead. On the 9th the 151st Brigade joined it, and on the 10th the two brigades fought their way into Gheel, only to be forced back next day. Bitter fighting continued, until, on the night of the 13th, the 15th (Scottish) Division, taking over the advance, secured a bridgehead across the Meuse-Escaut Canal another four miles on.[18]

Thus within three or four days of Student's heart-cry of the 4th, the German defences along the canal line were offering unexpectedly tough resistance. Repeated failures to blow bridges before they fell into enemy hands perhaps indicates a degree of residual disorganisation, but at each crossing the Germans counter-attacked strongly and persistently, often with the support of armour, shelled heavily, and fought hard to prevent further enemy advance. For the British, heavy casualties came as an unpleasant surprise after the days of 'swanning' ahead in the pursuit.

By 10 September, when Eisenhower, his leg still in plaster, arrived at Brussels airport to meet Montgomery, Operation Comet had been developed and renamed Market Garden, due to begin on the 15th. Eisenhower brought with him his deputy, Air Chief Marshal Sir Arthur Tedder, and his Chief Administrative Officer, Lieutenant General Sir Humfrey Gale. To save Eisenhower's leg the meeting was held in the aircraft, and, despite the demand he was making for absolute priority of supply, Montgomery insisted that Gale should be excluded from it.*

Accounts of what passed vary. Eisenhower agreed that Montgomery should postpone the opening of Antwerp until after Market Garden, that Montgomery should have the support of the First US Army on his right, and that the operation should have priority for supply over Patton's offensive south of the Ardennes, although not the absolute priority that Montgomery demanded. But, 'I instructed him that what I did want in the north was Antwerp working, and I also wanted a line covering that port' writes Eisenhower in *Crusade in Europe:*

> Beyond this I believed it possible that we might with airborne assistance seize a bridgehead over the Rhine in the Arnhem region, flanking the defences of the Siegfried Line . . . The target date was set for September 17, and I promised to do my utmost for him in supply until that operation was completed. After the completion of the bridgehead operation he was to turn instantly and with his whole force to the capture of Walcheren Island and the other areas from which the Germans were defending the approaches to Antwerp.[19]

Montgomery in his *Memoirs* quotes the last sentence to contradict it, saying that the point was never mentioned on 10 September, and that it was not until 9 October that Eisenhower for the first time gave the free use of Antwerp priority over all other missions.

Tedder says that Eisenhower explained to Montgomery the need to open Antwerp promptly for the advance into Germany. Gale, who may have been present for the latter part of the meeting, and who would in any case have heard from Eisenhower and Tedder what had passed, told Ramsay on the 13th that Montgomery was now impressed with the need to open Antwerp quickly.[20] Writing to Montgomery on the 13th, Eisenhower returned to the point. Referring to the reluctance of the First Allied Airborne Army to provide airborne troops for the attack on Walcheren, he wrote 'I consider

*Chester Wilmot says that, although Gale was excluded, Montgomery insisted on the presence of his own Major General, Administration, M.R.W.P. Graham; Eisenhower, that himself, Montgomery, Tedder and Gale were present; Ellis, the three former only. Wilmot also describes how after an outburst by Montgomery, Eisenhower laid a hand on his knee, saying 'Steady, Monty. You can't talk to me like that. I'm your boss.' It would be interesting to know his source.

42

the use of Antwerp so important to future operations that we are prepared to go a long way in making the attack a success.'

As he made clear in a directive to army group commanders also of the 13th, Eisenhower wanted both the Ruhr and the use of Antwerp. Realising that Antwerp was useless until the Scheldt had been opened, he was willing to let Montgomery try for the Ruhr first, but he remained convinced that Antwerp, or some other major deep-water port such as Rotterdam or Amsterdam, was an essential prerequisite for the final defeat of Germany. Montgomery is, therefore, correct in saying that it was not until 9 October that Eisenhower gave overriding priority to the opening of the Scheldt, but there is little excuse for his failure, if failure it was, to realise in September that Eisenhower attached great importance to opening the Scheldt without avoidable delay.[21]

On 11 September, still not satisfied that Eisenhower was giving Arnhem the priority for supply it needed, Montgomery signalled him that the new advance would have to be postponed until 23 September or possibly the 26th. This brought from Eisenhower a halt order to Patton — which he disobeyed — an order to Bradley to transfer logistic support from the Third Army to the First, and a visit to Montgomery by Eisenhower's chief of staff, Lieutenant General Walter Bedell Smith. Near Cherbourg three American divisions were grounded so that their transport could be used to ferry supplies forward to 21 Army Group.[22]

On 17 September the 101st and 82nd US Airborne Divisions dropped at Nijmegen and Eindhoven and the 1st British Airborne at Arnhem. The Second British Army advanced northeastwards from the Meuse-Escaut Canal to link up with them and reached the Americans, but failed to reach the British at Arnhem in time and strength enough to secure the bridge across the Rhine.

More remote from the heady prospects opened by the pursuit, Churchill, having on his return from Italy read an assessment by the Joint Intelligence Staff on the probability of an early German surrender, minuted his Chiefs of Staff on 8 September:

One can already foresee a lull in the magnificent advances we have made. General Patton's army is heavily engaged on the line Metz-Nancy. Field Marshal Montgomery has explained his misgivings as to General Eisenhower's future plan. It is difficult to see how the Twenty-First Army Group can advance in force to the German frontier until it has cleared up the stubborn resistance at the Channel ports and dealt with the Germans at Walcheren and to the north of Antwerp.[23]

Admiral Sir Andrew Cunningham in *A Sailor's Odyssey* describes in retrospect his feelings as First Sea Lord and Chief of Naval Staff at this time:

The approaching capture of Antwerp presented a tantalising picture, though Ramsay and myself agreed that it must be firmly pointed out to the Army Command that Antwerp lay well inland and about fifty miles up a river still controlled by the enemy. Before the port could be cleared for shipping the German defences must first be cleared.

Our forebodings were pretty well correct. By September 4th Antwerp was in our hands with its port facilities practically intact. In the paean of triumph at its capture the clearance of the approaches was not treated as a matter of urgency. For the time being one of the finest ports in Europe was no more use to us than an oasis in the Sahara desert.[24]

The powerful defences at the mouth of the Scheldt, he continues, would have to be eliminated before the mines that the Germans had laid in the estuary could be swept.

Cunningham writes that he presented the facts to his colleagues of the Chief of Staffs Committee. No mention of Antwerp appears in the minutes of the Committee at this time, but that does not necessarily mean that less formal representations were not made either at Chiefs' or lower levels. Cunningham understood that after their arrival in Quebec for the Octagon Conference, Brooke and General Marshall, Chief of Staff US Army, warned Montgomery and Eisenhower of their concern. Certainly on 12 September, the opening day of the conference, the Combined Chiefs of Staff, approving Eisenhower's proposal for the double thrust into Germany in a message drafted by Brooke, drew attention to the importance of the northern thrust and emphasised the need to open Antwerp and Rotterdam.[25]

By then the Second British Army was committed to the advance to Arnhem and the First Canadian Army to the attacks on Le Havre, Boulogne and Calais. The opportunity to push the pursuit north of Antwerp, across the Albert Canal to the South Beveland isthmus, thus trapping the German Fifteenth Army and opening the way to the north bank of the Scheldt, if it was to be taken, would have had to be taken earlier, either as a variant of the Arnhem plan, or as an alternative to the attack on the Channel ports.

On 26 September, when the last survivors of the 1st Airborne Division and the 1st Polish Parachute Brigade, which had dropped to its support, were withdrawn from Arnhem, any prospect of securing Rotterdam or Amsterdam as an alternative to Antwerp had vanished, the main part of the Fifteenth Army was safely back across the West Scheldt and in the process of taking over the canal line, and Antwerp still remained to be opened.

References

1 Colonel C. P. Stacey, *Operations in North-West Europe*, Vol III, *The Victory Campaign*, Ministry of National Defence, Ottawa, 1960, p.301.

2 Quoted by Sir Basil Liddell Hart, *The Other Side of the Hill*, revised edition, Cassell, 1973, p.429.

3 Martin Blumenson, *US Army in World War II: Break Out and Pursuit*, Office of the Chief of Military History, United States Army, Washington, 1961, pp.697-700; Charles B. MacDonald, *US Army in World War II, The Siegfried Line Campaign*, Washington,

1963, pp.99-108, 123-7 *et al.* Blumenson and MacDonald both use German records captured by the US Army now in the hands of the Chief of Military History, and MS prepared after the war by German commanders. P. E. Schramm, *Kriegstagebuch des Oberkommandos der Wehrmacht*, Vol IV, Part I, Bernard & Graefe Verlag fur Wehrwesen, Frankfurt am Main, 1961, pp.366-77; General Major G. Blumentritt, *Von Rundstedt; The Soldier and the Man*, (translation) Odhams, 1952, pp.253-4. Major L. F. Ellis, *History of the Second World War: Victory in the West*, Vol II, pp.10n, 31; Chester Wilmot, *The Struggle for Europe*, Collins, 1952, pp.479-80.

4   Quoted by Rear Admiral W. S. Chalmers, *Full Cycle: The Biography of Admiral Sir Bertram Home Ramsay, KCB, KBE, MVC*, Hodder & Stoughton, 1959, p.244; Ellis *op cit*, Vol II, p.5.

5   General Dwight G. Eisenhower, *Crusade in Europe*, Heinemann, 1948, p.320; Bradley *op cit*, p.399.

6   Ellis *op cit*, Vol I, p.459-460; Sir John Kennedy, *The Business of War*, Hutchinson, 1957, p.345.

7   Lord Avon, *The Eden Memoirs: The Reckoning*, Cassell, 1963, pp.568-9.

8   Stacey *op cit*, p.282; Ellis *op cit* I, p.465, omits the reference to 'Antwerp as a base'.

9   MacDonald *op cit*, p.30.

10 Montgomery, *The 21st Army Group in the Campaign in North-West Europe 1944-45*, Lecture at the Royal United Service Institute on 3 October 1945, Journal for November.

11 Montgomery, *Normandy to the Baltic*, Hutchinson, 1947, pp.128-9 (p.303 in the Barrie & Jenkins edition of 1973); Stacy *op cit*, p.323; Ellis *op cit*, II p.7.

12 Ellis *op cit*, II pp.9, 94-5; Montgomery, *Memoirs*, pp.265-6.

13 Stacey *op cit*, p.329.

14 Montgomery, *Memoirs*, pp.272-3; R. G. Ruppertal, *Logistic Support of the Armies*, Military History Department of the Army, Washington, 1958, II p.170; Eisenhower, *op cit*, p.335.

15 Montgomery, *Memoirs*, pp.272-3; Ellis, *op cit* II pp 16-17 which quotes the message in order sent rather than received.

16 Montgomery, *Memoirs*, pp.273-4.

17 Stacey, *op cit*, p.310.

18 Ellis, *op cit*, II pp.12-13; Major General G. L. Verney, *The Guards Armoured Division*, Hutchinson, 1955, pp.90-91; The Earl of Rosse, Colonel E. R. Hill, *The Story of the Guards Armoured Division*, Geoffrey Bles, 1956, pp.99-122, especially p.121 for estimate of German opposition.

19 Eisenhower, *op cit*, pp.335-7.

20 Montgomery, *Memoirs*. p.289, but see also p.285; Marshal of the Royal Air Force Lord Tedder, *With Prejudice*, Cassell, 1966, pp.590-1; Chalmers, *op cit*, p.249; Chester Wilmot, *op cit*, pp.488-8; MacDonald, *op cit*, pp.209-10.

21 MacDonald, *op cit*, pp.209-10; Ellis, *op cit*, II, pp.22-3; Forest C. Pogue, *The Supreme Command*, Dept. of the Army, Washington DC, 1954, pp.254-6.

22 Montgomery, *Memoirs*, p.276; Ellis, *op cit*, II, pp.21-4; Ruppertal, *op cit*, II, pp.18 & 169.

23 Winston S. Churchill, *The Second World War*, Cassell, 1948-54, VI, *Triumph and Tragedy*, pp.170-1; J. Ehrman, *Grand Strategy*, Vol V, HMSO, 1956, pp.397-403.

24 Admiral of the Fleet Lord Cunningham of Hyndhope, *A Sailor's Odyssey*, Hutchinson, 1951, p.609.

25 Ehrman, *op cit*, pp.525-6; Tedder, *op cit*, p.590; *Ellis, op cit*, II, pp.95-7.

4

Escape of an Army

General Gustav von Zangen, newly appointed to command the Fifteenth
Army at the end of August with orders to hold the line of the Somme, had
found Allied armour streaming past his southern flank where the Fifth
Panzer and Seventh Armies should have been. The Fifteenth Army, making
up with its six divisions and remnants of others nearly 100,000 men, had
continued its withdrawal at the best pace of marching men and horse-
drawn transport hoping to reach Holland through Antwerp and Brussels.
The news that Antwerp had fallen came as a stunning shock to von Zangen,
for it meant that his army was trapped by the West Scheldt. On the night of
4 September he made up his mind to break out between Antwerp and
Brussels and issued orders to that effect next day. But on the 6th Hitler's
order reached him that he should instead, after reinforcing the garrisons of
the Channel ports, establish a bridgehead south of the Scheldt covering
Breskens and the Cadzand batteries, secure Walcheren and South Beveland
and, bringing the main body of his army across the Scheldt to Flushing,
redeploy it north of Antwerp.[1]

Ordering the 245th and 711th Divisions, later reinforced by a large part
of the 70th from Walcheren, to hold a covering position along the Bruges-
Ghent Canal, von Zangen detailed the fresh 64th Division, newly arrived
from Germany, to defend the bridgehead, a line of canals and inundations
running from the sea at Zeebrugge to the West Scheldt near Terneuzen.

Von Zangen placed in charge of the ferry operation Lieutenant General
Schwalbe, described by Milton Shulman, who interrogated him a year later,
as serious minded and deaf, proud in retrospect of his achievement in
organising the escape of the Fifteenth Army. Getting together an improvised staff, he set up control posts on the main roads leading to Breskens
with orders to assemble units of the retreating divisions as they arrived,
telephone their numbers to his headquarters and hold them camouflaged
against air attack until he called them forward to embark. Meanwhile he
rounded up two large Dutch merchant ships, three large vehicle rafts and
sixteen Rhine barges each taking 250 men for the crossing.

Although there were apparently strong anti-aircraft defences at Breskens
and Flushing, the Luftwaffe could provide no fighter cover. Crossings were
in consequence mainly by night, although when the weather closed down,
Schwalbe took advantage of it to ferry in daytime and hasten the crossing.
Braskens and Flushing were attacked whenever the weather permitted, and
a number of troop-laden vessels caught in the Scheldt were hit.

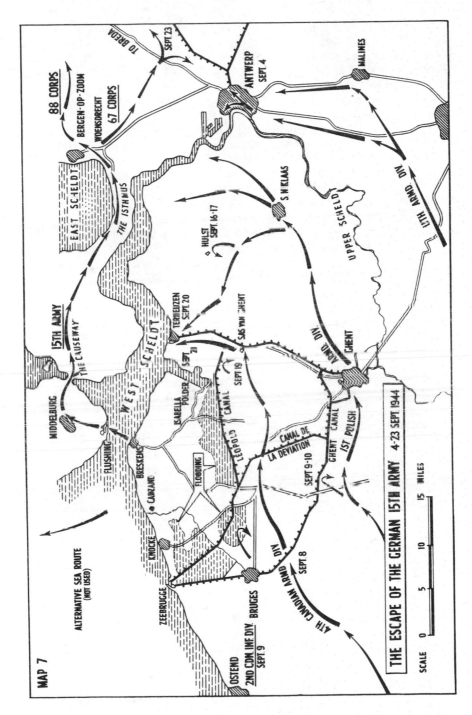

MAP 7

THE ESCAPE OF THE GERMAN 15TH ARMY 4-23 SEPT 1944

SCALE

MILES
0   5   10   15

88 CORPS

BERGEN-OP-ZOOM

67 CORPS

WOENSDRECHT

TO BREDA

SEPT 23

ANTWERP
SEPT 4

MALINES

11TH ARMD DIV

EAST SCHELDT

THE ISTHMUS

15TH ARMY

THE CAUSEWAY

MIDDELBURG

FLUSHING

BRESKENS

KNOCKE

ZEEBRUGGE

OSTEND

2ND CDN INF DIV
SEPT 9

BRUGES

4TH CANADIAN ARMD DIV

SEPT 8

SEPT 9-10

FLOODING

CADZAND

ISABELLA
POLDER

WEST SCHELDT

LEOPOLD CANAL

SEPT 19

SEPT 21

TERNEUZEN
SEPT 20

SAS VAN GHENT

HULST
SEPT. 16-17

S. N. KLAAS

UPPER SCHELDT

ARMD DIV

ARMD DIV

GHENT

GHENT CANAL

CANAL DE
LA DEVIATION

1ST POLISH

ALTERNATIVE SEA ROUTE
(NOT USED)

47

But what Schwalbe feared most did not happen. An Allied advance of twenty miles from Antwerp would have cut off the line of retreat of the Fifteenth Army at the South Beveland isthmus. In that event Schwalbe planned to evacuate troops by sea through the Dutch Islands to Dordrecht and Rotterdam, a twelve hour voyage far more dangerous than the three-quarters of an hour trip to Flushing, which at best would have meant abandoning guns and vehicles on embarkation.

Crossings began on 4 September, by the 8th 10,000 men had been ferried from Breskens to Flushing and by the 26th, when the ferry operation ended, 86,100 men, 616 guns, 6,200 horses and 6,200 vehicles had got away across the Scheldt.[2] Some eight divisions crossed at various strengths, or including the regiments of the 70th which made the double crossing, nine. Reaching Flushing, they marched across the causeway to South Beveland and then on to the mainland, where they took in reinforcements from the mixed bag of manpower being hurried forward from Germany and were put into the line on the right of the First Parachute Army.

The first division to cross, the 245th, was transferred to the First Parachute Army on 16 September to back up Battlegroup Chill. The next, the 59th, was in transit to the First Parachute Army on the 17th when the Allied parachutists dropped and on the 18th joined in the counter-attack on the American 101st Airborne Division at the bridge across the Wilhelmina Canal at Best. On the 19th von Zangen moved his headquarters from Middelburg to Dordrecht. On the 23rd 67 Corps with the 346th and 711th Divisions from across the Scheldt took over the 719th Infantry Division and became responsible for the line of the Turnhout Canal from Antwerp to Turnhout. Next day it repulsed the first Canadian attempt to force a crossing near Antwerp. The 59th, 245th and 712th Infantry Divisions from across the Scheldt went to 88 Corps which with the 89th Division now came under Fifteenth Army, whose front was extended to Nijmegen, freeing the First Parachute Army to concentrate on the eastern side of the Allied salient. At least three other divisions from across the Scheldt appeared in the Fifteenth Army or elsewhere.[3]

Prisoners from the Fifteenth Army gave harrowing accounts of their tribulations, marching long distances, attacked from the air, joined by half-trained men over or under military age, receiving scant rations irregularly and, as they were pushed in to strengthen the front, meeting Allied troops superior to them in numbers, fire power and organisation. On 10 September Himmler promulgated an order which in Shulman's opinion did more than anything else to hold them together,

'. . . every deserter will be prosecuted and will find his just punishment. Furthermore his ignominious behaviour will entail the most severe consequences for his family. Upon examination of the circumstances they will be shot.'[4]

Yet the command system of an army with trained and experienced divisional cadres capable of absorbing the men being sent forward from

Germany must have come as a godsend to the hard pressed German command. Among the reinforcements there were those such as the Luftwaffe aircrews and the Hitler Youth who were ready enough to fight and, given a lead from the more resolute of the men in the old divisions, would do so effectively. During the latter part of October the task of driving the Fifteenth Army back from its canal line to the Maas would absorb the main effort of 21 Army Group, temporarily diverting it, as the German command hoped, from Montgomery's original intention of pressing eastwards to the Ruhr.

On 6 September a captured order of 86 Corps told the First Canadian Army what was happening.[5] The previous day the army's Intelligence Summary had commented that, with Antwerp gone, the enemy was in a new pocket and could only escape through Flushing. It estimated that three divisions were 'in the bag' with the remains of at least three others. Then on the 6th, after commenting that the enemy seemed oblivious of the fact that escape through Antwerp was now impossible, the summary reported that according to the captured order the Germans were putting garrisons into Boulogne, Calais and Dunkirk and taking the rest of their troops in the 'Calais-Dunkirk pocket' out across the West Scheldt, leaving a screen of demolitions and mobile troops to cover embarkation.

On the 7th the Canadian summary said that, while there had been no tactical air reconnaissance that day, '. . . it is certain that the German scratch fleet of fishing boats and barges is plying busily to and fro in the West Schelde evacuating as many troops as possible for another, not far distant day.' On the 9th it forecast that the Germans would block the seaward approaches to Antwerp by holding Walcheren and South Beveland as a minimum and possibly the Dutch coast south of the Scheldt as well. On the 15th it remarked that the Scheldt front 'appeared to be moving more at the enemy's pace than our own', and on the 23rd that divisions of the Fifteenth Army were turning up north of Antwerp. Then on the 24th, 'his withdrawal across the Schelde . . . was a tremendous feat for a defeated and trapped army. Yet POW reports show it was done with poor troops'.

Hitler's order to the Fifteenth Army to escape across the Scheldt, issued on 4 September, had coincided with Montgomery's directive of the 3rd ordering the Second British Army to exploit the gap which had opened between the Fifteenth Army and the Seventh. On the Albert Canal the Second British Army, instead of continuing its advance northwards the twenty miles that would have cut the German escape route at the Beveland isthmus, turned eastwards for the Ruhr. Along the Channel coast the First Canadian Army, restricted in supply by the demands being made for the Arnhem offensive, instead of seizing the chance to catch von Zangen in the classic predicament of crossing a major water obstacle, directed its main weight against Le Havre, Boulogne, Calais and Dunkirk, leaving only its two armoured divisions to follow up the Fifteenth Army.

Explaining that maintenance problems prevented the full exploitation of the Allies' advantage and that a speedy and victorious conclusion of the war in consequence depended on the capture of the Channel ports, Crerar, in a directive of 9 September addressed to his two corps, continued:

'6. In view of the necessity to give first priority to the capture of the Channel ports, mentioned above, the capture or destruction of the enemy remaining NORTH and EAST of the GHENT-BRUGES Canal becomes secondary in importance. While constant pressure and close contact with the enemy, now withdrawing NORTH of R SCHELDE, will be maintained, important forces will not be committed to offensive action.'[6]

84 Group RAF was instructed to make every effort to interfere with and destroy the enemy ferrying himself across the Scheldt, and in response fighter bombers attacked ferries in transit by day, and medium bombers, Breskens, Terneuzen and Flushing night and day. Although the Luftwaffe offered no resistance, 40 aircraft were lost to German anti-aircraft fire.

After hard fighting in the Falaise Gap, the First Canadian Army had crossed the Seine almost level with the Second British Army. The 4th Canadian Armoured Division reached the Somme at Abbeville early on 2 September, after which the 1st Polish Armoured Division continued the pursuit. But thereafter the Canadian army had fallen behind, as Lieutenant General Sir John Crocker's British 1st Corps swung back for Le Havre and the two infantry divisions of Lieutenant General Guy Simond's 2nd Canadian Corps turned aside for Dieppe, Boulogne, Calais, Dunkirk and Ostend. Nevertheless Simonds's two armoured divisions were soon pressing on von Zangen's heels. The 1st Polish Armoured Division, meeting the 245th Infantry Division on the Ghent Canal west of Ghent tried to force a crossing on the 9th and again on the night of the 10th, but each time failed. On the 11th the Poles were ordered to give up the attempt and take over Ghent from the 7th Armoured Division and for the next two days were occupied in clearing the suburbs.

The 4th Canadian Armoured Division, after a day or two to rest and refit on the Somme, came up with the Fifteenth Army's covering position on the Ghent Canal at Moerbrugge at the junction of the 245th and 711th Divisions. On 8 September the Argyll and Sutherland Highlanders of Canada crossing the canal met unexpectedly severe opposition, but managed to hold on against determined counter-attacks until next day they could be reinforced and a bridge built. 'For the first time since we left the Falaise area the enemy was able to put down a truly effective concentration of fire with the result that the engineers could not get a bridge across in daylight' recorded the divisional war diary.[7]

Advancing eastwards from Bruges the division ran into more serious trouble on the 13th when it met the 245th Division holding the double line of the Canal de Derivation de la Lys and the Leopold Canal at Moerkerke. Supported by the concentrated artillery of the division, four companies of the Algonquin Regiment crossed in assault boats under heavy fire and dug in on the far bank, but then a storm of mortar and artillery fire inflicted heavy casualties on them, stopped the engineers working on a bridge and finally sank the boats so that supplies could not be brought across. At 10 o'clock next morning fresh German infantry attacked in strength, and at 11 the divisional commander ordered withdrawal. Some of the survivors escaped only by swimming the canal, and altogether in the action the Algonquins lost 35 killed, 53 wounded and 60 taken prisoner. Simonds now ordered the division not to incur further losses in forcing the twin canals, but to follow up any enemy withdrawals.

As the two armoured divisions pushed eastwards, the country had become increasingly unsuitable for armour. Much of it was nearly at sea level, polder, big open fields drained by a maze of waterways and liable to inundation. Several major canals crossed the area. Roads ran across the flat fields on raised embankments lined with trees. It was no country for tanks, and now the Germans were fighting with a new determination.

On the 16th the 1st Polish Armoured Division began to advance again. That day the 10th Dragoons crossed the Hulst Canal halfway to Terneuzen, but next day the Germans counter-attacked furiously and wiped out the bridgehead with heavy loss to the Poles. On the 18th the Polish 3rd Infantry Brigade renewed the attack. It established a strong bridgehead, and by the morning of the 19th the engineers had a bridge across. That day the brigade got within five miles of Terneuzen, and on the 20th reached the port, sinking and capturing many craft used by the Germans in their escape. Since the 10th the division had lost 75 killed, 191 wounded and 63 missing and had taken 1,175 German prisoners of war.[8]

Meanwhile the 4th Canadian Armoured Division, finding the Germans were withdrawing beyond the point of separation of the two canals, crossed the Canal de Derivation and pushed eastwards, south of the Leopold Canal. On the night of the 19th the Argyll and Sutherland Highlanders of Canada of the 10th Canadian Infantry Brigade took Sas van Ghent with a hundred prisoners and on the 21st reached the Scheldt west of Terneuzen. The Algonquin Regiment, however, striking northwest on the 22nd by the Breskens road around the Braakman inlet, found the Isabella Polder firmly held. They lost an entire platoon at the first attempt to cross, and subsequent attacks failed to dislodge the enemy. The Germans, it was becoming evident, were not giving up the Leopold Canal without a struggle!

That there was a feeling about that the war had been won as the pursuit from Normandy rolled eastwards is true and was natural. But, as the events so far related surely make evident, there was also an exhilarating feeling of great events in the making. No one wanted to get killed doing something stupid or unnecessary: many found they could call upon hidden reserves of courage, initiative, and energy to see and grasp fleeting opportunities when they knew what was wanted of them. At lower levels of idealism, if there were those too much concerned to save their skins, there were also those who looked for a final chance to win distinction or to prove themselves. The cheers of the crowd can call forth a final spurt or they can tell the runners that the race is won, and there were plenty of cheering crowds about in France and Belgium as August 1944 turned to September. More than ever in battle, everything depended on men knowing what was required of them and why. Those who miss that miss the essential spirit of the front-line in World War II.

That there was subsequently disappointment at what had been achieved is undeniable, but different people were disappointed about different things. At the top, Montgomery was disappointed that he was not given the means to reach Berlin and win the war. But that would have meant arriving on the Albert Canal in greater strength than that of the two armoured divisions which reached Brussels and Antwerp on 3 and 4 September. For that, as Montgomery says, Eisenhower would have had to make up his mind to concentrate everything on the northern thrust a month before in the event he agreed to give full support to the Arnhem attack.[10] Continuing to argue what, for better or worse, was a lost case, Montgomery relaxed his customarily firm grip on the battle being fought. Eisenhower was disappointed on two counts: that the pursuit did not reach the Rhine, and that it did not open Antwerp. He never believed it possible, he subsequently maintained, for the pursuit to reach Berlin and end the war,[11] and information which has subsequently become available on the whole supports him. Ramsay was disappointed that Antwerp was not opened quickly. He held at the time and subsequently that Montgomery should have cleared the Breskens Pocket, South Beveland and Walcheren before attempting Arnhem, and Brooke, on his return from the Quebec Conference, agreed with him.

At the next level down, Lieutenant General Sir Miles Dempsey, commanding the Second British Army, has since said that his mind was so set on Germany that he forgot Antwerp.[12] In contrast, Horrocks, at 30 Corps, has written in his memoirs that far from forgetting Antwerp, he remembered the influence of ports on the 8th Army's advance across the Western Desert, and made a serious mistake in ordering Roberts to go straight through Antwerp to capture the docks before the Germans could carry out large scale demolitions. Roberts, he says, had not the strength to seize the docks, clear the city and secure a bridgehead across the Albert Canal, and Horrocks himself, with his eyes set on the Rhine, failed to realise that the Scheldt would be mined, and the port in consequence useless, or that the Fifteenth Army would be able to escape across the estuary. Had he instead ordered Roberts to by-pass Antwerp to the east and make for isthmus, he might have hindered or even stopped the escape.

The 4th September, Horrocks continues, was the key date. On the 3rd his corps still had a hundred miles of petrol per vehicle and a further day's supply within reach. The 50th Infantry Division was strung out to the rear protecting the left flank of his corps and collecting thousands of prisoners who were attempting to break out from the coastal belt behind the armoured divisions to reach Germany. The 43rd Infantry Division had on the 2nd been transferred to 8 Corps. So if anyone was to break for the Rhine on the 4th, it had to be the 11th Armoured Division or the Guards. But, with Brussels and Antwerp in his hands, Horrocks was ordered to halt and not released to continue the pursuit until the 7th.[13]

By then, as we have seen, the Antwerp docks had been secured largely intact, and the trapped Fifteenth Army had begun its escape across the Scheldt. The KSLI's bridgehead in the Schijnpoort area offered little promise, but, unrealised by the British, two chances to reach the isthmus remained open. In the docks the Monmouths on the 7th held a toehold across the entrance to the Albert Canal, and Colson's Resistance groups on the 6th and subsequently patrolled unsupported across Leopolddok towards Wilmarsdonck and into the northwestern corner of Merxem. And at Wijnegem, to the east of Merxem, Pilaet's men held the bridge they had captured on the night of the 5th, which they did not lose until the Germans counter-attacked on the night of the 17th. In deciding, as he must have done on 6 September at the latest, to make his thrust for the Rhine on the right and centre of the Second British Army's front rather than on its left, Montgomery, as well as narrowing his options in pursuit, abandoned the chance of intercepting the Fifteenth Army.

A single battalion, even if not primarily responsible for the docks, could hardly have opened the way for an advance west of Merxem, but, as Colson's success on the 20th showed, a fresh infantry brigade together with the rested 29th Armoured Brigade and followed perhaps by another brigade from the 50th Infantry Division, threatening Merxem in flank and rear and seizing 12 Sluiskens to control the water level around Wilmarsdonck, would earlier in September have had an excellent chance of shouldering aside the 719th Division and advancing the 15 or 20 miles needed to reach the South Beveland isthmus, whence the 11th Armoured and 50th Infantry divisions could as Operation Market Garden developed have joined in on the left of the Guards Armoured Division instead of on the right. Cut off at the isthmus, and attempting the long and dangerous sea passage to Dordrecht and Rotterdam, the divisions of the Fifteenth Army, if they arrived at all, would have arrived too late to fight in the Arnhem battle.

Depriving Model of the Fifteenth Army would certainly have increased the strain on the German defence both at the time of Arnhem and later. Whether bottling up that army at the mouth of the Scheldt would have hastened the opening of Antwerp is another matter. Crowded into the Breskens Pocket and the islands, all three areas flooded to a greater or lesser extent, and cut off from supplies and reinforcements, the battered German divisions from Normandy would hardly have fought as well as in the event did the fresh 64th Division in the Pocket, or even as well as the much-abused 70th in South Beveland and Walcheren. That a débâcle on the sea route would have been followed by another at the mouth of the Scheldt is very much less certain.

Montgomery's failure to press the pursuit west and south of the Scheldt is more remarkable. Instead of urging Crerar to strain every nerve and if necessary, like Patton, run his petrol tanks dry to catch the Fifteenth Army astride the Scheldt, Montgomery held the First Canadian Army back, so that supply might be concentrated on the Second British Army, and diverted its main effort, together with that of Bomber Command in support of the land battle, to the capture of the Channel ports.* Then, when Le Havre had been taken, he grounded 1 Corps so that the advance of the Second British Army might be maintained.[14]

In his instruction of 26 August, Montgomery had given the First Canadian Army the tasks of seizing Dieppe and Le Havre and of destroying enemy forces in the coastal area as far east as Bruges. On 3 September, having the previous day released 30 Corps for Brussels and Antwerp, he addressed to the First Canadian Army in his written instruction for the advance on the Ruhr what the Canadian official historian has described as a single bleak sentence:

> 5. Canadian Army will clear the coastal belt and will then remain in the general area Bruges-Calais until the maintenance situation allows of its employment further forward.[15]

It was hardly an order, in the aftermath of three months hard fighting, to spur an army to relentless pursuit.

On the 6th Montgomery sent the signal to Crerar forecasting delay in the opening of Antwerp and emphasising the need to open Boulogne. On the 9th Crerar issued his own instruction directing 2 Canadian Corps against Boulogne and Calais and restricting the commitment of important forces further east. By the 12th Montgomery had begun to think again about Antwerp, but by then it was too late, for the infantry divisions of 2 Canadian Corps were committed and the opportunity had passed.

It has recently been revealed that Simonds, who had at this time not yet taken temporary command of the First Canadian Army, suggested to Crerar that 2 Canadian Corps should continue the pursuit unrelentingly along the coast to Breskens and then turn east to cut off the Fifteenth Army from the Scheldt. To ease the transport difficulties, he proposed that his corps should be supplied with bridging, ammunition and petrol by landing craft along the coast. 'He [Simonds] would have given anything for ten minutes with Montgomery, who would have seen the possibilities in a flash. Antwerp would have been opened quickly and the delay in opening the Channel ports, even if it had been more than a few days, would not have affected the situation.'[16] But Crerar would not question the orders he had received from Montgomery.

Whether Montgomery would in reality have been so easily persuaded is open to doubt. Montgomery's signals to Crerar at this time do indeed show

*Exact figures are not available, but on a rough calculation Bomber Command dropped a total of some 20,000 tons on Le Havre, Boulogne, Calais and the Gris Nez batteries in support of the First Canadian Army's successful attacks on them. Between 17 September and 30 October it dropped a total of 10,219 tons on Walcheren, its only contribution to the opening of Antwerp.

uncharacteristic signs of vacillation between the Channel ports and Antwerp. He thought highly of Simonds and might have been more receptive to a suggestion from a younger subordinate than from a superior, with whom, despite professions of loyalty, he was in a state of ill-suppressed mental rebellion. Yet his mind was strongly set on early advance into Germany, and he did in the event persistently ignore suggestions from others besides Eisenhower that he should give higher priority to Antwerp.

Had Montgomery adopted Simonds's idea, the two Canadian infantry divisions at a minimum would have been able to support the two armoured divisions in the attack on the German bridgehead. In view of the difficulties subsequently experienced by the 3rd Canadian Infantry Division in its attempts to break through the German position on the Leopold Canal, the pursuit might have run into trouble east of Bruges, especially if landing craft or amphibians had not been available, but the German 64th Infantry Division had not at this time taken over the defence of the bridgehead. [17] Ostend, captured on 9 September, was not open for cargo until the 21st, but earlier beach landings might have been possible.

It is impossible to be sure, but, given Simonds's energy and resource and the backing that Ramsay would undoubtedly have given him, the attempt might well have succeeded. Had someone had the forethought to ask the navy rather sooner, say towards the end of August, to be prepared to support the pursuit along the coast, the chances would have been further improved. As will be seen in the next chapter, little would have been lost by delay in opening Boulogne and Calais.

References
1 Shulman, op cit, pp.178-80.
2 MacDonald, op cit, p.219; Stacey, op cit, p.300; cf Ellis, op cit, II, p.69 giving a lower total for the period 5-22 September.
3 Shulman, op cit, p.180; Ellis, op cit, II p.31; Stacey, op cit, p.366; Schramm, op cit, pp.366-8; MacDonald, op cit, pp.129, 144-7; First Canadian Army Intellegence Summaries for September 1944.
4 Shulman, op cit, p.218.
5 First Canadian Army Intelligence Summaries Nos 68-86, 5-24 September.
6 GOC-in-C 1-0-4 of 9 September, quoted Stacey, op cit, p.330.
7 Stacey, op cit, pp.326-7.
8 ibid, p.361-4.
9 ibid, p.392 and map p.424; Ellis, op cit, II, p.68.
10 Montgomery, Memoirs, p.282; Ellis, op cit, II, p.83.
11 See p.III/12 above.
12 Robert Lewin, Montgomery as a Military Commander, Batsford, 1971, p.233.
13 Lieutenant General Sir Brian Horrocks, A Full Life, Collins, 1960, pp.203-6; Ellis, op cit, II p.4n. Horrocks perhaps underestimates the German 719th Division which repeatedly turned up at times and places inconvenient to British plans.
14 Ellis, op cit, II, p.13.
15 Quoted Stacey, op cit, p.324.
16 E. K. G. Sixsmith, Eisenhower as a Military Commander, Batsford, 1973, p.170. My own enquiry to General Simonds on this point was unhappily overtaken by his fatal illness.
17 On 8 September the 1st Polish and 4th Canadian Armoured Divisions met the 245th and 711th Divisions east of Bruges, see p.50 above; part of the 70th Division was at this time holding the German line near Ghent.

5

Supply Famine

The logistic problem that faced Montgomery and Eisenhower and suddenly became urgent at the end of August as the armoured spearheads raced ahead for Antwerp, Brussels, Aachen and Nancy was this: how far could the supply system of their armies be stretched in exploiting the Normandy victory before the armies must stop and establish bases further forward?

Montgomery, tempted by the collapse of German resistance in France and Belgium, thought that, if he could stretch his supply system still further, he could break through the hurriedly improvised German defence in Holland and end the war either by reaching Berlin, or, failing that, at least the Ruhr, the main source of German arms. The extra range he needed could be achieved, he believed, by concentrating the whole of the logistic resources available for 12 and 21 Army Groups on a single thrust into northern Germany, and perhaps at some later stage by opening Rotterdam, Amsterdam or ports in Germany.

Eisenhower, influenced to some extent perhaps by national feelings but much more by the facts of command of a great force of three army groups to which new divisions from America and from the reborn French Army were being added faster than they could be maintained, had to take a longer view. He still hoped by stretching his logistics to the limit to squeeze everything possible from the Normandy victory by seizing the Ruhr and breaching the Siegfried Line, but he did not believe that he could reach Berlin and had therefore to think ahead to the logistic requirements for final victory later, for which he believed a major deep water port in northern Europe to be essential. Early in September, tempted like Montgomery by the German collapse, he authorised Bradley to release the First and Third US Armies for the Siegfried Line and shortly afterwards agreed that Montgomery should try for Arnhem and the Ruhr before opening Antwerp. Unlike Patton and Montgomery, however, he realised that the final advance deep into Germany must come later. At a meeting of his principal staff officers and senior commanders on 22 September, which Montgomery was unable to attend, he took pains to insist that they should differentiate clearly between the logistic requirements for seizing the Ruhr and breaching the Siegfried Line and those for the final offensive. Two days later he made the same point in writing to Montgomery, concluding 'Of course, we need Antwerp.'[1]

The difference was then that Montgomery in September believed that he saw a chance, if he were given full logistic support at the expense of all else, to win the war quickly and need not make plans beyond that*: Eisenhower, while eager to exploit the present advantage to the full, thought it essential to make provision for the longer term. Running through and confusing this issue, but not in essence part of it, were the earlier differences between Montgomery and Eisenhower on the subjects of command and of broad versus narrow front strategy.

Maintenance plans for the invasion had inevitably had to be made well in advance of the June landings, and logistic calculations based on estimates of the positions which the armies would reach at a series of subsequent dates. Because the Germans had not withdrawn when they could still have saved the Fifth Panzer and Seventh Armies, the advance in June and July had fallen behind these estimates, and supplies had piled up in the beachhead. But then, as the German armies disintegrated and the Allied armies streamed castwards in pursuit, they ran far ahead of schedule. They reached the Seine 11 days before predicted and freed Paris 55 days ahead of forecast. Now in mid-September three armies were closing the German frontier, which they had not been expected to reach until May 1945, and a supply famine was developing. Moreover, because the Third US Army had been switched from Brittany to the pursuit eastwards, of the Brittany ports scheduled to land 14,000 tons a day for the American armies by D+90, all except St Malo were still in German hands.[2]

It was in this situation that Eisenhower had to choose between Patton's plan for a thrust in the centre and Montgomery's for one in the north. Patton's plan was logistically practicable, but it would take his army through terrain unsuitable for armour, would open no ports and would strike at no vital part of Germany. Montgomery's plan offered more attractive prizes. As well as opening Antwerp or Rotterdam and striking at the Ruhr, it would take him into the North German plain, well suited to the massive deployment of armour. It had, in fact, been part of the pre-invasion plan. At Supreme Headquarters, Eisenhower's planners estimated that an advance into northern Germany by five corps, of which three divisions would reach Berlin, was logistically practicable, but only if ten American divisions were grounded elsewhere and twelve others relegated to quiescence, and provided also that the Rhine was reached and Antwerp opened by 15 September.[3]

In neither army group was there in September any anxiety about shortage of supplies in the Normandy beachhead maintenance areas. The problem was to get supplies forward to the fighting fronts along lines of communication which had suddenly to be reckoned in hundreds of miles rather than in tens, and by roads and railways damaged first by Allied bombing and then by German demolitions. Meanwhile the liberation of great areas of friendly territory had brought with it responsibility for providing the civilian population with at least the necessities of life.

*Although in August Montgomery had advocated a single thrust in the north, at that time his intention seems to have been more limited, see pp.39, 40 above.

57

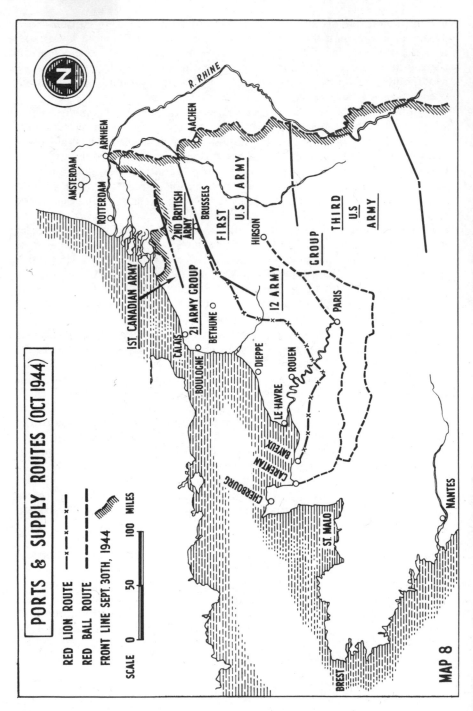

PORTS & SUPPLY ROUTES (OCT 1944)

RED LION ROUTE —x—x—x—
RED BALL ROUTE — — — —
FRONT LINE SEPT. 30TH, 1944

SCALE

0   50   100   MILES

MAP 8

N

R. RHINE

AMSTERDAM
ARNHEM
ROTTERDAM
AACHEN
BRUSSELS
2ND BRITISH ARMY
FIRST U.S ARMY
HIRSON
THIRD U.S ARMY
21 ARMY GROUP
12 ARMY GROUP
1ST CANADIAN ARMY
BETHUNE
CALAIS
BOULOGNE
DIEPPE
ROUEN
LE HAVRE
PARIS
BAYEUX
CARENTAN
CHERBOURG
ST MALO
NANTES
BREST

A British divisional slice, that is a division together with its share of corps and army supporting and administrative troops, required when engaged in active operations 520 tons a day delivered at road or rail head and 180 tons further back. The equivalent American figures were similar.[4] As airfields for them were established in France and Belgium, the tactical air forces had to be supplied with petrol, ammunition, spares and food. Engineers building new airfields had to be supplied with construction stores. Bridging had to be brought forward to the numerous water obstacles as the advancing armies reached them and provided in anticipation of the advance across the Maas, the Waal and the Rhine in the north and across the Moselle in the centre. Further back engineers continued their work of building bridges and improving communications. As for the civilian population, Paris alone needed 2,400 tons a day. No figures appear to be available for the total tonnages required, and if they were available they would be so complicated by distances and delivery points as to defy generalisation, but perhaps enough has been said to give an idea of the scale of the problem.

For 21 Army Group the distance from the Bayeux base to the fighting front had in a week increased from 80 miles to the Seine to over 300 to Louvain, almost twice the distance for which the allotment of road transport was calculated, and Arnhem lay another hundred miles further forward. Something in the nature of 5,500 tons had to be delivered daily to the road head of the Second British Army, by mid-September close to Brussels, and perhaps about 3,000 tons to the road head of the First Canadian Army, some of whose divisions were grounded, at Bethune.

Air supply from Britain was an obvious alternative to road and rail supply from the beachhead, but it could handle only limited tonnages and had to compete for airlift with projected airborne operations. It began in August, and the main tonnages were lifted by the US 9th Troop Carrier Command with assistance from the US 9th Air Service Command, the US Strategic Air Forces and 46 Group RAF. (see Table 1)

In the week ending 26 August some 4,500 tons were delivered. On 28 August SHAEF authorised withdrawal of all troop carrier aircraft assigned to the First Allied Airborne Army in anticipation of airborne operations during the pursuit, but next day ordered that all C-47 transport aircraft not required by the 8th and 9th Air Service Commands should be made available for air supply and 100 B-17 Flying Fortresses and B-24 Liberators should be converted for use as cargo planes. By these means the tonnage lifted during the week ending 2 September was maintained at substantially the same level as for the previous week. Then, after the troop carriers were released on 3 September, the level was raised to 7,000 tons in each of the next two weeks. After that the tonnage fell abruptly as the aircraft allocated to the First Allied Airborne Army were finally withdrawn for the Arnhem operation.

Of these supplies 21 Army Group, which had in the first two weeks

Table 1 — Airlift Tonnages

		Week ending			
Flown by	26 Aug	2 Sep	9 Sep	16 Sep	Total
US Forces					
9th Troop Carrier Command	3,599	2,480	6,119	5,300	17,498
9th Air Service Command	586	630	0	0	1,216
US Strategic Air Forces (B-24s)	0	443	975	235	1,653
Total US	4,185	3,553	7,094	5,535	20,367
British Forces					
46 Group RAF	350	917	184	1,395	2,849
Total	4,535	4,470	7,278	6,933	23,261
Received by					
12 Army Group	4,185	1,877	3,316	3,221	12,799
21 Army Group	350	917	2,787	3,712	7,776
Paris	0	1,676	975	0	2,651

after Ruppertal *op cit* Vol 1, p.581.

received only the smaller tonnages lifted by the RAF, received 6,500 tons in the next two weeks, of which 2,000 tons, mainly petrol, were delivered at airfields near Amiens in the week ending the 9th, and 3,300 tons, mainly ammunition, at airfields near Brussels in the week ending the 16th. 12 Army Group, having received 6,000 tons in the first two weeks, received another 6,700 in the next two.[5]

Meanwhile the First Canadian Army had begun its task of opening ports along the Channel coast closer to the front. (see Table 2 for dates of opening, capacity and distances) The 2nd Canadian Infantry Division found Dieppe abandoned by the Germans on 1 September. The first ship entered on the 7th, and by the end of the month the port was handling 6-7,000 tons a day. On 8 September one brigade from the same division reached the outskirts of Dunkirk to find the town held by the enemy, and on the 9th another entered Ostend unopposed, but owing to demolitions and mining the port would not be fully usable until the 28th. By the end of October it would be discharging 5,000 tons a day. On 12 September, after heavy air and sea bombardment, Le Havre fell to the attack of the 49th Infantry and 51st (Highland) Divisions of 1 Corps. The port was allocated to the American Communications Zone, but owing to German demolitions and British bombardment would not be usable until 9 October. [6]

Supported by the 2nd Canadian Armoured Brigade, the 3rd Canadian Infantry Division attacked Boulogne, which fell on 22 September, but did not become usable until 12 October, and Calais, which fell on the 30th but did not become usable until November, when it was used only for train ferries and personnel. Thus during September and for the Arnhem offensive 21 Army Group remained, with the exception of Dieppe and airlift, dependent for supplies on its Bayeux base served by the surviving Mulberry harbour and by the beaches.

Exceptional efforts were made to solve the resultant transport problem. 8 Corps was grounded so that its second line transport could be used to bring supplies to the roadheads, as were the divisions of 1 Corps, after they had taken Le Havre. Lorries were taken from reserve and from beach unloading and the War Office sent across additional transport companies. Tank transporters were converted to carry supplies by welding sections of airfield tracking to their sides. The American Red Lion Express, which undertook to supply the Second British Army with 500 tons a day, half for the 82nd and 101st US Airborne Divisions, bettered the estimate and averaged 650 tons a day. 800 British three-tonners were diverted to bring up bridging

Table 2 — Ports: Dates of Capture and Opening, Capacity and Distance

	taken	open	capacity tons/day	distance from Brussels km	miles
Bayeux maintenance area	—	—	—	467	292
*Dieppe	1 Sep	7 Sep	6-7,000 by end Sep	292	182.5
Le Havre	12 Sep	9 Oct	3,650 by mid-Oct 5,000 in Nov	220	235
*Boulogne	22 Sep	12 Oct	11,000 later POL by PLUTO	209	137.5
Calais	30 Sep	Nov	personnel & LST only	209	130.5
Dunkirk	—	—	—	167	104
Ostend	9 Sep	25/28 Sep	1,000 by end Sep 5,000 by end Oct plus POL	113	70.5
Antwerp	5 Sep	26 Nov	19,000 by 7 Dec 80-100,000 later	45	29

*Coasters and LST only

from Bayeux. Despite piston failure at this critical time in 1,400 British lorries of one type and in all the spare engines for them, the Arnhem offensive went forward and did not lack for supplies. A justifiable risk had been taken to gain an important tactical advantage, and administrative resources, although strained to the limit, had survived.[7]

By late September the transport crisis in 21 Army Group was largely over. A railway bridge across the Seine had been completed joining up the line from Bayeux to Brussels, and road bridges had been improved. With its flank on the Channel coast and with its lines of communications on the whole rather shorter than those of 12 Army Group, 21 Army Group had its supply problem reasonably well in hand.[8]

At Headquarters Communications Zone, ComZ, responsible for supplying the American armies, and at Supreme Headquarters, the limitations of port and beach discharge caused more concern than in either 12 or 21 Army Groups. Cherbourg, although it had surrendered on 29 June, had been found to be very seriously damaged, mined and obstructed. Although the first loads were discharged there on 15 July, port clearance was not completed until 29 September. In November the port would discharge some 15,000 tons a day, but during September it averaged only 10,000 tons, nearly half of which was transportation stores and rolling stock. Omaha and Utah Beaches together did better, averaging in September 10,500 tons a day. In October Le Havre and Rouen would make important contributions to the American tonnage and Cherbourg would improve, but the American total, except for Marseilles supplying 6 Army Group, remained almost exactly the same. Significantly for the onset of winter, discharges over the beaches and through minor ports were heavily down.[9]

But for the Americans, as for 21 Army Group, transport was in September the immediate problem, and to the Americans, with their longer hauls from the Channel, the end of the pursuit brought little relief. The Red Ball Express, the first and best known of the Color Routes, starting to run on 25 August, completed its initial task on 5 September, having delivered 75,000 tons to the Chartres area. Now it was decided to continue it indefinitely, extending its route and branching it to deliver to the First US Army at Hirson, fifty miles south of Brussels, and to the Third US Army at Sommesous, near Chalons. In September it averaged 6,891 tons a day, and in the last week, 8,209 tons a day in 1,542 lorries. The average round trip was 714 miles and took 71 hours. As rail transport improved, the route was successively shortened, and on 16 November, the same day that the Normandy beaches closed, it ceased operation. The White Ball Route, from Le Havre and Rouen to the two American armies, opened on 6 October and ran until 10 January, but it was less effective than the Red Ball Express.[10]

To provide 550 tons a day for each division in 12 Army Group and meet the needs of the Ninth US Air Force required in mid-September 13,000 tons a day, in addition to which it was estimated that 150,000 to 180,000 tons were needed in the forward area to re-equip fighting units, build up reserves and provide winter clothing. ComZ, however, was only able to lift forward 11,000 tons a day, of which 4,000 tons went to the Ninth Air Force and the rest to the two armies, leaving reserves in the forward area sufficient only for two or three days supply. At the end of August the First US Army had been getting more tonnage than the Third, but on 5 September, as Montgomery was quick to detect, Bradley ordered the 7,000 tons available to be shared equally between the two armies. On the 14th the total tonnage lifted was increased by grounding three divisions in Normandy and Brittany and using their transport, and on the 22nd Bradley issued orders, which took effect on the 27th, allotting the First Army 5,400 tons a day and the Third 3,100.[11]

The capture of Antwerp, it had been assumed when it was announced early in September, would solve both the immediate problem of transport and the future threat of inadequate port discharge. But as it began to be realised that Antwerp was not about to be opened, the outlook became bleaker. At the beginning of October 12 Army Group had twenty divisions, ten in the First Army, eight in the Third and two in the Ninth at that time still in Normandy and Brittany, where there were also another seven divisions, only one of which was engaged in active operations. By mid-October twenty-five divisions could be available for 12 Army Group, but if the additional divisions were brought forward, over 22,000 tons a day would have to be delivered to support the army group and the Ninth Air Force. By 1 November the total could rise to twenty-eight divisions, but that would call for delivery of 22,700 tons day. On this basis Supreme Headquarters calculated that the strength of 12 Army Group in the forward area should not exceed twenty divisions, and informed Bradley that he could only move forward the additional divisions if he withdrew a corresponding number from the line and rested them. Bradley moved the divisions forward and brought his strength in the line up to twenty-three divisions, but supply remained only fully adequate for thirteen and strict rationing had to be imposed.[12]

In these circumstances it is easy to understand that Eisenhower should have insisted to Montgomery throughout September and October on the urgency of the need to open Antwerp, and that Bradley and Patton should have resented what seemed to them Eisenhower's weakness in giving way to Montgomery's demands for priority for his Arnhem offensive. Montgomery was no easy team mate, and he must have been a singularly exasperating subordinate. Bradley can be criticised for failing to give the First US Army the priority for supply that Eisenhower had promised, but the frustration of the situation in which the Americans found themselves has been too little recognised in this country. Owing to the relative geographic positions of the two army groups, Bradley was dependent on Montgomery to open the ports that would enable the Americans to deploy the continually increasing might of their armies. Meanwhile Montgomery, more comfortably situated for supply, procrastinated in the execution of this essential task.

Hitler had counted on lack of ports holding up the invaders, but hardly in this way. He had a passion for fortifications, and when he realised early in 1942 that he was in for a long war with Russia and began to feel anxious about the West, he had set Organisation Todt to work to build an impregnable defence line along the entire 1500-mile coastline of Holland, Belgium and France. But the resources of the Reich and the conquered countries, even under a dictatorship, were quite inadequate either to build or to man defences on such a scale. Faced by this, Hitler had seized upon the idea that the western Allies would be unable to invade successfully unless they could take a large port quickly. He had therefore nominated a number of ports, or in some cases their seaward approaches, as fortresses.[13] These were to be defended by a comprehensive system of concrete and steel structures, some to Hitler's personal design, and the rest of the coastline defended only by single strong points too far apart for mutual support.

Von Rundstedt, appointed Commander-in-Chief West in March 1942, thoroughly disliked the system. The enemy, he believed, would not be so foolish as to attack the fortresses frontally, but would land on the open coast and take them from landward. Anyway he had not enough men for his task of defence without locking up in the fortresses the large garrisons which would be needed to hold them adequately. Nor were the fortress commanders, sworn to hold the fortresses in their charge to the death, in a happy position. Their garrisons were too small, and they had only limited control over naval and Luftwaffe units in their areas.[14] But Hitler was not entirely wrong, for it was their realisation of the need for ports and of the difficulty of taking them quickly that led the British to devise and construct the Mulberry artificial harbours. As it was, things turned out much as Von Rundstedt had predicted, and the only immediate return Hitler got for the manpower and engineering effort expended on some dozen fortresses was at Cherbourg and Brest.

Now Hitler saw a new chance to exploit the fortresses. They had failed to prevent invasion, but they might still be made use of to hold up the victorious invaders as they pursued the defeated German armies towards Germany. On 4 September Hitler issued a new directive:

> Because of the breakout of enemy tank forces towards Antwerp, it has become very important for the further progress of the war to hold the fortresses of Boulogne and Dunkirk, the Calais defence area, Walcheren Island, the bridgehead at Antwerp, and the Albert Canal positions as far as Maastricht.

The Fifteenth Army was therefore to bring the garrisons of Boulogne, Dunkirk and Calais up to strength, and the commanders at Calais and Walcheren to be given the same authority as fortress commanders.[15] On 6 September the Naval General Staff ordered the mining and obstruction of the Scheldt.[16]

In contrast von Rundstedt, when he was re-appointed Commander-in-Chief West on 4 September, seems to have failed to appreciate the extent to which

Top: Antwerp Docks in 1944. View taken from the vicinity of Royerssluis looking north to northwest across the exit of the Albert Canal to the Schledt at what was at the time the newer and larger part of the docks. Albertdok can be seen in the middle distance centre; Kattendijkdok behind camera. The few ships visible may indicate that the port had just been opened when the photograph was taken./ *Imperial War Museum (IWM).* Resistance Leaders. *Above:* Lieutenant Urbain Reniers, *Reamur*, Chef du Comité de Coordination de la Resistance d'Anvers, centre./ *Centre de Recherches et d'Etudes Historiques de la Seconde Guerre Mondiale, Brussels (CR)*

Top: Edouard Pilaet, *Francois*, after the
liberation in uniform as commandant
(major), receiving the British Officers
bringing FM Montgomery's citation./ *Pilaet.*

Above: Eugene Colson, *Harry*, with Belgian
generals after the liberation./ *CR.*

Top: **Armée Secrete (Zone 5) Oath taking ceremony by 5th Section, Group D, August 1944./ CR.**

Above: The 11th Armoured Division reaches Antwerp. A Cromwell of the 15th/19th Hussars, 11th Armoured Division, crosses the Seine early on 28th August 1944./ *IWM.*

Top: Moment of triumph. Colonel Silvertop's Sherman reaches the cross-roads leading from Avenue Reine Elisabeth into the Malines Chaussée one kilometre from the Central Park. Silvertop stands in the turret hatch. Vekemans left and Pilaet right stand on the hull./ *Pilaet.*

Above: "A welcome none of us ever dreamt was possible" Half-track in Grote Marckt in the Old City./ *CR.*

Above: Sherman and children in Groenplaats, Old City, probably 5 September when the main body of the 3rd RTR had concentrated leaving C Squadron and G Company, 8th Rifle Brigade, in the docks./ *CR.*

Below: German prisoners being marched out of Antwerp on 5 September./ *IWM.*

Right: Admiral Sir Bertram Ramsay, Commander-in-Chief Allied Naval Expeditionary Forces. He was responsible under Eisenhower for all naval aspects of the Normandy landings and subsequent fighting in NW Europe. As Flag Officer Dover, he had commanded Operation Dynamo, the Dunkirk evacuation; later, as Deputy Commander Allied Expeditionary Force under Cunningham, he had commanded the naval task force which landed Montgomery's Eighth Army in Sicily. "Antwerp is useless unless the Scheldt estuary is cleared of the enemy", he wrote in his diary on 5 September./*IWM*.

Below: Mounting Operation Market Garden, the advance to Arnhem. Montgomery with, left, Major General Adair (Guards Armoured Division) and, right, Lieut General Horrocks (30 Corps) and Major General Roberts (11th Armoured Division), 15 September 1944. "It looks as if the port of Antwerp may be unusable for some time" said Montgomery in a signal to Crerar on 6 September./ *IWM*

Above: General Eisenhower, Supreme Commander Allied Expeditionary Force, with, left, Lieutenant General H. D. G. Crerar, GOC First Canadian Army, and, right, Lieutenant General Sir John Crocker (1 Corps) "While we are advancing we will open the ports of Havre and Antwerp, which are still essential to sustain a powerful thrust into Germany" Eisenhower said in a signal which reached Montgomery on 7 September./ *IWM.*

Centre left: Montgomery and Horrocks on the Albert Canal 15 September 1944. Horrocks's 30 Corps spearheaded the advance of the Second British Army in its attempt to cross the Rhine at Arnhem./ *IWM*

Bottom left: Montgomery with Lieutenant General Guy Simonds. In the First Canadian Army, Simonds's 2 Canadian Corps was given the task of clearing the Scheldt estuary while Crocker's 1 Corps took Le Havre. But for a large part of September Simonds's two infantry divisions were engaged at Dunkirk and Ostend (2nd Canadian Infantry Division), Boulogne, Calais and Gris Nez (3rd Canadian Infantry Division). On 26 September Crerar was invalided to England and Simonds temporarily appointed to the command of the First Canadian Army./ *IWM.*

Above: Naval Force T. Captain Pugsley RN and officers of Naval Force T. Pugsley (centre) with captain's four rings, Commander Masterman immediately left, Commander Sellar immediately right./ *Daily Sketch/ Graphic Photo Union.*

Centre right: Outflanking the Breskens Pocket from the Scheldt. Buffalo of the 5th Assault Regiment Royal Engineers bringing troops of the 3rd Canadian Infantry Division to reinforce the bridgehead behind the German defences of the Breskens Pocket on 13 October 1944./ *Canadian Archives (CA).*

Bottom right: M-19 self-propelled anti-tank gun of the 3rd Anti-Tank Regiment Royal Canadian Artillery on a Bailey raft with two Buffaloes in attendance on its way from Terneuzen to the bridgehead under cover of a smoke screen. 15 October 1944./ *Canadian War Museum (CWM).*

Left: "... it has at last come home to him that Antwerp is the first priority of all, and he has moved back to Brussels to give it his attention", wrote Ramsay in his diary of Montgomery. Montgomery with Major General H. W. Foster, commanding the 4th Canadian Armoured Division, at divisional headquarters near Calmpthout, 28 October 1944./ CA.

Below: The Fifteenth Army withdraws. German prisoners pass Kangaroos (armoured personnel carriers converted from Churchill tanks) and troops of the 15th Scottish Division near Tilburg late October 1944./ IWM

Above: Willemstadt below the junction of the Maas and Waal captured by the 49th Infantry Division on 4 November 1944./ *IWM.*

Below: Sherman tank of the Fort Garry Horse, 2nd Canadian Armoured Brigade, supporting the 2nd Canadian Infantry Division, on the way to cross the South Beveland Canal, 29 October 1944./ *CA.*

Top: Tanks of the Fort Garry Horse cross the South Beveland Canal by a Class 40 Bailey bridge, while a supply lorry returns by a Class 9 bridge. These bridges were built near the main road and rail bridges across the broken spans of which men of the Sasketchewan Regiment had scrambled to secure a bridghead on the night 27/28 October. By the afternoon of the 28th the Royal Canadian Engineers had a bridge across./ *CA*

Above: Carriers universal (usually known as Bren carriers) of the Canadian Scottish Regiment near Breskens, 28 October 1944. In the background may be seen the sort of country over which the Canadians had to fight in the Breskens Pocket even when clear of the main floods along the Leopold Canal./ *CA*.

Top left: **Landing Craft Tank Mark III** (in foreground) Slow, shallow-draft, designed to carry armour, they were also able to carry Buffaloes and if need be allow them to swim out without beaching./ *IWM.*

Centre left: **Landing Craft Infantry** (Small). Fast and manoeuvrable, they beached badly, had shaky plank gangways and plywood hulls which gave no protection against bullets and shell splinters./ *IWM.*

Bottom left: **The Westkapelle Gap.** High oblique air photograph taken on 18 October 1944. The gap was made by bombing on 3 October when much of the village was laid in ruins./ *Crown Copyright (CC).*

Top: Vertical taken later. As the tide rose twice daily, the water reached the bottom of the gap and rushed through in a torrent./ *IWM.*

Above: Gun in Battery W17 with control tower behind. The guns in this battery were in open emplacements, those in W11, W13 and W15 were in thick concrete casemates and therefore much less vulnerable to bombing and shellfire. Yet on 1 November the *Warspite* fired over 300 15-shells at W17 without putting any of its guns out of action./ *IWM.*

Top: Flushing — the waterfront and esplanade taken after the battle. The bunker in the angle of the esplanade (centre) blocked the way along the waterfront past Spuikom.

Above: Flushing from the Air. Taken in 1951 this photograph shows clearly the scenes of the fighting in 1944. Uncle Beach left foreground, Merchants' and Fishers' Docks left middle distance, Schelde Yard right middle distance, Spuikom far right./ *KLM*.

Above: Flushing from the harbour entrance, Breskens. Photograph dated 1 November 1944, but might have been taken the previous evening. Two smoke floats may be seen in what appears as an ineffective attempt to screen the harbour from observation across the Scheldt. ". . . it was a miserable, grey day, and it was not possible to make out many of the landmarks. The forest of cranes in the shipyard, however, stood out clearly against the skyline."/ *CA*

Below: Breskens, 1 November 1944. One of the two KOSB battalions of the 156th Infantry Brigade marches through the ruined town to embark for Flushing./ *Associated Press (AP).*

Top: Uncle Beach (Dock Harbour) under shellfire, 1 November 1944. The photograph is taken from the entrance breakwater close to the point where 4 Commando landed./*IWM.*

Above: Uncle Beach later. Landing craft assault beached with stores being unloaded, Oranje Mill behind./*AP.*

the opening of Antwerp would relieve the supply famine developing in the Allied armies. Rather than hold out to the last at the mouth of the Scheldt, he wanted to save manpower by shortening his front and withdrawing from west Holland to the line of the Yssel from the Zuyder Zee to Arnhem.[17] This would have meant abandoning not only the Scheldt but Rotterdam and Amsterdam also to the Allies, or at best leaving them weakly garrisoned and isolated to attack. But as von Rundstedt might have guessed, Hitler, who had insisted on much less valuable positions being held to the last, would have none of it.

It is sometimes suggested that, had the British and American armies been less lavishly equipped and supplied, they would have been able to stretch their logistics the extra that was needed to break through to Germany in the critical early days of September. Compared to the 520 tons a day at roadhead required for each divisional slice of the British armies and the 550 for the American, a German division, it is claimed, needed only about 200 tons.[18] On that scale the support of the Second British Army or of the Third US Army would hardly have presented any problem. But the comparison is inexact, for it is not clear at what strength the German division is taken in this calculation — even at full strength the German divisions tended to be smaller than the Allied and they were certainly not at full strength as they fell back from France in September 1944 — nor is it clear whether the German figure refers to a division or to a divisional slice.

Leaving that aside, the speed of the pursuit from Normandy depended on two things, mobility and fire power, petrol and ammunition, one to some extent balancing the other as the resistance encountered varied, but both essential at all times. The German infantry divisions withdrawing from Normandy, except for those for whom trains could be provided, marched and their first-line transport was horse drawn. They did not need much petrol, but they were completely outpaced and out-manoeuvred by the mechanised onrush of their enemies. Even in 1940 the bulk of the German infantry had marched, and the armoured divisions which broke through at Sedan were not only lightly armed and armoured in comparison whith those of 1944, but also able to find stocks of petrol on their way.

Then too in 1944 the Germans were withdrawing. If at Caen a British and a German tank were both knocked out, the British replacement had only to trundle some twenty miles or so from the beaches; the German replacement, if it came at all, had to come some 600 miles from the Ruhr factories. If the same thing happened at Arnhem, the situation was reversed. The British replacement had to come 400 miles from the Bayeux base; the German, 60 miles from the Ruhr. The Germans withdrawing were blowing up bridges: the British and Americans pursuing, building new ones. The Luftwaffe, such of it as remained, now operated from home airfields: the RAF and the USAAF tactical air forces came forward to airfields in Belgium and eastern France, many of which had to be built for them, others repaired, and all supplied with petrol, ammunition and spares from the beachhead base areas.

The strategist is always tempted to evade the hard facts of logistics — a few have indeed won fame by contriving to do so without paying an excessive penalty — and most sophisticated armies could with advantage learn to be more frugal in their demands on the supply services. It remains that Eisenhower, in saying 'Of course we need Antwerp' is more likely to have been right than those German generals who, criticising the slow down of the Allied advance in September, saw only their own difficulties in the catastrophic situation of their armies.

Among these von Rundstedt was not numbered. 'Any suggestion that the Allies could have advanced faster than they did in September is nonsense. On the contrary they went much faster than was actually expected.' he said at his War Office interrogation in July 1945, '. . . There is only one possibility by which things might have been speeded up and that would have been a second landing in the north rather than in the Mediterranean.'[19] After the redeployment of landing craft and other amphibious resources to the Mediterranean, there remained off the coast of Normandy and in harbour in southern England sufficient to mount the amphibious assaults on Flushing and Westkapelle on 1 November. Had the need been foreseen, there seems no reason to believe that some similar operation could not have been mounted earlier. Whether an operation or operations on that scale, much more modest than envisaged by von Rundstedt, could by hastening the opening of the Scheldt have done something to speed up the advance of the main armies must remain a matter for speculation in the light of the events attending the mounting of the operations that actually took place.

References
1   Ruppertal, *op cit*, II p.15; Ehrman, *op cit*, p.527.
2   Ruppertal, *ibid*, pp.6-7.
3   *ibid*, pp.10-11.
4   Brigadier Ravenhill OBE, *The Influence of Logistics on Operations in North-West Europe 1944-45*, Journal of the Royal United Service Institute, November 1946; Ruppertal, *op cit*, p. 169.
5   Ruppertal, *op cit*, I pp.597-583, II p.161.
6   *ibid*, II pp.45-105; Stacey, *op cit*, pp.355-6.
7   *The Administrative History of 21 Army Group 6 June 1944-8 May 1945*, Headquarters British Army of the Rhine, Germany, 1945, p.37; Chester Wilmot, *op cit*, pp.472,602; Stacey, *op cit*, p.388; Ruppertal, *op cit*, II pp.139-40.
8   Admin 21 AG, p.63.
9   Ruppertal, *op cit*, II pp.70-97.
10 *ibid*, pp.134-137.
11 *ibid*, pp.18-19, 169.
12 *ibid*, pp.18-19.
13 H. R. Trevor-Roper (ed) *Hitler's War Directives*, Sidgwick & Jackson, 1964, pp.110-116, Directive No. 40 of 23 March 1942; Albert Speer, *Inside the Third Reich*, Weidenfeldt & Nicolson, 1970 pp.476-7.
14 Blumentritt, *op cit*, pp.122 & 153.
15 Stacey, *op cit*, p.301.
16 Ellis, *op cit*, II p.10.
17 Blumentritt, *op cit*, pp.245 & 248.
18 Sir Basil Liddell Hart, *History of the Second World War*, Cassell, 1970, p.564.
19 Shulman, *op cit*, p.206.

6

An Assault Across Water Cannot be Ruled Out

Whether it was his own assessment of the supply situation, Eisenhower's insistence at the Brussels airport meeting of 10 September, or the message sent by Brooke on behalf of the Combined Chiefs of Staff that in mid-September turned Montgomery's attention to the opening of Antwerp can only be conjectured. Whichever it was, Montgomery, having heard on the 12th that his requirements for the Arnhem offensive were to be met, wrote next day to Crerar:

'3. The things that are now very important are:
(a) Capture of Boulogne and Dunkirk and Calais.
(b) The setting in action of operations designed to enable us to use the port of Antwerp.

Of these two things, (b) is probably the most important. We have captured a port which resembles Liverpool in size, but we cannot use it; if we could use it, all our maintenance troubles would disappear. I am very anxious that (a) and (b) should both go on simultaneously if you can possibly arrange it, as time is of the utmost importance.'

A great deal of air support would be needed for the opening of Antwerp, and Montgomery had given orders that bombing to destroy the forts on Walcheren Island should begin at once, while '. . . on the day concerned we can lay on for you the whole weight of the heavy bomber effort from England, both Bomber Command and Eighth Air Force.' Airborne forces would be available for the capture of Walcheren.

'8. The really important thing is speed in setting in motion what we have to do. I hope very much that you will be able to tackle both your tasks simultaneously, ie the Pas de Calais Ports *and* the Antwerp business.'

An exchange of signals, in one of which Montgomery offered to give up operations against Calais and Dunkirk to speed the opening of Antwerp, took place the same day. On the 14th Montgomery conferred with his army commanders and then issued his directive for Arnhem, the Channel Ports and Antwerp. '. . . our real objective is therefore the Ruhr' said that part of the new directive which dealt with the First Canadian Army, but that would merely be the first step for an advance into Germany, to support which

Antwerp and Rotterdam would be needed. While the Second British Army made its thrust for Arnhem and beyond and the First US Army advanced on Bonn and Cologne, 'The whole energies of the [First Canadian] Army will be directed towards operations designed to enable full use to be made of the port of Antwerp,' but the Canadian army was also to capture Boulogne and Calais, mask Dunkirk and send Headquarters 1 Corps and the 49th (West Riding) Division to take over Antwerp from 12 Corps, which was needed for the Arnhem offensive. After opening the Scheldt, the First Canadian Army was to open Rotterdam, then advance into Germany on the northern flank of the Second British Army.[1]

After conferring with Simonds on the 14th, Crerar decided to make 2 Canadian Corps responsible for opening Antwerp and issued a new directive the following day. The early use of Antwerp for the maintenance of 21 Army Group, Crerar now said, was a matter of paramount importance, for which 2 Canadian Corps was forthwith to assume responsibility. The 2nd Canadian Infantry Division was to take over from the 53rd (Welsh) Division in Antwerp by 18 September, leaving the 4th Special Service Brigade to mask Dunkirk. The 3rd Canadian Infantry Division, by now committed to the attack on Boulogne, was to capture that port on the 16th or as soon thereafter as the necessary heavy air support became available, and would then take the Gris Nez batteries and Calais. Should Calais prove stubborn, however, 1 Corps, leaving the 51st (Highland) Division grounded at Le Havre, would take over at Calais with the 49th Division. This would free the 3rd Canadian Infantry Division, presumably to clear the German pocket south of the Scheldt, although no specific mention was made of that task. If not required for Calais, 1 Corps would move up to the Albert Canal between 2 Canadian Corps and the Second British Army.[2] On the 19th, in a further directive, Crerar confirmed that 1 Corps should carry out the latter task.

The 3rd Canadian Infantry Division took Boulogne on the 22nd, the Gris Nez batteries on the 29th and Calais on the 30th. On the 28th the 1st Polish Armoured Division went to 1 Corps for operations east of Antwerp, leaving the 4th Canadian Armoured Division facing the German 64th Division, until in the second week of October the 3rd Canadian Infantry Division arrived to resume the attack on the Pocket. Thus during September only the two armoured divisions were directly occupied in clearing the seaward approaches to Antwerp, and they from the 9th onwards had orders not to commit important forces to offensive action.

Behind the ambiguities in Montgomery's directive of 14 September and the lack of incisiveness in Crerar's of the 15th lay the emphasis on Walcheren in Montgomery's letter of the 13th. To Montgomery, thinking in terms of an advance to the Ruhr and on into Germany, neither the clearance of whatever troops the Fifteenth Army, portrayed in intelligence reports as demoralised, had intentionally or unintentionally left south of the Scheldt, nor the advance from the Albert Canal to the isthmus leading to South Beveland could have appeared as demanding tasks. The embattled island of Walcheren, strongly fortified and inaccessible, was a different matter, as might be, should the Germans hold the isthmus in strength, South Beveland.

Thus when the Planning Section of the First Canadian Army made the appreciation of the problem facing 2 Canadian Corps, which it produced on 19 September, it assumed that it had only to deal with Walcheren and South Beveland, and that by the time the question of attacking these arose the whole south bank of the Scheldt would be in Canadian hands.

Another assumption was that a full-dress amphibious assault on Walcheren would be impracticable. The Royal Navy had said that it could provide 70 Landing Craft Assault and 20 Landing Craft Tank at Ostend, whence it might be possible for the LCA to reach the West Scheldt either by tank transporter or by canal, but it was very doubtful if the LCT could do so at all. Moreover the navy had pointed out that the crews available for the landing craft were not trained to carry out a set piece operation. Meanwhile the 5th Assault Regiment, Royal Engineers, of the 79th Armoured Division, recently equipped with amphibians, was by 24 September expected to have available near Ghent 100 Buffalo tracked amphibians and 40 Terrapin wheeled amphibians.

While not ruling out lesser 'water-borne' operations in the West Scheldt, the planners considered:

'It is reasonable to discard at the outset the possibility of mounting a successful combined [ie amphibious] operation to capture WALCHEREN island by assaulting the only possible beaches, which are on the North West and South West coasts, because this could only be done after considerable time spent on combined training and preparation.'

The assumption, undoubtedly a legacy from the long period of planning and training which had preceded the Normandy assault landings, is also evidence of the extent to which the possible requirements for further amphibious operations had been ignored once the Normandy assaults were over.[3]

Montgomery had said in his directive of the 14th that airborne forces were available for the opening of the Scheldt. Now, the planners said, Headquarters First Allied Airborne Army was making a study of the assault on Walcheren and South Beveland, for which two parachute regiments (brigades) of the 17th US Airborne Division might be available, or, if the attack were not to be made until after 1 October, two brigades of the more experienced British 6th Airborne Division.

The appreciation recommended that a firm base should first be established by securing the area between Antwerp, Bergen-op-Zoom and Roosendaal, and a thrust should then be made westwards across the isthmus into South Beveland as far as the South Beveland ship canal, some ten miles from the mainland. Next a parachute brigade should drop to take the canal in rear and secure the small port of Hoedenskerke for build-up forces crossing the Scheldt. Thereafter a second parachute brigade should drop in Walcheren to secure a bridgehead across the causeway leading from South Beveland for an advance to capture the island. The planners strongly recommended the employment of airborne troops, but, if these should not be available, waterborne flanking operations should be used to assist both the capture of South Beveland and the forcing of the Walcheren causeway.

Captain A. F. Pugsley RN was at home on leave after taking part in the Normandy assault and build-up, when he was hurriedly recalled for a 'short planning job that will take you a few days only.' He would not, as it turned out, get home again until after the Rhine crossing next March. He reached Headquarters First Canadian Army at St Omer on 20 September after preliminary briefing on the way and was given the appreciation to read in draft. Next day he told Crerar's Chief of Staff, Brigadier C. C. Mann, that an amphibious assault on Walcheren was certainly a possibility and would probably be essential. Mann replied that Simonds held the same view. Pugsley immediately rang Ramsay, who had sent him to the Canadians, and began assembling a naval planning staff.[4]

On the afternoon of the 21st Simonds sent Crerar his written comments on the appreciation, injecting a new note of reality and urgency. 'As I understand it' he began;

> the object of the operation is NOT "to capture the islands of WALCHEREN and SUID BEVELAND" but "to destroy, neutralise or capture enemy defences which deny us free passage through the WEST SCHELDT to the port of ANTWERP."'

Clearing the enemy-held area between the Leopold Canal and the southern shore of the Scheldt might be a major operation. The Germans were strongly posted on the canal, along which they had already made extensive inundations.

> 'A German document in our possession makes it clear that the conditions most advantageous to the defence and most disadvantageous to us are those of "ground saturation". This denies to us the use of the ground to exactly the same extent as if it was completely flooded but allows the enemy the use of his roads, and avoids the flooding of buildings, stores and many works which must be of importance to him.'

Attack across such an area sacrificed all the normal advantages of the offensive, for, while the attackers could only move along the raised roads, which would be heavily mined and obstructed, the defenders in the dry area could concentrate their fire on the roads without exposing troops. Attack by land on South Beveland, although it appeared attractive, might turn out to be an advance down a single stretch of road, five miles long and bordered by impassable ground on either side, the equivalent of an assault landing in which it was only possible to beach one craft at a time at a point known to the enemy.

'I consider that the project of an assault across water cannot be ruled out if WALCHEREN ISLAND must be taken. It may be the only way of taking it. Though it would be a last resort and a most uninviting task, I consider it would be quite wrong to make no preparation for it, and to be faced at some later time with the necessity of having to improvise at very short notice. I am strongly of the opinion that the necessary military and naval forces should now be earmarked, married up and trained against the contingency that they may be required.'

Much of Walcheren lies below sea level, and Simonds suggested that the dykes should be broken by bombing to flood completely all parts of the island below high water level. This, he considered, would not increase the difficulties for airborne troops, who would in any case find it impossible to operate over ground flooded by the Germans to 'saturation' point, but would seriously handicap the defence. The part of the island that remained above water should be systematically bombed by day and by night to destroy the concrete defences and wear down the garrison. As soon as patrols sent across the Scheldt found the enemy ripe for surrender, airborne and waterborne troops should be landed immediately after a bombing raid had driven the defenders to ground. Meanwhile the 2nd Canadian Infantry Division should push northwards from Antwerp to cut off South Beveland and test the possibilities of the land approach to Walcheren. The 3rd Canadian Infantry Division, as soon as it could be released from the attack on Boulogne and Calais, should relieve the 4th Canadian Armoured Division on the Leopold Canal with two of its brigades, while the third started to train with the navy for seaborne operations against Walcheren.[5]
Earlier that afternoon at a meeting with Crerar at St Omer also attended by Major General Sir Francis de Guingand, Montgomery's Chief of Staff, Ramsay had confirmed that there would be no obstacle to mounting an amphibious assault on Walcheren, subject to a detailed examination of the feasibility of such an operation, and on the 23rd Crerar outlined the plan for opening the Scheldt to a full conference of his senior staff together with representatives of 21 Army Group, First Allied Airborne Army, 2 Canadian Corps, the Royal Navy and the RAF. He told them that Eisenhower had decided against the employment of airborne troops, although there was a possibility that he might change his mind. Meanwhile operations should go forward to clear the south bank of the Scheldt and to secure the Roosendaal-Bergen-op-Zoom area as a preliminary to an advance westwards into South Beveland. Attack across the Scheldt might be needed to secure Hoedenskirke and possibly a minor amphibious operation against the southwest coast of Walcheren.[6]

On 11 September Lieutenant General Lewis Brereton, the American airman commanding the First Allied Airborne Army, had noted in his diary that the stage was set to deal the Germans a knock-out blow and that his airborne forces were available for a bold stroke in the enemy's rear. Of ten operations projected:

'I refused Operation Infatuate [Walcheren] because of intense flak on Walcheren, difficult terrain which would prevent glider landings, excessive losses likely because of drowning, non-availability of US troops, and the fact that the operation is an improper use of airborne forces.'[7]

Brereton's final objection came perhaps from his vision of an airborne knock-out blow. Although he had written 'Our big problem is supply', Walcheren may have seemed a side-show, not the massed descent on the enemy rear that he and others envisaged as the true role of the airborne army. But the tactical objections were genuine enough. The three airborne divisions landed in the Normandy assault had all suffered losses from flak and by drowning in the flooded rivers and marshes that flanked the beachhead. Sticks of parachutists had often been dropped and gliders landed miles from their intended dropping and landing zones. The well-defined coastline of Walcheren would have made pathfinding easier there, but, especially after the Normandy experience, the prospect for airborne assault of intense anti-aircraft fire and watery terrain was not one to be lightly faced.

Eisenhower, warning Montgomery on 12 September of Brereton's unwillingness to provide airborne troops, said he thought the difficulties might be overcome. 'I consider that the use of Antwerp is so important that I am prepared to go a long way to make the attack a success', he had written, and Montgomery in turn had told Crerar that airborne troops would be available.[8]

On the 17th Brereton's representative, visiting St Omer, heard that the projected attack on Walcheren was not intended as an exclusively airborne operation. On this he held out hopes that the two parachute brigades required might be provided. But Brereton was not to be persuaded. On the 21st, after Montgomery had made an urgent request to Eisenhower for a definite statement on the subject, Eisenhower called Brereton to his head-quarters. Brereton continued in his objections and was backed by Air Chief Marshal Sir Trafford Leigh-Mallory, commanding the Allied Expeditionary Air Force. Eisenhower signalled to Montgomery that airborne forces would not be available and, perhaps seeking subconsciously to clear himself on any charge of lacking ruthlessness, added that the question of losses did not arise. He would, he said, have been willing to accept heavy losses if he thought that doing so would have contributed to the rapid conclusion of these vital operations. Instead a priority demand would be made on Bomber Command and the Eighth US Air Force for complete saturation bombing of targets selected by Montgomery. De Guingand raised the question again next day, and Eisenhower directed the airborne army to re-examine the problem, but nothing came of it.[9]

There the matter rested until on 21 October, with the 2nd Canadian Infantry Division involved in a bitter struggle at the eastern end of the isthmus, the First Canadian Army made a last appeal for a parachute brigade to be dropped in South Beveland. The airborne army refused to consider it. Since 15 October, Brereton's staff replied, the airborne army had been withdrawn from support of the northern group and it now planned to use all available airborne troops in support of the central group.[10]

Simonds was more successful in his request for air bombing to break the dykes. At least two objections were at once made to the proposal, technical and ethical. On 24 September the Chief Engineer, First Canadian Army, submitted a memorandum which concluded that it was not possible to flood the island by bombing the Westkapelle dyke. The dyke was one of the oldest and solidest in Holland, 200 to 250 feet wide with a very flat profile. It was improbable that even the most accurate bombing would produce a clear channel. If it did, there would be insufficient depth of water over the flooded parts of the island for assault landing craft to operate, while amphibians would not be able to get through the gap. Few technical forecasts can have been more quickly and completely proved wrong.[11]

The ethical objection was more cogent. Some of the bombs intended for the dyke would inevitably fall on the village of Westkapelle, and if the dyke were broken, the village would probably be overwhelmed by the rush of incoming water. Casualties and damage to friendly towns and villages in enemy occupation were unhappily far from unprecedented. But at Walcheren, it was feared, perhaps not quite logically in view of the depth of water argument, that the spreading floods would drown large numbers throughout the island, while the salt water would undoubtedly poison the fields for future crops. The traditional disaster of the Dutch lowlands, indeed, seemed about to be brought down on the inhabitants of the island. In retrospect it is perhaps possible to discount the more extreme of the fears. Historically defence by inundation is as old as the dykes themselves, and the Germans would have no hesitation in opening dykes as it suited the defence. But it would be as wrong to suggest that the decision to break the dykes should have been taken lightly as it would be untrue to imply that it was.

Simonds expected to gain several advantages from flooding the island. The floods would compel the Germans to concentrate their forces, making it easier to attack them. They would impose serious difficulties in supply to the naval and anti-aircraft batteries disposed about the island, and German reserves would be immobilised. Finally, despite the Chief Engineer's conclusion, he hoped that amphibians might be able to enter the flooded area and give to the attackers the mobility denied to the defenders. As acting army commander he therefore asked Bomber Command that the plan to break the dykes should be put to the test.[12] Pugsley, believing it impossible to beach landing craft on the Westkapelle dyke, was relieved to learn that it was to be destroyed.[13]

Bomber Command agreed to make the attempt, and on 1 October Eisenhower, apparently without consulting the Dutch government in exile, approved. Warning leaflets were dropped on the 2nd, and on the afternoon of the 3rd 259 Lancasters and Mosquitoes dropped 1,270 tons of bombs aimed at the Westkapelle dyke. Despite the care and overall accuracy of their aim, some bombs fell in the village which was laid in ruins as well as being partly flooded, but the dyke was quickly broken. Even as the bombing went on, reconnaissance aircraft reported that water was flowing through a gap 100 yards wide, and twelve Lancasters carrying 12,000 lb Tallboy bombs were in consequence ordered to return without dropping them. Air photographs that evening showed the sea flowing through a 75-yard gap, which under the action of the tide filling and emptying the flooded area inland later became a mill-stream. Subsequent photographs showed an emergency dam being built to contain the floods. On the 7th the bombers returned and broke the dyke on both sides of Flushing, and on the 11th again a mile north of Veere, and the task of containing the floods became impossible.[14]

The first bombs had already been dropped on Walcheren when on 22 September Eisenhower made his promise to Montgomery of saturation bombing. On 17 September 96 aircraft of Bomber Command attacked batteries near Flushing, Biggeskerke and Westkapelle. On the 23rd 49 aircraft attacked the coastal battery at Domburg, bringing the total weight of bombs dropped on the island to that date to 616 tons. Between 1 and 23 October Bomber Command and the 2nd Tactical Air Force despite bad weather made rocket attacks and between them dropped a further 1,600 tons of bombs mainly on radar stations, ammunition stores and batteries near Flushing which were firing across the Scheldt, losing seven aircraft in doing so. Little if any damage was done to the main coast defence batteries, but the bombing during September had some effect on the Fifteenth Army escaping through Flushing.

On 28 September Leigh-Mallory protested to Montgomery against the diversion of bomber effort to Walcheren from the German forces opposing the advance to the Ruhr and from the strategic air offensive against Germany. Montgomery, despite his letter of the 12th to Crerar, replied the same day outlining a programme for Walcheren: early flooding of the island, continued sporadic harassment, 'Then 3 or 4 days before D-Day we should fairly let them have everything we have got.'[15]

So much had hung on the success of the Normandy assault that the British and American governments had felt it impossible to refuse Eisenhower's request that the strategic air forces as well as the tactical should be placed under his command. But there was a distinction. Under Eisenhower, Leigh-Mallory commanded the tactical air forces — the British Tactical Air Force and the Ninth US Air Force: but Eisenhower retained command of the strategic air forces — Bomber Command and the Eighth US Air Force — delegating control of both tactical and strategical air forces to his deputy, Air Chief Marshall Sir Arthur Tedder. This worked well, but the strategic air offensive had suffered during the preparations for the landings and the battle in Normandy.

By September the fate of the invasion no longer hung in the balance, and the claims of the strategic offensive were in consequence more difficult to resist. On the 13th it was decided at the Quebec Conference that command of the strategic air offensive should revert to the Combined Chiefs of Staff Committee exercised through its air members, who in turn delegated the task to Air Marshal Sir Norman Bottomley, Deputy Chief of Air Staff, and General Carl Spaatz, Commander US Air Forces in Europe. Eisenhower's requirements were still to receive priority over others.[16]

This left Tedder and Leigh-Mallory doing the same job, so Leigh-Mallory was removed, closing his headquarters on 15 October. Tedder fully endorsed Eisenhower's insistence on opening the Scheldt, but felt even more strongly than Leigh-Mallory that Bomber Command was being mis-employed in support of the army. Asking for a paper on the subject, Air Chief Marshal Sir Charles Portal, Chief of Air Staff, wrote to him 'I believe that the constant application of the heavy bombers to the land battle, when it is not essential and its only purpose is to save casualties, must inevitably lead to demoralisation of the army.' In reply Tedder wrote:

'We are now, I am afraid, beginning to see the results in precisely that demoralisation of which you speak. The repeated calls by the Canadian Army for heavy bomber effort to deal with a part-worn battery on Walcheren, and the evacuation of Breskens because of intermittent harassing fire from this battery, is in my opinion only too clear an example. It is going to be extremely difficult to get things back on a proper footing.'[17]

It would be hard to deny that there was something in this criticism, ill-informed and unfeeling though this expression of it was. Compared to its casualties over Germany, Bomber Command lost few aircrews in support of the army, but the bombing was sometimes counter-effective, producing obstacles to the attacker without silencing the machine and anti-tank guns which held up the assault. In Eisenhower's opinion, the new command system was 'a clumsy and inefficient arrangement, but so far as our operation was concerned made no difference.' It was however, Leigh-Mallory who had agreed with Montgomery the bombing programme for Walcheren.

On 24 October Tedder forbade further bombing of the dykes, which had by then became unnecessary, and ordered the First Canadian Army and 2nd Tactical Air Force, which in turn delegated the task to 84 Group, to prepare a joint air plan for the assault, calling on Bomber Command as needed.[18] 'Experience in Normandy and at the Channel Ports suggests that if it had been possible to deal direct with Air Chief Marshal Harris,' writes the Canadian official historian, 'the bomber effort at Walcheren might have been heavier and lives might have been saved.'

On 24 September Ramsay appointed Pugsley naval commander for the amphibious attack on Walcheren and authorised him to draw on what was left of Force J, the British naval assault force which had landed the 3rd Canadian Infantry Division and subsequent troops on Juno Beach in Normandy, now lying at Southampton, for landing craft to form a new force for Walcheren, Naval Force T. For bombardment in support of the assault he would have the *Warspite* and the monitors *Erebus* and *Roberts* and, for close support, he now asked for the Support Squadron Eastern Flank.

A destroyer captain with a long fighting record, Pugsley had in the Normandy landings commanded one of the naval assault groups in Force J and had had his headquarters ship sunk under him. Returning to the Normandy coast in another headquarters ship, he had become Senior Naval Officer Afloat in the British sector, responsible for the defence of the anchorage against the almost nightly attack from Le Havre by E-boats, midget submarines, human torpedoes and explosive motor boats. In addition to the destroyers, minesweepers, motor gun- and torpedo-boats of his command, a group of some seventy support and flak landing craft — most of them adaptions of Landing Craft Tank hulls with 4.7-inch guns, rockets or Oerlikons added — had co-operated in the protection of the anchorage. Under Commander K. A. Sellar, formerly well-known as a Rugby international, these had formed each night the Trout Line running seawards from the coast well within range of the German coast defence guns east of the beachhead. Anchored a few hundred yards apart, these craft were the first line of detection and defence against intruders and saw much action. Most of them had now to be rejected as unserviceable, leaving twenty-three which could be ready in time for the attack on Walcheren* to which would be added two Landing Craft Gun (Medium), a new experimental type which had not yet been in action, two landing craft headquarters and a motor launch.[19]

The landing craft Pugsley took from Force J were mostly Landing Craft Assault for Flushing and Landing Craft Tank for Westkapelle with a number of other types for special tasks. With the mouth of the Scheldt closed by German batteries, there could be no question of getting major landing craft such as the LCT to Terneuzen; and to get minor landing such as the LCA there was a complicated process requiring the co-operation of a number of naval and army authorities. From Portsmouth the LCA were shipped by Landing Ship Dock to Ostend. At Ostend they were loaded on two trains and taken by rail to Ghent. There they were off-loaded into the canal by crane and proceeded under their own power to Terneuzen. At Terneuzen a dam was built by means of which they were locked out into the Scheldt. By this route a small number of LCA were made available for the

---

*The Support Squadron Eastern Flank had been formed from surviving support craft from all three British assault forces and had remained under direct command Flag Officer British Assault Area, although co-operating closely with Pugsley, the Senior Naval Officer Afloat. The detailed composition of the Support Squadron at Walcheren was as follows:

Landing Craft Headquarters (LCH)	2
Landing Craft Gun (Large) (LCG(L))	6
Landing Craft Gun (Medium) (LCG(M))	2 *
Landing Craft Flak (LCF)	6
Landing Craft Tank (Rocket) (LCT(R))	5
Landing Craft Support (Large) (LCS(L))	6
Motor Launch (ML)	1 *

Landing and support craft are described in Appendix II.   * Not from original SSEF.

9th Canadian Infantry Brigade's operation of 9 October and two flotillas for the 156th Infantry Brigade's of the 26th.[20]*

The alternative to LCAs for operations in the Scheldt were the tracked amphibians usually known in Europe as Buffaloes, but more correctly called Landing Vehicles Tracked (LVT). They were of two types: Mark 2 without a ramp, carrying 24 passengers, and Mark 4 with a stern ramp and able to carry a jeep, bren carrier, 25-pounder field gun or similar loads. Developed by the US Navy and US Marine Corps primarily for beach maintenance, they had in November 1943 been used to solve the problem of assault across the coral reefs of Tarawa and Makin.[21] Their success there led to a great demand for them in the Pacific, and they did not reach Europe in quantity until too late for the Normandy assaults. In August the 5th Assault Regiment, Royal Engineers, previously equipped with AVREs was re-equipped with Buffaloes and trained with them in the Orne Canal. They reached Ghent on 7 October and on the night of the 8/9th landed the 9th Canadian Infantry Brigade from the Scheldt beyond the Leopold Canal. Commander R. D. Franks RN who first saw them at Ghent writes 'They were very well trained and raring to go.'

The 79th Armoured Division, which had been responsible for the specialised armour in the Normandy assaults, provided a number of other units for the Scheldt operations, which it will be convenient to describe here. Two other units operated Buffaloes: the 6th ARRE and the 11th Royal Tanks, the latter after a very quick conversion from Shermans. The 6th ARRE also provided a squadron of Terrapins, the not very successful British version of the DUKW. The Staffordshire Yeomanry, converted after Normandy to swimming DD Shermans, provided a squadron to cross the Scheldt with the 156th Infantry Brigade. The 1st Lothians and Border Yeomanry, the 6th ARRE and the 149th Assault Park Squadron RE provided specialised armour for Westkapelle. The 141st Regiment Royal Armoured Corps (The Buffs) provided Crocodiles, Churchill tanks converted to flame-throwers, in support of the 3rd Canadian Infantry Division in the Breskens Pocket.[22] Major General Sir Percy Hobart, the divisional commander, took an enthusiastic interest in providing his specially equipped units when and where wanted. Brigadier C. N. Barclay, whose 156th Infantry Brigade was committed at very short notice to the Scheldt crossing, says of Hobart who arranged the details of the embarkation of the 156th Brigade which Barclay himself, then being briefed for the operation, had no time to do, 'Hobo was a tower of strength all the time.'

Simonds had suggested that one brigade of the 3rd Canadian Infantry Division should start training with the navy in case assault from the sea

*The Landing Craft from Naval Force J took part in either the assault on Flushing or that at Westkapelle:

Landing Craft Tank (LCT)	36	Landing Craft Infantry (Small) (LCI(S))	10
Landing Craft Assault (LCA)	72	Landing Craft Personnel (Large) (LCP(L))	12

and a number of auxiliary craft including Landing Craft Personnel (Survey) (LCP(Sy)) became necessary. At the conference on 21 September, however, Ramsay said that he could see no objection to the use of the 4th Special Service Brigade for the attack on Walcheren, and Crerar adopted his suggestion.

The 1st and 4th Special Service Brigades had both taken part in the Normandy assault and had then served under command of the 6th Airborne Division in defence of the eastern flank of the beachhead. On reaching the Seine in August, the 6th Airborne Division and the 1st Special Service Brigade had been recalled to the United Kingdom, but the 4th Special Service Brigade had remained in the Canadian army and had taken over the Dunkirk position from the 5th Canadian Infantry Brigade. On 26 September it was ordered to hand over at Dunkirk to units detailed from the 51st (Highland) Division and move on eastwards to the coast beyond Ostend to prepare for an amphibious assault on Walcheren. Shortly afterwards 4 Commando joined it from England in exchange for 46 (Royal Marine) Commando which left to join the 1st Special Service Brigade. A little later 10 (Inter-Allied) Commando and a small reconnaissance party from the Commando Mountain Warfare Training Unit at St Ives, Cornwall, were attached to the 4th Special Service Brigade for the Walcheren attack.

4 Commando, raised by Lord Lovat in 1940, had distinguished itself in the Dieppe raid, capturing a flanking coast defence battery in exemplary fashion. For Normandy it had been made up to strength by the inclusion of the two French troops from 10 (IA) Commando, and these troops thereafter became to all intents an integral part of 4 Commando. 10 (IA) Commando was formed at the end of 1942 with French, Belgian, Dutch and Norwegian troops and as well a troop of German speakers, Austrians or Germans who had escaped from the Nazis. For Walcheren, its Dutch and German speaking troops were distributed to the four other commandos as fighting interpreters; the Belgian and Norwegian troops under the commanding officer of 10 (IA) Commando, Lieutenant Colonel D. S. Lister, formed as small additional unit within the brigade.[23] Keepforce, the reconnaissance party, comprised seven officers and 19 other ranks trained to land on a hostile coast from the 18-foot dories and rubber dinghies they brought with them. They were primarily intended for the reconnaissance of the Westkapelle dyke.

The commandos, which had remained much below strength since the June assaults, now received their first large drafts, bringing them up to rather less than full strength, and, after a week or two general training to absorb the newcomers, started on special training, using the abandoned defences along the Belgian coast to work out means of dealing with the defences of Walcheren. Except for discussions with the landing craft officers who would be taking them to Walcheren or supporting them on the way, they were to have no opportunity for amphibious training or rehearsals, but there can be no doubt that they greatly benefitted from what was to turn out to be five weeks of rest, reinforcement and retraining before the attack on Walcheren. The Canadian infantry, which after 6 June had been more heavily engaged than the commandos and was also below strength at this time, had no such respite. But owing to the availability of the commandos for Walcheren the 3rd Canadian Infantry Division was now able to go on to its demanding task south of the Scheldt as a full division of three brigades.

Very unwisely the commandos had been told before the Normany landings that as specialised troops they would be withdrawn after the successful assault of the beaches. It would be wrong to say that morale had been affected when they found themselves instead retained to hold the line, but there had been some grumbling. It is a mistake to imagine that specialised infantry can be worth their keep if they are not available to fight in a general purpose role. Yet it could also be said that a mistake had been made by the higher command which, knowing the need that would arise to open ports in Holland to support the advance into Germany, made no provision to retain, or to reassemble at short notice, a joint force capable of assault from the sea.

References
1   Stacy *op cit*, pp.336, 358-9.
2   *ibid*, p.360.
3   War Diary Plans Section Headquarters First Canadian Army, September 1944, Appendix 17, quoted in part Stacey *op cit*, pp.369-370.
4   Rear Admiral A. F. Pugsley, *Destroyer Man*, Weidenfeldt & Nicolson, 1957, pp.175-9 and correspondence.
5   Lieutenant General Simonds, GOC 8 of 21 September 1944 to GOC-in-C First Canadian Army quoted in part in Stacey *op cit*, pp.370-2.
6   Headquarters First Canadian Army Notes on Conference 1400 hours 21 September 1944; Stacey *op cit*, p.373.
7   Lieutenant General Lewis H. Brereton, *The Brereton Diaries*, William Morrow, New York, 1946, p.340.
8   Ellis *op cit*, p.23.
9   Stacey *op cit*, p.373-4, Eisenhower makes no reference in *Crusade in Europe*.
10 Stacey *op cit*, p.374.
11 *ibid*, p.375.
12 *ibid*, p.375.
13 Pugsley, *op cit*, p.179 and correspondence.
14 Ellis, *op cit*, p.115; Stacey, *op cit*, p.376.
15 Stacy, *op cit*, pp.374-8. Staccy (p.378) quotes Air Commodore T. N. McEvoy, SASO 84 Group, visiting Headquarters 2 Canadian Corps: 'AEAF have specified that heavy bomber support should be provided only when ground troops are going to assault the bombed position immediately afterwards.'
16 Tedder, *op cit*, p.603-4.
17 *ibid*, pp.605-6.
18 Eisenhower, *op cit*, p.337; Stacey, *op cit*, p.409.
19 Pugsley, *op cit*, p.168 et seq; discussion with Commander K. A. Sellar.
20 Captain R. D. Franks RN, papers and correspondence.
21 J. A. Iseley & P. A. Crowl, *The US Marines and Amphibious Warfare*, Princeton University Press, 1951, pp.208-212, 227-8.
22 Anon, *The Story of the 79th Armoured Division: October 1942-June 1945*, privately printed in Germany, 1945.
23 Hilary St George Saunders, *The Green Beret*, Michael Joseph, 1949, pp.217-222.

7

Antwerp while we are Going for the Ruhr

Handing over the watch on Dunkirk to the 4th Special Service Brigade, the 2nd Canadian Infantry Division reached Antwerp between 16 and 19 September and took over from the 53rd (Welsh) Division. To the Canadians the city seemed a strange contrast to the Normandy battlefields they had recently left.

> Ordinary urban life went on in Antwerp much as in peacetime. The trams continued to run; night clubs remained open; and the shops sold a reasonable assortment of goods. Two bands played each night at the Century Hotel — 'J'attendrai' and 'La Vie en Rose' were probably the most popular numbers — and the Belgian girls in their elegant evening dresses were certainly (or did it, after all, only seem so?) the most beautiful in the world.' [1]

In the docks and along the Albert Canal Resistance groups were nightly grappling with the enemy, but under enemy occupation there had been no obligation to contribute more to the war effort than the Germans could extract, the reverse in fact, and, with the Germans gone, life took on an aspect noticeably less austere than that of wartime Britain.

The 4th Canadian Infantry Brigade, taking over in the city and in the docks, found people in the city still going about their business, at one place alighting from the tram to cross the canal on foot and pick up another on the German side. In the docks things were tougher. The low lying ground was under close observation from the buildings of Merxem and any movement or failure of camouflage attracted shell and mortar fire, and Colson's patrols, pushing steadily forward into Merxem, Oorderen, Wilmarsdonck and towards 12-Sluiskens, frequently clashed with the Germans. On the night of the 20th, a strong German fighting patrol from Merxem, covered by intensive shell and mortar fire, crossed the railway embankment and attacked a company position of the Essex Scottish Regiment on the Groenendaallaan. After a sharp action lasting two hours it was driven off. Meanwhile the Royal Hamilton Light Infantry, holding the northern side of the docks, after a number of patrol encounters in and around Oorderen and Wilmarsdonck, moved its line forward on the 22nd to include the two villages.

On the front of the 5th Canadian Infantry Brigade to the east of Merxem, a strong patrol of the Black Watch of Canada tried on the 20th to establish a lodgement across the canal but failed. The following night the Calgary Highlanders managed to secure a footing across the canal a mile or two beyond Antwerp, beating off counter-attacks of the 743rd Grenadier Regiment of the 719th Division. Crossing the canal, Le Regiment de Maisonneuve drove the Germans back to the Turnhout Canal, which east of the city branches off the Albert Canal to the northeast.

Following up the 5th Brigade's success, the 6th Canadian Infantry Brigade was now directed to secure a bridgehead across the Turnhout Canal, held here by the 346th Division, at Lochtenberg with the intention of reaching Brasschaet on the Breda road. Two battalions attacked in assault boats at 7am on the 24th. On the right Les Fusiliers Mont-Royal got across without difficulty, but on the left the South Saskatchewan Regiment, meeting heavy machine-gun fire from Lochtenberg, did not get across until 1 o'clock. The Fusiliers were held up 300 yards beyond the canal and the crossing remained under fire, so that a bridge could not be built. During the afternoon seven or eight German half-tracks, thought at first to be tanks, overran many of the Fusiliers' positions, while two others got into the small bridgehead gained by the Saskatchewans. Realising that the attempt had failed, the divisional commander authorised withdrawal. The operation cost the Canadians 113 casualties, most among the Fusiliers, and Pilaet's Resistance group, which had crossed in their support, 27. The brigade tried again on the 28th, but despite effective support by rocket-firing Typhoons and Spitfires, this attempt, in which the brigade had been ordered not to incur heavy losses, also failed. [2]

Meanwhile, 1 Corps with the 49th (West Riding) Division had come up from Le Havre to the Albert Canal near Herenthals. Finding that the Germans were withdrawing, the division followed them up to the Turnhout Canal and occupied Turnhout. On the night of the 24th, in pouring rain, the 4th Lincolns of the 146th Infantry Brigade surprised a crossing north of Oostmalle, and by the 29th, despite heavy counter-attacks, again by the 719th Division, all three brigades were across, holding a bridgehead at Rijkesvorsel, a mile deep and two miles wide. [7]

On the 26th 1 Corps temporarily took over the 2nd Canadian Infantry Division from 2 Canadian Corps, and the 5th Canadian Infantry Brigade, crossing the canal immediately west of the bridgehead with help from the 49th Division, began to fight its way back towards the roads leading north from Antwerp, but Brecht, two miles from the bridgehead, did not fall until 1 October. Meanwhile the 1st Polish Armoured Division, having joined 1 Corps in the area southeast of Antwerp, was ordered to break out of the bridgehead for the Wilhelmina Canal, 20 miles to the northeast. It met heavy resistance and by the 30th had got no further than Merksplas, four miles beyond the Turnhout Canal.

General Crerar, suffering from dysentery which was found to require further diagnosis and treatment in England, temporarily gave up command of the First Canadian Army on 26 September. On his recommendation and with Montgomery's approval, Simonds took over from him and was thus to become responsible for the successful conclusion of the battle just beginning for the opening of the Scheldt. Major General C. Foulkes moved up from the 2nd Canadian Infantry Division to command 2 Canadian Corps, and Brigadier R. H. Keefler from Commander Royal Canadian Artillery of the division to its command.

Meanwhile the Second British Army had fought the battle of Arnhem. Although it had failed to win a bridgehead across the Rhine, it had won a salient which now stuck out slightly east of north like a thumb, fifty miles long and fifteen across, its base at Eindhoven and its tip across the Waal at Nijmegen. This salient, now threatened with German counter-attack, Montgomery hoped to use for a drive southeastwards to the Ruhr. He issued his directive for it on 27 September.[4]

The Second British Army, while holding the salient firmly, was 'to operate strongly with all available strength' from Nijmegen and Gennap, the upper phalanx of the thumb, southeastwards towards the Ruhr and Krefeld. The opening of Antwerp, fifty miles westwards from Eindhoven, was, Montgomery said, 'absolutely essential before we can advance deep into Germany,' but it was still only one of the tasks which he set the First Canadian Army. These his directive listed as: to complete the capture of Boulogne and Calais, to develop operations to open Antwerp, and to thrust strongly northwards to 's-Hertogenbosch to free the Second British Army from the defence of its long flank facing west. The early opening of Antwerp was vital, the directive said, but it was important for the right wing of the Canadian army to reach 's-Hertogenbosch as soon as possible. This meant that the bulk of 1 Corps, which Crerar had intended should strike northwest for Bergen-op-Zoom and Roosendaal to seal off the South Beveland isthmus, must instead strike northeast, along the back of the thumb. For the 'vital' task of opening Antwerp, Simonds would still have only the 2nd Canadian Infantry Division, north of Antwerp, and the 4th Canadian Armoured Division, on the Leopold Canal, to which would be added after Calais fell on 30 September the 3rd Canadian Infantry Division. For the second time, Montgomery had issued a contradictory directive. In saying Antwerp was vital, he had in reality given it a low priority in his plan of attack.[5]

By now von Zangen's Fifteenth Army was responsible for the canal line from Antwerp to Nijmegen. The 49th Division, after its successful surprise of the Rijkesvorsel bridgehead, had had to fight hard to hold and extend it. In this fighting Corporal Harper of the Hallamshire Regiment in the 146th Infantry Brigade won a posthumous Victoria Cross, leading an assault on a strongly defended position in the dykes near Merksplas and playing an important part in its defence until he was killed. Passing through the 49th Division a few days earlier, the 1st Polish Armoured Division found Merksplas and the farms around it strongly held, heavily mined and booby-trapped, but finally cleared the area on 2 October. Thrusting down the line

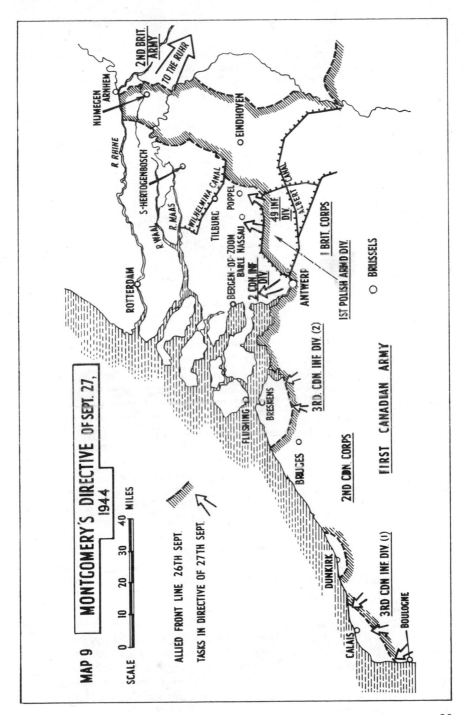

MAP 9 MONTGOMERY'S DIRECTIVE OF SEPT. 27, 1944

SCALE

MILES
0 10 20 30 40

ALLIED FRONT LINE 26TH SEPT.

TASKS IN DIRECTIVE OF 27TH SEPT.

2ND BRIT. ARMY

TO THE RUHR

ARNHEM
NIJMEGEN

R RHINE

S-HERTOGENBOSCH

R. WAAL

R. MAAS

WILHELMINA CANAL

TILBURG

EINDHOVEN

POPPEL

49 INF DIV

ALBERT CANAL

I BRIT. CORPS

BERGEN-OF-ZOOM

BAARLE NASSAU

2 CDN INF DIV

ANTWERP

IST POLISH ARM'D DIV.

BRUSSELS

ROTTERDAM

3RD. CDN. INF DIV (2)

FLUSHING

BRESKENS

2ND CDN. CORPS

BRUGES

FIRST CANADIAN ARMY

DUNKIRK

3RD CDN INF DIV (I)

CALAIS

BOULOGNE

of the railway towards Tilburg, the Polish armour reached Barle-Nassau on the 3rd and Alphon, six miles short of Tilburg, on the 5th.

On either side of the Poles the 49th Division with the 27th Canadian Armoured Regiment in support covered the twenty-mile gap opening between the Second British Army and the 2nd Canadian Infantry Division. Advancing along the road from Turnhout towards Tilburg, the 146th Infantry Brigade and the Canadian armour took Poppel against light opposition on the 4th and on the 5th got within two and a half miles of Tilburg. The 147th Infantry Brigade supported the Poles in the centre, and a mixed force based on the 49th Division's reconnaissance and anti-tank regiments linked up with the Canadians at Brecht on the left. But the Germans, who had counter-attacked the Poles on the 4th, counter-attacked much more strongly on the 6th both at Alphen and on the Tilburg road. The Poles and the 49th held their ground, but the Poles lost heavily both in men and tanks. There was then a check, and for the next ten days both divisions remained stationary as 1 Corps regrouped in accordance with a further directive issued by Montgomery on the 4th.[6]

With effect from the 7th, 1 Corps was now to take over from 12 Corps additional frontage stretching northeastwards to the Maas, so that it became responsible for most of the west face of the salient, receiving for this extra responsibility the 51st (Highland) Division from Le Havre and the 7th Armoured Division from 12 Corps, while the 2nd Canadian Division reverted to 2 Canadian Corps.[7] The effect of this was, certainly, to increase the total strength of the First Canadian Army, but it also increased its frontage and its effort continued to be split along two divergent axes: 1 Corps on its right advancing on 's-Hertogenbosch protecting the rear of the Second British Army; 2 Canadian Corps on the left struggling to open the Scheldt.

Early in September Lieutenant General Kurt Chill, an outstandingly able and determined soldier, had taken command of a miscellaneous collection of troops in full retreat and, as the British reached Brussels and Antwerp, had on his own initiative deployed them on the line of the Albert Canal. Battle Group Chill, also known as the 85th Division, now comprised the remnants of the 84th, 85th and 89th Divisions, part of the Hermann Goering Training Regiment and the crack 6th Parachute Regiment. Under 88 Corps it was ordered to the Tilburg area to mount a counter-attack on the Nijmegen salient, then switched to 67 Corps and used to reinforce the 719th Division's counter-attack on the Poles and the 49th Division south of Tilburg. From that it was ordered away to deal with the Canadian threat to the South Beveland isthmus.[8]

On 2 October the 2nd Canadian Infantry Division began its advance for the South Beveland isthmus. The 6th Canadian Infantry Brigade, passing through the 5th's extension of the 49th Division's bridgehead across the Turnhout Canal, took Lochtenburg that day, Camp de Brasschaet the next, and on the 4th one of its battalions, Les Fusiliers Mont-Royal, took Capellen. Advancing from the Antwerp docks, the 4th Brigade, having with

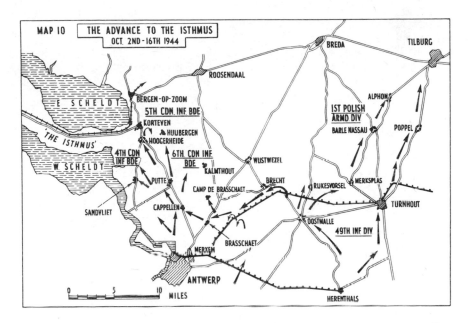

MAP 10 THE ADVANCE TO THE ISTHMUS
OCT. 2ND - 16TH 1944

the Resistance cleared Merxem on the 2nd and 3rd, gained six miles towards the Dutch frontier on the 4th, crossed it and took Putte on the 5th and Ossendrecht and Sandvliet on the 6th. That night, as the 2nd Canadian Infantry Division reverted to 2 Canadian Corps, the isthmus, some three miles away to the west of Woensdrecht, seemed within easy reach.[9]

Woensdrecht, between a spur of rising ground and the flooded polder, and Hoogerheide, three quarters of a mile to its east on sandy heathland, were the turning points around the floods for the isthmus. A village road through Woensdrecht connected with the railway station of that name, three-quarters of a mile to the north on the isthmus line, while the main isthmus road branched off a mile north of Woensdrecht and Hoogerheide at Korteven. The 2nd Division now planned to pass the 5th Brigade through the 4th at Ossendrecht and down the road to Korteven, while the 6th Brigade covered the lengthening open right flank of the division. On 7 October the Calgary Highlanders of the 5th Brigade got into Hoogerheide after a stiff fight, but Le Regiment de Maisonneuve on its right was held up short of Huijbergen, three and a half miles further east, and the 6th Brigade made little progress.

At five o'clock next morning, however, Les Fusiliers Mont-Royal surprised the Germans holding the village of Kalmthout, well out on the right flank, and in heavy fighting secured the village and crossroads. That evening they were joined by a Resistance company of 350 men under Pilaet. Isolated as the German counter-attacks developed in the days that followed, the French Canadians and the Resistance, with a language in common, fought as one unit. 'Use him as you would a Canadian officer; he knows his stuff', wrote Major J. A. Dextrase, commanding the Fusiliers, in a handover note of 20

85

October 1944, and in 1976, as a general, he adds, 'Had it not been for Pilaet and his men, I doubt very much that I would be sitting here writing to you.' Two other Resistance companies, one of them under Colson, were also deployed on the long, exposed flank of the division, helping to ease the shortage of infantry.

On the morning of the 8th the Black Watch of Canada passed through the Calgaries in an attempt to take Korteven, but after violent fighting in and around Hoogerheide were pushed back to their start line. That evening air reconnaissance reported a large German force massing in the woods between Korteven and Bergen-op-Zoom, which Dutch civilians confirmed. Battle Group Chill had arrived from Tilburg, and the Black Watch had already met part of it in the attack on Korteven. The 5th Brigade called down air strike on the woods and went over to defence expecting counter-attack.

The first came in that night, and they continued all through the 9th, mainly against the Calgaries in Hoogerheide. Prisoners taken turned out to be young parachutists. Except for local withdrawals, the Canadians held their ground, but Battle Group Chill had for the moment halted the 5th Brigade's advance towards Korteven and Bergen-op-Zoom.[10]

Meanwhile on the 8th the Royal Regiment of Canada, guided by the Resistance, had found a way by a side road across the floods westwards from Ossendrecht towards the isthmus.

For some 800 yards on both sides of the straight road the polders were flooded to a depth of about eight feet, with only the road and a few feet of verges above water. The whole area was overlooked by the Woensdrecht feature, which was held in strength by the enemy, but the riflemen got over the ground quickly.[11]

D Company, the first to cross, surprised a German outpost on dry ground beyond the floods, then pushed on in a series of platoon attacks with strong artillery and mortar support nearly to the sea dyke. A Company followed across the floods, and together the two companies secured an extensive bridgehead in dry polders south of the isthmus. Next day D Company took the sluice gates on the sea dyke. On the 10th the remainder of the battalion crossed and turned north for the isthmus. By 5pm B and C Companies were on their objectives covering by fire the isthmus road and railway.

So far casualties had been light, but when on the afternoon of the 11th B and C Companies attacked again to reach the road and railway, they lost heavily, and later under counter-attack from the mainland and from South Beveland, were forced to withdraw to their earlier positions. Nor were other units of the 4th Brigade, attacking that day from Hoogerheide, able to make progress, and for the next two days they were heavily counter-attacked.

By now units of the 4th Canadian Armoured Division were beginning to reach Antwerp as the 3rd Canadian Infantry Division took over on the Leopold Canal. On the 9th the 29th Armoured Reconnaissance Regiment and a company of the Algonquin Regiment had taken over from the 6th Brigade the task of guarding the 2nd Division's exposed eastern flank. On the 10th the 4th Brigade with the South Saskatchewan Regiment of the 6th under command had relieved the 5th in Hoogerheide and in the heathland to its east, so that the latter could make a concentrated attack to close the isthmus.

On the 13th the Black Watch of Canada of the 5th Brigade, passing through the Royal Regiment of Canada in an attempt to reach the road and railway, found the Germans well dug in and strongly supported by mortars. Despite fighter air strikes, strong artillery support and, in the afternoon, tanks and flame-throwers, they could make no progress. By one o'clock next morning, when the brigadier called off the attack, the Black Watch in a long day of heavy fighting had lost 56 killed, 62 wounded and 27 taken prisoner.

On the 14th the Calgary Highlanders of the 5th Brigade relieved the Royal Regiment of Canada, while the 4th Brigade prepared to attack Woensdrecht from Hoogerheide. A German counter-attack coming in as the new dispositions were being made, however, forced postponement of the attack until the 16th.

At 3.30 that morning the Royal Hamilton Light Infantry attacked Woensdrecht and the spur to its north. Supported by tanks, by the whole divisional artillery and three medium regiments and one heavy anti-aircraft regiment, they fought their way into and through Woensdrecht and on to the rising ground, and there they stayed. Before long the counter-attacks began. One company of the Hamiltons was overrun, but a company of the Essex Scottish and more tanks came forward, and the Hamiltons held on. 'It is close hard fighting — the enemy is not giving up here the way he has in the past' the Hamiltons reported. The turning point came when the 4th Medium Regiment, Royal Canadian Artillery, brought down a heavy concentration very close to the Canadians. 'The fire caught the enemy troops right out in the open whereas our men were deep down in their slit trenches having been warned before hand. Our troops cheered; the slaughter was terrific.'[12]

In two days, the 16th and 17th, the Hamiltons lost 21 killed with 140 other casualties. Commenting the Hamiltons war diary said:

'We did not have enough bodies on the ground to completely control the Woensdrecht Feature and it was possible for the enemy to infiltrate. The enemy appeared to suffer very heavy casualties from our artillery fire which was used unsparingly, but he continued to reinforce his positions. We were prevented from probing forward as the average company strength was forty-five and casualties amongst our officers and NCOs and older men were very heavy. The bulk of the men in the battalion at the present time had not had very much infantry training, but had been remustered from other branches of the service.'

These and other losses had come at a time when the Canadian army was suffering from a general shortage of infantry reinforcements. Like the Hamiltons, the Black Watch complained that recent arrivals had had very little infantry training, some less than a month, a few none at all.

The German paratroops whom they were fighting, though their ranks now contained many young reinforcements, were a corps d'elite as was the Hermann Goering Regiment, but the ordinary German line divisions were in much worse case than the Canadians. Their ranks, too, were filled by half-trained or untrained reinforcements, many of them boys or old men combed out and sent to make up strength. They often went short of food, and over all of them hung the constant menace of deadly air attack.

By now von Rundstedt had given up hope of recovering the isthmus. In the war diary of his headquarters there appeared on the 16th the entry:

'In the area of the Scheldt Estuary a permanent recapture of the land connection with Walcheren can no longer be expected. C-in-C West therefore consents to the flooding of the area.'

At Woensdrecht both sides were for the moment exhausted, and an uneasy lull brooded over the mud and blood of the battered villages of the isthmus.[13]

Known to the Germans as Scheldt Fortress South and to Canadians and British as the Breskens Pocket, the area held by the German 64th Infantry Division south of the Scheldt measured some 25 miles from east to west and 20 at its greatest depth from the coast to the Leopold Canal. Its front ran southwards from the coast at Zeebrugge through seven miles of floods to Moerkerke. After that the floods stopped, but the flat coverless country was dominated by the formidable double obstacle of the two canals raised above the level of the surrounding countryside, until, after another five miles, the canals separated just beyond the village of Eede and the floods began again. They continued eastwards for eleven miles along the north bank of the Leopold Canal, then came a single dry polder, the Isabella, and the Braakman inlet, a mile wide and six miles long, leading to the Scheldt. About five miles behind this line and clear of most of the floods ran a second line, and about half the area between the two lines was flooded.

The 64th Infantry Division, commanded by Major General Knut Eberding, had been formed during the latter part of July from experienced soldiers on leave from the Russian and Italian fronts and from Norway. Some of its artillery and engineers had been detached for the defence of Boulogne, but the Fifteenth Army had handed over to it additional weapons, ammunition and rations for protracted defence, and with naval and air force elements the Germans in the Breskens Pocket now mustered about 11,000 officers and men, over 500 machine guns and mortars, some 200 anti-tank and anti-aircraft guns including 23 of the formidable 88s, and about 70 other guns from 75-mm calibre upwards. To cover the mouth of the Scheldt there were six naval batteries between Breskens and Knocke-sur-Mer. In all this would have been an inadequate force to hold so extensive a position, had it not been for the floods and canals which channelled the approach of

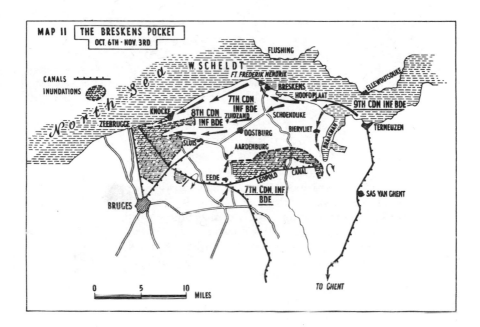

MAP II THE BRESKENS POCKET
OCT 6TH - NOV 3RD

CANALS
INUNDATIONS

FLUSHING

W. SCHELDT
FT. FREDERIK HENDRIK
BRESKENS
HOOFDPLAAT
ELLEWOUTSDIJKE

North Sea

KNOCKE
8TH CDN INF BDE
7TH CDN INF BDE
ZUIDZAND
SCHOENDIJKE
9TH CDN INF BDE

ZEEBRUGGE
OOSTBURG
BIERVLIET
TERNEUZEN

SLUIS
AARDENBURG
BRAAKMAN

EEDE
LEOPOLD CANAL
7TH. CDN. INF BDE
SAS VAN GHENT

BRUGES

0   5   10
MILES
TO GHENT

attackers into two defiles: a small area immediately east of Eede between the separation of the doubled canals and the floods beyond; and the Isabella Polder, already the scene of the first repulse of the Algonquins.[14]

The 3rd Canadian Infantry Division, commanded by Major General D. C. Spry, took Calais on 30 September. At first light on 6 October its 7th Canadian Infantry Brigade with one battalion of the 8th under command, having moved forward 90 miles, attacked at Eede. And in the early hours of 9 October, after a 24-hour postponement for the Buffaloes which were to take it into the Scheldt and around the mouth of the Braakman, the 9th Brigade embarked to land behind the German line on the other flank. To support these two attacks, the divisional artillery of the 3rd Division was reinforced by that of the 4th Canadian Armoured Division and by two field and one medium regiment from the army artillery groups. This large force of artillery was to concentrate to support each brigade in turn. To avoid loss of surprise there would be no preliminary bombardment. Meanwhile the Algonquins on the 5th made a new attempt at the Isabella. Like the earlier attack, it failed, but may well have served its main purpose in drawing the enemy's attention from the attacks which were now about to be delivered.

At 5.30 am on 6 October, twenty-seven Wasp flame-throwers in the angle of the canals flamed across the 100-foot wide Leopold Canal. Simultaneously the artillery opened fire and the leading companies of the Canadian Scottish on the right and the Regina Rifle Regiment on the left clambered up the bank of the canal to launch their assault boats. Three of the four assaulting companies got across before the flame died down and the Germans recovered from the shock, but the right-hand company of the

Reginas was caught by close-range German fire and driven back. The battalion crossed behind its left-hand assaulting company, the Army Headquarters Defence Company of the Royal Montreal Regiment temporarily exchanged into the Reginas to get battle experience, but this left a gap between the shallow bridgeheads secured by the two battalions. Rapidly recovering the Germans replied with intense mortar and small arms fire and counter-attacked the bridgeheads repeatedly. The Canadians held on supported by intensive artillery fire and in the course of the day by 200 fighter sorties from 84 Group RAF, but they could not extend their bridgeheads or join up the ground they had won.

On the front of the Canadian Scottish the 16th Field Company, Royal Canadian Engineers, had got a kapok assault bridge across within twenty minutes, and in the evening, after an earlier failure, they got another across to the Reginas. During the night the Royal Winnipeg Rifles crossed to join the Canadian Scottish in the righthand and larger of the two bridgeheads. Early next morning the Germans counter-attacked viciously and the whole area remained under heavy fire for days and was shelled from the Cadzand batteries and others. The ground was waterlogged, so that slit trenches could only be dug a foot or two down and, except on the actual bank of the canal, rapidly filled with water. The Regina war diary said:

'. . . the past few days have seen some of the fiercest fighting since 'D' Day. Lobbing grenades at enemy 10 yards away and continued attempts at infiltration have kept everyone on the jump. Ammunition has been used up in unbelievable quantities, men throwing as many as 25 grenades each a night. Artillery laid 2000 shells on our front alone in 90 minutes on 10 October and our own Mortar Platoon expended 1064 rounds of HE in 3 hours. ' [15]

Gradually the Canadians got the upper hand. After three days, the Winnipegs early on the 9th succeeded in closing the gap between the bridgeheads. After three more, a company of the Canadian Scottish, passing through the Reginas, early on the 12th got astride of the road to the left of the bridgehead leading past the floods toward Aardenburg, while the Winnipegs had troops in the hamlet of Graaf Jan on the very edge of the floods north of the bridgehead. Next day the Canadian Scottish gained a foothold in Eede. That evening, the 13th, the 8th and 9th Field Squadrons from the 4th Armoured finished bridging the two canals on the line of the Aardenburg road, and next day tanks of the British Columbia Regiment crossed into the bridgehead. By then the worst was over, and the attack of the 9th Brigade was making itself felt. In the first seven days the three battalions had lost 533 officers and men of whom 111 were killed, and there must have been other casualties among the engineers and other supporting arms. The Regina Rifle Regiment had suffered the worst; including the company from the Royal Montreal Regiment the battalion lost 280, of whom 51 were killed.

At last light on the 18th the 157th Infantry Brigade from the 52nd

(Lowland) Division began to relieve the 7th Brigade in the bridgehead, and on the 19th it occupied Aardenburg and Middelbourg without opposition. The Germans had fallen back to their second defence line, and that day the 7th Canadian Reconnaissance Regiment, having crossed the Leopold Canal at the Isabella Polder and passed north of the floods, made contact with the 157th Brigade in Aardenburg.

The attack at Eede had been intended as the 3rd Division's main attack with the 8th Brigade following the 7th into the Breskens Pocket. In the event it was the 9th Brigade's attack from the Scheldt which was to unlock a way into the pocket, and in doing so to show the battle-winning possibilities of the waterborne attack.* A hundred Buffaloes manned by the 5th Assault Regiment, Royal Engineers, and forty-two Terrapins manned by the 6th Assault Regiment were allocated to the 9th Brigade. They reached the brigade near Ghent on 7 October. After demonstrating these strange new vehicles to the men whom they were to take into battle, the engineers took the two assaulting battalions on board and after dark set off with them down the canal to Terneuzen.

Along the canal obstructions had been marked by lights, but at Sas van Ghent there was a delay in passing through the lock due to difficulty in steering the Buffaloes at low water speeds. This was followed by a more serious and dangerous delay at the lock at Terneuzen leading from the canal into the Scheldt. The lock had been damaged and was unusable, and two wooden ramps had therefore been built to allow the amphibians to climb out of the canal and into the Scheldt. After a few had done so, the ramps gave way, and thereafter the Buffaloes had to be winched up out of the canal by bulldozers, with the result that only thirty were ready to leave at the time set and the operation had to be postponed 24 hours. All signs of the Buffaloes were hurriedly obscured, the gaps in the locks netted over and the Buffaloes withdrawn out of sight of an observation post in Elleswoutsdjik church across the Scheldt before daylight could reveal them to the Germans.

The following night things went much better. The remaining Buffaloes entered the Scheldt, and, guided by a motorboat navigated by Commander Robert Franks, a naval officer recently attached to the First Canadian Army, and by Bofors firing tracer from the shore, they set off in two columns, one carrying the North Nova Scotia Highlanders for Green Beach, two miles from Hoofdplaat and six by water from Terneuzen, and the other with the Highland Light Infantry of Canada for Amber Beach, close to the mouth of the Braakman. H-hour, at which they were to 'beach' on the dyke was set for 2 am on 9 October. At H minus 15 minutes artillery fired coloured marker shells on the beaches, shifted to fire more marker shell

---

*Although amphibians were used, they did not on this occasion go further inland than the Scheldt dyke. Captain R. D. Franks, who navigated the assault, believes that, had they been available at this time, landing craft assault would have been a better choice. LCA were quieter, faster and more seaworthy than Buffalows, but, on the other hand, the LCA Mark 1 of World War II could not take vehicles, while the Buffalo could take Jeeps, Weasels and field guns.

elsewhere so that the Germans should not realise what was happening, then at H minus 5 minutes returned to mark the beaches again. The leading Buffaloes arrived five minutes late, and beach parties called the rest in by lamp. Some failed to climb the dyke, but all were able to retract.* Except for a few shots at Amber Beach, there was no opposition. Later the Germans, who had been taken completely by surprise, opened harassing fire on the beaches and after daylight shelled Terneuzen, but neither was effective.

Under cover of a screen of smoke floats, a ferry service began, taking the Stormont, Dundas and Glengarry Highlanders in brigade reserve to land on Green Beach. Although now under shellfire, the ferry service had the battalion and a machine gun and mortar company ashore by half past nine that morning, and the advance began, the Stormonts along the coast towards Hoofdplaat and the other two battalions directly inland.[16]

Taken by surprise Eberding scraped together what reserves he could, and surprisingly enough two companies of the 70th Division in Walcheren came across the Scheldt, possibly under cover of the smoke from the floats, to help him. Artillery in Breskens and naval guns from across the Scheldt joined in and progress was slow. The Stormont Dundas and Glengarry took Hoofdplaat on the 10th, but Biervliet, three miles inland on the road back to the head of the Braakman, did not fall to the Highland Light Infantry of Canada until the next day. Meanwhile the ferry service continued, with the Terrapins joining in with the Buffaloes to supply the brigade.

The success of the amphibian-borne attack from the Scheldt contrasting with the bitterly fought stalemate at Eede led Spry to alter his plans for the employment of his reserve brigade. On 9 October he gave orders for it to attack by the Isabella to link up with the 9th Brigade. But a renewed attack by the Algonquins that day failed to break through the German defence and a patrol from the Argyll and Sutherland Highlanders of Canada found the village of Watervliet, four miles further west at a narrow part of the floods, also firmly held. Meanwhile the 9th Brigade as it gained ground from its beachhead was becoming over-extended. Reinforcing success, Spry sent first the 7th Reconnaissance Regiment and then the 8th Brigade by amphibian to join the 9th. By the 12th the 8th Brigade had completed its move to the beachhead and next day took over on the left of the 9th Brigade. On the 14th patrols from the Algonquins made contact with patrols from the Queen's Own Regiment of Canada coming south from the beachhead, and it was discovered that the Germans had abandoned both their Isabella and their Watervliet positions. A land supply route around the Braakman was opened, and the amphibian ferry service could at last close down.

The Buffaloes were released on the 10th and the Terrapins on the 14th. In this first tactical employment of amphibians in the European theatre,

*Buffaloes frequently had difficulty in climbing out of the water, but they were usually able to get back into the water for another attempt.

92

Buffaloes and Terrapins between them had carried 880 loads, including 600 vehicles and guns as well as the fighting personnel of two infantry brigades. Their casualties had been light: four killed and 22 wounded in the 5th Assault Regiment. Three Buffaloes had been lost, one by collision two by shellfire, but almost all of them now needed mechanical servicing before they could be used again.[17]

References
1   Major D. J. Goodspeed, *Battle Royal: A History of the Royal Regiment of Canada 1862-1962*, Royal Regt. of Canada Association, Ottawa, 1962; p.490; author's impression at the time was similar.
2   Stacey, *op cit*, pp.365-8; War Diaries of Headquarters, 6th Canadian Infantry Brigade and of Les Fusiliers Mont-Royal.
3   Ellis, *op cit*, **pp.60**, 69-70.
4   Stacey, *op cit*, pp.380-1; Ellis, *op cit*, pp.100-1.
5   Stacey, *op cit*, p.379; Ellis, *op cit*, p.80.
6   Lieutenant Colonel F. K. Hughes, *A Short History of the 49th West Riding and Midland Division, Territorial Army*, Stella Press (printers), 1957, pp.33-4.
7   Ellis, *op cit*, pp.83,98,101.
8   *ibid*, p.12n.
9   Goodspeed, *op cit*, p.495; Stacey, *op cit*, p.382.
10 Stacey, *op cit*, p.383.
11 Goodspeed, *op cit*, p.495.
12 Stacey, *op cit*, pp.383-5.
13 *ibid*, p.386.
14 Shulman, *op cit*, p.200; Ellis, *op cit*, p.104.
15 Stacey, *op cit*, pp.394-5; Ellis, *op cit*, p.105; 'The Canadian Scottish: From Mobilisation to the Nijmegen Salient', article in *The Thistle*, Quarterly Journal of the Royal Scots (The Royal Regiment), April 1946, p.73.
16 Stacey, *op cit*, pp.396-7; *79 Armd Div*, pp.142-6.
17 *79 Armd Div*, p.146.

8

Belated Priority

On 5 October Eisenhower held a meeting of his army group and naval and air commanders, which was also attended by Brooke just back from Quebec, one of the very few people, possibly the only person, to whose military judgement Montgomery would defer with good grace when it differed from his own. Montgomery had in his directive of 27 September described the opening of Antwerp as essential before his armies could advance deep into Germany, but had in effect given it a lower priority than the operations of the Second British Army. Now he announced to the meeting that the Allies could take the Ruhr without first opening Antwerp. 'This afforded me the cue I needed' wrote Ramsay in his diary.

> '. . . to lambast him for not having made Antwerp the immediate objective of highest priority, and I let fly with all my guns at the faulty strategy we had allowed. Our large forces were practically grounded for lack of supply, and had we now got Antwerp and not the corridor we should be in a far better position for launching the knock-out blow. CIGS Brooke told me after the meeting that I had spoken his thoughts, and it was high time someone expressed them.' [1]

Ramsay's outburst had wide support, and Brooke wrote in his diary:

> 'I feel that Monty's strategy for once is at fault. Instead of carrying out the advance on Arnhem he ought to have made certain of Antwerp in the first place . . . Ike nobly took all blame on himself as he had approved Monty's suggestion to operate on Arnhem.' [2]

Ramsay believed that it was his intervention, supported by Brooke, that now led Montgomery to give higher priority to the opening of Antwerp.

And indeed on 9 October Montgomery issued a new directive. Certain commitments, it said, must be eliminated before the Second British Army could be launched towards the Ruhr: the Nijmegen bridgehead must be securely held and maintained; the area west of the Maas (ie beyond the bend east of Nijmegen) must be cleaned up and the enemy forced back eastwards across the river; and operations to open Antwerp, the use of which was vital to the Allies, must have priority 'as regards troops, ammunition and so on' — the wording seems significant of residual reluctance. The Second British Army would carry out the first two tasks, and the First Canadian Army concentrate all available resources on the third — but it had also to ensure that there was no enemy interference from the west with the Second Army's supply route through Eindhoven to Nijmegen. The Canadian army would be reinforced by the 52nd (Lowland) Division, the first of whose brigades would be available at Ostend on 13 October, and by the 104th US Division now moving up from Cherbourg.[3]

Two days before this directive was issued one of the most outspoken of the exchanges between Montgomery and Eisenhower had begun. Restrictions of supply continued to affect both the Second British and the First US Armies, and on the 8th Montgomery met Bradley and agreed with him that the tempo of their drive for the Ruhr would have to be reduced. Warned by Montgomery the day previously of the likely outcome of this meeting, Eisenhower had addressed a message to the two army group commanders pointing out that, while it might have to be postponed, the advance to the Ruhr remained their primary mission and must be carried out as soon as humanly possible.

Eisenhower's logistic planners were, however, becoming increasingly anxious about the delay in opening Antwerp. 'The failure to open Antwerp is jeopardising the administrative soundness of our entire winter campaign' wrote Colonel Whipple, Chief of SHAEF Logistic Plans Branch, in a memorandum dated 8 October. It was in his view imperative that '21 Army Group be directed to place the clearing of Antwerp as highest priority and make such other adjustments as are essential to insure it will not be further delayed.' On the 9th Eisenhower sent another message to Montgomery. Quoting a report from a naval source that the First Canadian Army would be unable to move until 1 November unless properly supplied with adequate ammunition, he continued:

The recent gale has materially reduced the intake at Cherbourg, while Arromanches, which we count on to assist materially in supply for US forces, has been severely damaged. This re-emphasises supreme importance of Antwerp . . . Unless we have Antwerp producing by the middle of November, entire operations will come to a standstill. I must emphasise that, of all operations on our entire front from Switzerland to the Channel, I consider Antwerp of first importance and I believe operations to clear up entrance require your personal attention.'[4]

Montgomery replied saying that the First Canadian Army's operations were going well — which as we have seen was not entirely so — and reminded Eisenhower that he, Eisenhower, had prescribed the attack on the Ruhr as the main effort.

In his *Memoirs* Montgomery accuses Eisenhower of fundamentally altering his plan in this message, but says that now at least all were agreed about what had to be done. If he thought that, he had failed to make it plain in his reply, for it drew from Eisenhower on the 10th an uncompromising rejoinder:

'In everything we try to do or plan, our intake of supplies in the Continent looms up as the limiting factor and it is for this reason that no matter how we adjust missions and objectives for both groups in their offensive action towards the east, the possession of the approaches to Antwerp remains with us as an objective of vital importance. Let me assure you that nothing I may ever say or write with respect to future plans in our advance eastwards is meant to indicate any lessening of our need for Antwerp which I have always held as vital, and which has grown more pressing as we enter the bad weather period.'[5]

On the same day, and before Eisenhower's message reached him, Montgomery addressed a long memorandum to Eisenhower's chief of staff, Bedell Smith, on his perennial theme of command. To this Eisenhower replied by letter on the 13th, beginning, 'The questions you raise are serious ones and I will discuss them later in this letter. However they do not constitute the real issue now at hand. That issue is Antwerp.' Eisenhower acknowledged that in his latest communication Montgomery had said that he was giving priority to Antwerp and continued:

'I do not know the exact state of your supply, but I do know in what a woeful state it is throughout the American and French forces extending all the way from your southern boundary to Switzerland. By comparison you are rich! If you could have a similar clear picture of that situation you would understand why I keep reverting again and again to the matter of getting Antwerp into a workable condition. I have been informed both by the Chief of Imperial General Staff and by the Chief of Staff of the United States Army that they seriously considered giving me a flat order that until the capture of Antwerp and its approaches were fully assured, this operation should take precedence over all others . . . the Antwerp operation does not involve the question of command in any slightest degree. Everything that can be brought in to help, no matter of what nationality, belongs to you.'[6]

As 21 Army Group appeared to have insufficient forces to open Antwerp while also thrusting eastwards, Eisenhower proposed to assign the capture of the Ruhr to 12 Army Group, giving 21 Army Group a supporting role on its northern flank. But he did not propose to alter his command system.

On the 16th, as the 3rd Canadian Infantry Division, clear at last of the floods along the Leopold Canal, followed up the German withdrawal to their second line, as the 2nd Canadian Infantry Division in the polders around Woensdrecht grappled with Battle Group Chill, both close to exhaustion, and as von Rundstedt, abandoning hope of recapturing the isthmus, consented to the flooding of South Beveland, Montgomery, chastened, replied to Eisenhower '. . . you will hear no more from me on the subject of command. I have given Antwerp top priority in 21 Army Group and all energies and efforts will now be devoted towards opening up that place.'

That same day Montgomery met his army commanders and issued them with a new directive. It began:

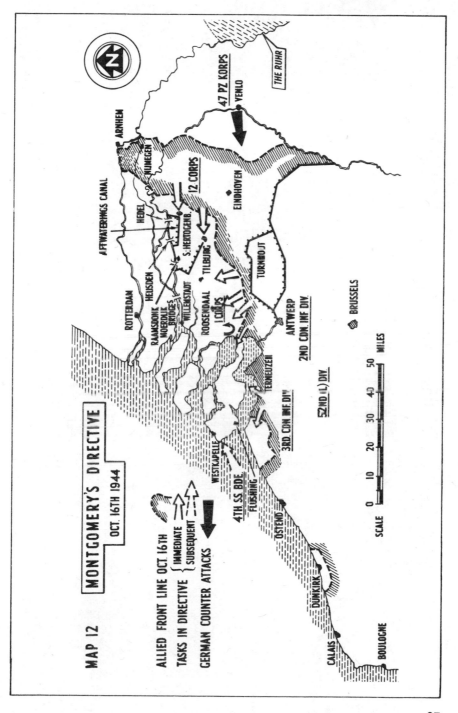

MAP 12 MONTGOMERY'S DIRECTIVE
OCT. 16TH 1944

ALLIED FRONT LINE OCT. 16TH
TASKS IN DIRECTIVE { IMMEDIATE
                     SUBSEQUENT
GERMAN COUNTER ATTACKS

THE RUHR

47 PZ KORPS
VENLO

ARNHEM

NIJMEGEN

AFTWATERINGS CANAL

12 CORPS

EINDHOVEN

HEDEL

S. HERTOGENB.

TILBURG

TURNHOUT

ROTTERDAM

HEUSDEN

RAAMSDONK
MOERDIJK
BRIDGES

WILLEMSTADT

ROOSENDAAL

I CORPS

ANTWERP
2ND CDN. INF. DIV.

BRUSSELS

TERNEUZEN

52ND (L) DIV

3RD. CDN INF. DIV.

WESTKAPELLE

4TH S.S. BDE.

FLUSHING

OSTEND

DUNKIRK

CALAIS

BOULOGNE

SCALE

0   10   20   30   40   50
MILES

97

Infantry Brigade with supporting armour arrived. Its counter-attack having failed, the 245th was now ordered to hold the Breda road against Allied advance northwards. That day, the 22nd, the 4th Canadian Armoured Division took Esschen after an air strike by Typhoons of 84 Group. Swinging further to the west, the Canadians now headed for Bergen-op-Zoom and the East Scheldt, threatening the rear of the paratroopers at Korteven. The Germans fought hard, but on the 26th were given permission to withdraw to avoid being cut off. Next day the 10th Canadian Infantry Brigade, after overcoming opposition from the 6th Parachute Regiment, enter Bergen-op-Zoom. Meanwhile the 49th Division, moving through Esschen behind the Canadians, advanced on Roosendaal, taking it after a two-day battle on the 30th. The 104th US Division, coming up on the 49th's right, took Zundert on the Breda road from Wuustwezel, and the 1st Polish Armoured Division, coming in from the southeast, took Breda on the 29th.[10]

On 12 Corps front, the 51st (Highland) Division and the 7th Armoured Division with strong artillery and air support forced the Aftwaterings Canal on 4 November, and the Germans blew the Heusden bridge. On 1 Corps front the 49th and 104th Divisions, with similar support, established bridgeheads across the Mark on the 2nd and on the 6th, as the 1st Polish Armoured and the 104th US divisions converged on Moerdijk, they heard the Germans blow the great bridges there. That day the 49th Division entered the ancient fortified town of Willemstadt, now surrounded by floods. Refusing demands to surrender, the Germans had escaped by boat. On the 9th at the other end of Hollandsch Diep where the Maas and Waal combine, the last Germans abandoned the ruins of Moerdijk. The Fifteenth Army in the fighting south of the Maas had lost 8,000 prisoners and an unknown number of killed and wounded, but it had held out for three weeks against the main effort of two Allied armies before, for a second time escaping across a major water obstacle.[11]

In his Memoirs Montgomery writes:

'And here I must admit a bad mistake on my part — I underestimated the difficulties of opening up the approaches to Antwerp so that we could get free use of the port. I reckoned that the Canadian Army could do it *while* we were going for the Ruhr. I was wrong.'[12]

But, as we have seen, during the Arnhem offensive the First Canadian Army had not been permitted to direct more than a fraction of its strength towards opening up the approaches. Until the end of September the infantry divisions essential for advance into the polders of the Breskens Pocket and the Beveland isthmus were engaged by Montgomery's orders with the Channel ports. During the first half of October 2 Canadian Corps was able to set to in earnest to clear the Pocket and to reach the isthmus, but 1 Corps, acting on Montgomery's directive of 27 September, had to protect the left flank of the Second British Army rather than threaten the flank and rear of the Germans facing 2 Canadian Corps at the isthmus. This remained essentially unchanged in Montgomery's directive of 9

October, despite its wording. Then, in his directive of the 16th, Montgomery halted his thrust for the Ruhr and directed the main effort of both his armies to opening the Scheldt. So it is difficult to identify the period to which Montgomery's admission of error refers. Had he from the start unequivocally directed the First Canadian Army to employ its whole effort to opening Antwerp, then the preliminaries at least might have been concluded in shorter order.

But the opening of Antwerp was not simply a matter for 21 Army Group. It was needed for the supply of 12 Army Group as well, and the Royal Navy was involved, for until Antwerp was opened it had to supply the armies through smaller ports and over the Normandy beaches. The reluctance with which Montgomery turned his attention to it was reflected in the attitude of his staff. When on 1 October Ramsay withdrew five LCT from the Ostend ferry service in order to prepare them for the assault on Westkapelle, Headquarters 21 Army Group objected, saying that doing so would interfere with operations of greater priority. Ramsay replied that he knew of no such operations and that Eisenhower had confirmed that there were none. On the 3rd Ramsay, visiting Headquarters First Canadian Army, in a long telephone conversation with de Guingand in the end referred him to Eisenhower's conference about to be held next day. There, as we have seen, the position was made abundantly clear.

A last shot came, however, on 23 October, when Montgomery took Ramsay to task for planning the opening of the Scheldt direct with First Canadian Army. Ramsay replied that he had done so because of Montgomery's apparent reluctance to concern himself with the operation. In his diary he wrote of the incident:

'The fact is that it has at last come home to him that Antwerp is the first priority of all, and he has moved back to Brussels to give it his attention. And high time too. I said I would be happy to deal with him in future.'[13]

References
1 Chalmers *op cit*, p.252.
2 Arthur Bryant, *Triumph in the West*, Collins, 1959, p.291.
3 Stacey *op cit*, p.388.
4 quoted Stacey *op cit*, p.388; Ellis *op cit*, p.85; F. C. Pogue, *The Supreme Command*, Dept of the Army. Washington, 1954. p.296-7. Ruppertal, *op cit*, p.107 for Whipple's report. Stacey says the naval report was not from Ramsay; Thompson, *op cit*, p.96, attributes it to Pugsley; both Pugsley and Franks, at the time Naval Liaison Officer at Headquarters First Canadian Army, disclaim all knowledge; but Masterman's appreciation (see Chapter 11 below) refers to the ammunition shortage. Whipple's memorandum seems to indicate a more substantial basis for Eisenhower's apprehension.
5 Stacey *op cit*, p.388.
6 Ellis *op cit*, II pp.88-91.
7 Stacey *op cit*, p.389; Ellis *op cit*, p.91.
8 Stacey *op cit*, pp.398-90; Ellis *op cit*, 123-4.
9 Ellis *op cit*, II pp.124-7.
10 Hughes *op cit*, pp.34-5; Stacey *op cit*, p.390.
11 Stacey *op cit*, p.424; Ellis *op cit*, II p.127; Hughes *op cit*, p.36.
12 Montgomery *Memoirs*, p.297.
13 Chalmers *op cit*, p.254.

The 2nd Canadian Infantry Division returned to the attack on the 23rd. That day both the 6th Brigade, attacking the high ground south of Korteven, and the 5th, pushing forward to complete the closure of the isthmus, met fierce resistance. But on the 24th the Germans, threatened in rear by the advance of the 4th Canadian Armoured Division on Bergen-op-Zoom, withdrew hurriedly beyond Korteven.

Without waiting for the German withdrawal northwards, the 4th Brigade attacked westwards along the isthmus at 4.30 on the morning of the 24th, hoping to seize the crossings of the ship canal ten miles away. Supported by a heavy concentration of artillery, the Royal Regiment of Canada overran the German defences at the eastern end of the isthmus, but was then held up by mud and mines. It had been planned that the Essex Scottish in armoured 15-cwt trucks, escorted by tanks of the 10th Armoured Regiment from the 2nd Canadian Armoured Brigade, and by armoured cars of the 2nd Division's 8th Reconnaissance Regiment, should make a dash for the canal. But the only way through the floods was by the railway embankment alongside the road, and there well placed German anti-tank guns knocked out a number of tanks and armoured cars. The plan had to be given up. Once again the infantry would have to make its way forward on foot through the floods and the mines, the machine gun fire and the sniping. On the 26th when the 4th Brigade reached Krabbendijke, half way to the canal, very tired after 48 hours continuous fighting, the 6th passed through to take up the advance.[2]

The South Beveland Ship Canal varies in width from 190 to 290 feet. Its banks are raised well above the surrounding countryside, which like most of the central part of the island is below sea level. Drainage canals alongside the main canal make subsidiary obstacles. The main road and railway cross by swing bridges rather more than a mile from the south coast of the island, there is another road bridge further north, and there are locks at each end.

The 6th Brigade approached the canal on a three-battalion front. On the right, the Queen's Own Cameron Highlanders of Canada reached the canal that night, and in the centre the South Saskatchewan Regiment did so early on the 27th. That day several attempts by the Camerons to cross were beaten back, but during the night the Saskatchewans, scrambling across the broken spans of the road and rail bridges, secured a small bridgehead and beat off several counter-attacks. Next morning Les Fusiliers Mont-Royal got across at the locks at the southern end of the canal, and the Camerons were ordered to call off further attempts. During the afternoon of the 28th the engineers finished a bridge on the line of the main road, and the Royal Hamilton Light Infantry, coming up at about the same time, led the advance of the 4th Brigade into the southern part of the island. Next day they met the 156th Infantry Brigade from the 52nd (Lowland) Division at 's-Gravenpolder. To the battleworn Canadians, the Scottish troops entering their first battle seemed spick and span and rather formal. Meanwhile the Black Watch of Canada led the advance of the 5th Brigade into Goes, the capital town of South Beveland. 'The men had to kiss babies and sign autographs all the way through the town.'[3]

That German resistance had since the 26th been patchy and disorganised and had given the 6th Brigade on its way to the canal less trouble than the floods and the mines was partly due to the fact that the Canadians were now meeting elements of the German 70th Infantry Division rather than the fiery young paratroopers of Battle Group Chill, but it was also due to the fact that early on the 26th the two brigades of the 52nd Division had landed on the south coast of the island, threatening the take the Germans in rear and to cut off their retreat to Walcheren.

The 52nd (Lowland) Division had in 1942 been designated as a mountain division, the only one in the British Army, and for eighteen months had trained as such in the Cairngorms and Grampians. In June 1944 it had gone to the Combined Operations Training Centre at Inveraray for a short period of amphibious training, then in July it had handed over its special mountain equipment, except for its Jeep first line transport, and had re-organised as an air portable division with a Seaborne Echelon based on Headquarters 157th Infantry Brigade and one of its battalions. During September the Seaborne Echelon, having crossed to Normandy and moved eastwards in anticipation of meeting the division airlanded at Arnhem, became involved in the fighting in the salient.[4] In mid-October the Seaborne Element moved to the Ghent-Courtrai area preparatory to the arrival of the rest of the division crossing via Ostend, and on 18 October, as we have seen, the reconstituted 157th Infantry Brigade temporarily relieved the 7th Canadian Infantry Brigade in the bridgehead across the Leopold Canal at Eede. Then, as they arrived, the 156th and 155th Infantry Brigades were detailed respectively for the attacks across the Scheldt on South Beveland and on Flushing, the 157th withdrawn from Eede to follow up the 156th to South Beveland, and finally on the 23rd the division warned that it would assume responsibility as soon as practicable for operations in South Beveland and subsequently for those in Walcheren.[5]

On 21 October the 156th Infantry Brigade received a warning order that it might be required for an assault landing on South Beveland, which was confirmed next day. On the 23rd, as the brigade moved up to Axel, brigade headquarters was told that the attack was to be made on the night of the 24th. Feverish planning with the staffs of 2 Canadian Corps and of the 1st Assault Brigade from the 79th Armoured Division began at once. Although some administrative planning had been done by the 5th Canadian Infantry Brigade, no loading tables had been made out. The newcomers were unfamiliar with the ground and with the capabilities and performance of the Buffaloes. Before the men who were to make and support the assault could get their orders, officers at their different levels had to study air photographs, decide on tactical plans, convert these into loading tables and issue their orders. Military units are trained to do as much as possible of all this simultaneously at different levels, but there are obvious limits to what can be done. When at 6 pm on the 24th the order came postponing the attack for 24 hours, the war diarist wrote in capitals after the entry 'Thank

God!' Had the earlier timing been adhered to, he records, the battalions could not have been tactically loaded, the men would not have been properly briefed and the 7th Cameronians and 5th HLI would still have been without their transport, mortars and anti-tank guns. As it was many of the key personnel went into the assault on the night of the 25th having had practically no sleep the two previous nights.[6]

Brigadier C. N. Barclay, commanding the brigade, was told the detailed plan of attack at Headquarters 2 Canadian Corps on the 23rd as the battalions were moving up. His task was to seize the small port of Ellewoutsdijke at the southernmost corner of the island, from which an attack would be developed to threaten the rear of the Germans holding the South Beveland Ship Canal. He would have one battalion of the 157th Brigade under command and full artillery support from across the estuary. Barclay pointed out, first, that his brigade could not be ready by the night of the 24th, and, second, that, judging by the Canadians' experience at Dieppe in 1942, direct assault of a port was likely to be a risky and costly proceeding. After some argument, especially about the delay, it was agreed that the operation should be postponed 24 hours and the landing should be made to the east of Elleswoutsdijke to secure a beachhead from which to take the port from landward.

Like the Canadians at the Braakman seventeen days earlier, the brigade was to cross mainly in amphibians: Buffaloes for the initial landing, Terrapins and some assault landing craft for the follow up. But this time there were to be two further innovations. Eighteen DD Shermans of B Squadron, Staffordshire Yeomanry, were to swim the Scheldt, and, at Barclay's suggestion, as many Buffaloes as possible, instead of dropping the infantry when they reached the dyke, were to exploit their amphibious capability and go on inland taking the infantry to objectives on the beachhead perimeter. This latter would greatly speed the seizure of the beachhead, and with luck save casualties, for although the Buffaloes had only boiler plate sides, their sudden appearance might persuade the Germans that they were being overrun by tanks. But the Buffaloes were very vulnerable to anti-tank guns, which might not matter much in the dark, and to mines, which might matter a great deal if they had the bad luck to run into them. With the general intention of reaching the beachhead as quickly as possible it was therefore left to the infantry and sapper officers or NCOs in each Buffalo to decide together when to drop the infantry.[7]

The Buffaloes would also carry Jeeps and Weasels with mortars, anti-tank guns, ammunition, wireless sets and other necessaries for the infantry advancing inland, and a few bulldozers for the engineers accompanying the brigade. Later, it was hoped, they would bring mountain artillery across the Scheldt.

Two 'beaches' were designated about a mile and a half apart: Green Beach on the right, Amber Beach on the left about three and a half miles to the east of Elleswoutsdijke, and the order of landing would be:

First Wave

Green Beach — 4/5th Royal Scots Fusiliers in A Flotilla, 78 Buffaloes of
the 5th Assault Regiment RE.

Amber Beach — 6th Cameronians in B Flotilla, 59 Buffaloes of the 11th
Royal Tank Regiment.

Second Wave

Amber Beach — B Squadron, Staffordshire Yeomanry, 18 DD Shermans.
7th Cameronians in C Flotilla, 37 Buffaloes of the 11th Royal Tank
Regiment, 27 Terrapins of the 5th Assault Regiment RE and 25 LCA of
the 509th, 550th and 552nd Flotillas.

Follow Up

5th Highland Light Infantry under command of 156th Brigade until 157th
Brigade landed, mountain artillery, etc.

Starting from Terneuzen the Buffaloes would swim eastwards up the
Scheldt for three miles, then turn to cross it diagonally making for Green
Beach another four miles away, and Amber Beach, two and a half. Fifteen
minutes before the Buffaloes were due to arrive medium and field artillery
would give intensive fire on the beach area, lifting after ten minutes. Spare
LCAs of the three flotillas would provide navigational leaders and smoke
layers for the First Wave. Leading lights on the near shore would mark the
turning point and the direction of the beaches. Bofors would fire tracer,
field artillery, marker shell, and Commander Franks would navigate, all as
for the Canadians earlier.

The morning of the 26th was calm, and at 2.45 when the first flight left
Terneuzen, very dark with no moon and some mist. The leading lights
showed up well, as did later the tracer marking the far limit of Green
Beach. At 4.30 the artillery opened fire. 'It was most accurate and
heartening' wrote Franks, 'We were very close, not more than 200 yards
away, and we could smell the explosive, but no shells fell short and I felt
quite safe, although the noise was a bit disturbing.'

As the bombardment lifted, the first Buffaloes went in.

'There was still no opposition and the LVTs roared in ashore. They had
great difficulty in negotiating the dyke which was pretty steep. I watched
the leader wavering nearly at the top and then running back again. Most
of the infantry [at Green Beach], I think, disembarked at the dyke
although it had been intended to carry them on inland. I believe the LVT
carrying vehicles eventually did get up and over . . . About five minutes
after landing a certain amount of fire from rifles and machine guns broke
out from the HOEDEKENSKERKE area, but it went over our heads.'

Buffaloes with one company, in fact, did manage to climb out and took
their infantry about a mile inland, and later Green Beach was mortared
fairly heavily.[8]

At Amber Beach Germans fired a few shots then fled, and the Buffaloes

107

took the forward companies inland. Mortar fire was less intense than at Green Beach, but the dyke, like that at Green, was steeper and higher than expected, and engineers had to blow part of it down to form a ramp. The two battalions quickly secured all but one of their immediate objectives, but owing to mortar fire and the difficulty of the dykes, it was some time before both were complete ashore.

By 6.35 the beaches had been joined up, and it was decided to close Green Beach in favour of the more practicable Amber. At 10 o'clock the DD Shermans arrived in good formation, but the dyke was too steep and muddy for them to climb out at their designated landing place, and only four or five managed to get ashore using the ramp prepared by the engineers for the Buffaloes. They were followed half an hour later by the 7th Cameronians, and by nightfall the 156th Brigade was firmly established in a beachhead a mile deep and three miles wide and had taken 200 prisoners at the cost of 60 casualties.[9]

Meanwhile Lieutenant Colonel A. N. Gosselin, who had temporarily handed over command of the 4/5th Royal Scots Fusiliers to take charge of the whole of the first wave, had had an extraordinary adventure. The Buffalo carrying him and his command party, after apparently losing its way, was hit by a mortar bomb and caught fire and sank. Gosselin, burnt and wounded, rapidly lost consciousness and floated away in his lifejacket, to be picked up some time later by a naval motor boat, also lost and like him carried upstream by the tide.[10]

On the afternoon of the 27th the 7th Cameronians, supported by the four Shermans and by artillery firing across the Scheldt, attacked Elleswoutsdijke, which fell to them the following morning. Build up and maintenance continued through the 26th by ferry service from the Oossnisse peninsula, upstream from Terneuzen, taking about five hours for the round trip. That night fog caused many Buffaloes to lose their way and delayed the service, and on the 27th and 28th heavy rain made the mud still worse, forcing the service back to Terneuzen. About this time most of the Buffaloes had to be withdrawn for the assault being mounted on Westkapelle, leaving two squadrons of the 11th Royal Tanks, which provided twelve trips every two hours until the 30th when the ferry was discontinued. In all over 700 Buffalo and Terrapin loads were carried across the Scheldt during the operation.

On the 28th patrols of the Royal Regiment of Canada made contact with the 4/5th Royal Scots Fusiliers at 's-Gravenpolder, and on the 30th the 157th Brigade, having crossed the Scheldt on the 28th and 29th, joined the 5th Canadian Infantry Brigade near the western end of the island. In view of the steepness of the dyke and the mud, no attempt was made to land artillery, which continued to support the two brigades across the Scheldt until it could join them via the isthmus.

In the course of the operation 600 prisoners were taken, mostly by the 156th Brigade, and the appearance of the two brigades in South Beveland west of the canal rather more than 24 hours before the Canadians reached it from the east can hardly have failed to have shaken the German defence. That the landing had failed to trap a larger proportion of the 70th Infantry Division, more than half of which was at the time deployed in South Beveland, was partly attributable to the fact that the two brigades landed in a part of the island widely inundated by the Germans and suffered thereafter from miserable weather, and that so few of the DD Shermans had managed to climb the dyke.* The landing had first been conceived of as a means to secure a port for the development of operations in South Beveland, which led to time being wasted on the capture of Elleswoutsdijke, and later appears to have been undertaken mainly in order to dislodge the German defence of the South Beveland Canal. No mention was made in the instructions to Brigadier Barclay of the possibility of cutting off a German withdrawal to Walcheren, and, indeed, the German action in largely denuding Walcheren for the defence of South Beveland was aberrant and hardly to be foreseen. In these circumstances it was not to be expected that the newcomers would see what everyone else had missed, the fleeting chance to cut off in South Beveland a major part of the German garrison of Walcheren.

To the weary men of the 2nd Canadian Infantry Division it must have seemed by now that for them the gruelling struggle for the Scheldt was all but over. To keep them going, Brigadier Keefler told the 4th and 5th Brigades that whichever first reached the eastern end of the causeway leading to Walcheren would stop there, leaving to the other the uninviting task of crossing to secure a bridgehead in Walcheren for the 52nd Division.

On the 30th the Essex Scottish advanced twelve miles, all the way on foot, from Kapelle through Nisse to Nieuwdorp on the western coast south of the causeway. Patrols, which had come under fire as they approached the bunkers guarding the end of the causeway, reported the enemy were holding a strong position about a quarter of a mile in radius. Ferried forward in all available transport on the 30th, the Royal Regiment of Canada attacked at two o'clock on the morning of the 31st. Advancing northwards along the sea dyke, A Company took the Germans in rear, while B attacked frontally. By 2.50 A Company had reached the causeway, and by first light all companies were on their objectives, the bunkers cleared and 153 more prisoners in Canadian hands.

So that was the end of the battle for the 4th Brigade.

'On 1 November 1944 a long line of weary, muddy infantrymen plodded slowly back down the road that would take them to a new area in Hofstade, a sleepy little Dutch village near Mechelen. The men were indescribably dirty. They were bearded, cold as it is only possible to be

*The orders for the attack warned the 6th Cameronians to be ready as an exploitation task to advance northwestwards with B Squadron, Staffordshire Yeomanry. When on the 29th they attempted to do so without armour and out of range of artillery support, D Company was caught on flooded ground and lost 10 killed and 28 wounded before it could be extricated.

cold in Holland in November, and wet from having lived in water-filled holes in the ground for 24 hours a day. Their eyes were red-rimmed from lack of sleep, and they were exhausted from their swift advance on foot under terrible conditions. Yet all ranks realised with a certain grim satisfaction that a hard job had been well and truly done.' [11]

But for the 5th Brigade the job was not yet done, for it now faced the prospect of crossing the 1,200 yard long road and rail causeway, 40 yards wide and dead straight, with no cover, partly mined and flanked on either side by sodden reed-grown marshes and muddy tidal creeks, in order to reach Walcheren. Five hundred yards from the far end the Germans had blown a large crater, and on the Walcheren side they held infantry positions with at least one 88-mm anti-tank gun firing straight down the causeway. Brigadier W. J. Megill, commanding the brigade, thought about using amphibians for the crossing, but rejected the idea, believing they would find the mud flats impassable. So infantry again must lead the way.

One company of the Black Watch of Canada tried on the afternoon of the 31st. It met heavy machine gun, mortar and artillery fire and suffered many casualties. Two heavy guns, probably from Domburg, were firing at the causeway, raising plumes of water 200 feet high, and armour piercing anti-tank shells were ricocheting down the causeway. At 3.35, however, it was reported that the leading troops were 25 yards from the far end of the causeway and still working forward. But they could make no further progress and were withdrawn that evening. At 11 o'clock that night a company of the Calgaries made an attempt, but meeting the same sort of opposition were withdrawn. At 6.05 next morning the Calgaries made another attempt, this time with strong artillery support. Their leading company reached the far end and seemed to be about to break through the German defences. About noon a second company crossed and passed through and the others began to move up. But 88-mm fire down the causeway stopped the engineers bulldozing the gap, vehicles could not cross, and about 5.30 pm, despite close air support, a determined counter-attack drove the two companies 300 yards back along the causeway.[12]

Early on the 2nd Megill sent in his last battalion, Le Regiment de Maisonneuve, supported by three field and three medium regiments, while the 1st Glasgow Highlanders from the 157th Infantry Brigade waited to take over before dawn the bridgehead the Maisonneuve hoped to gain for the advance into Walcheren. D Company of the Maisonneuve got across and by 6.30 was reported to be 200 yards north and south of the western end of the causeway, but meanwhile the remaining companies had been held up by the intensive fire coming down on the causeway and were ordered out to make way for the Glasgow Highlanders. At 5.20, however, Brigadier J. D. Russell, commanding the 157th Brigade, ordered that although the relief of D Company was to continue, no more men should be sent than necessary for that purpose. During the course of the forenoon two platoons of the Glasgow Highlanders managed to get along the causeway and reach the Maisonneuves who were holding a house and railway underpass some 500 yards west of the far end, while the remaining companies of the Glasgow Highlanders held the eastern end. The operation ended that evening as the remnants of D Company and the two Glasgow Highlander platoons withdrew under the cover of smoke fired by the Canadian artillery and rocket attacks by Typhoons. In the three days of this heartbreaking attempt, which had once seemed to come so close to success, the 5th Canadian Infantry Brigade suffered 135 casualties. [13]

Meanwhile in an almost bloodless operation A Squadron, the 8th Reconnaissance Regiment, had taken North Beveland. Reaching the Oosterkerke ferry terminal on the afternoon of the 31st, it sent a patrol across to Kortgene by motor boat. There the Dutch Resistance told them that there were 250 Germans waiting evacuation from Colinsplaat on the northern coast of the island. Next morning the Canadians reached Colinsplaat and the Germans surrendered. Turning their attention next to Kamperlant on the west coast, the Canadians mortared the town during the night and next morning entered it taking the surrender of another 357 Germans, and cutting off withdrawal from the eastern corner of Walcheren. [14]

By then the amphibious assaults on Westkapelle and Flushing were firmly ashore and making progress. The 2nd Canadian Infantry Division, on top of its heavy fighting in Normandy, had since crossing the Turnhout Canal lost 207 officers and 3,443 other ranks and taken over 5,000 prisoners. Now it could be withdrawn into well-earned rest.

In the Breskens Pocket, where the 9th Canadian Brigade's amphibian-borne attack on 9 October had shaken loose the German hold on the Leopold Canal, the German 64th Division had fallen back to its second line running from Breskens inland to Schoondijke, then through Oostburg and Sluis and along the Sluis Canal to the floods and the twin canals south of Zeebrugge.

Breskens was needed as the harbour from which to launch the assault against Flushing, and the area west and south of it, as well as that to the east already in Canadian hands, was needed for the deployment of the mass of artillery that would support both the assault on Flushing and that on Westkapelle. General Spry planned to attack from the east, using specialised armour from the 79th Armoured Division to help his infantry deal with the minefields and concrete defences which abounded in the area remaining to the Germans. On the 20th an explosion of flame-thrower fuel caused 87 casualties and destroyed ten AVREs, intended to carry fascines and bridging for the attack on Breskens. Nevertheless, after a preliminary bombardment by heavy and super-heavy artillery, the Stormont, Dundas and Glengarry Highlanders attacked next day supported by Crocodile flame-throwers from the 141st Regiment, Royal Armoured Corps, and by Typhoons of 84 Group attacking in clear weather Breskens and the Flushing batteries firing across the Scheldt. By noon the town was taken, and patrols were pushing westwards towards Fort Frederik Hendrik. Further south the Highland Light Infantry of Canada attacked Schoondijke on the 22nd. They met tenacious opposition and did not take the town until the 24th.

Fort Frederik Hendrik, lying on the coast a mile or so west of Breskens, was an ancient ruin guarded on the landward side by twin moats. These remained an effective obstacle, and behind them the Germans had built modern concrete defence works. It looked a hard nut to crack, and indeed on the 22nd two companies of the North Nova Scotia Highlanders attempting to take it were beaten back. Plans were made to attack it again on the 25th after bombardment by artillery and medium bombers, but on the night of the 24th a deserter got through and told the Canadians that there were only twenty-three Germans in the fort. He was sent back to threaten them with destruction if they did not surrender, which thereupon they did, leaving the North Nova Scotia to occupy the fort and round up other prisoners.

The 7th Brigade now advanced through the 9th along the coast, hoping to outflank Cadzand from seaward. On the 27th a German counter-attack, effectively supported by guns in Walcheren firing across the Scheldt, overran a company of the Canadian Scottish. But then the Germans pulled back across the canal there, leaving Cadzand to the Canadians. Meanwhile the 8th Brigade, much hampered by sodden ground, strong points and minefields, but assisted by Flails, AVREs and Crocodiles, took Oostburg on the 26th and Zuidzande on the 29th. As late as the 27th, however, the Germans in the Pocket maintained touch with Walcheren, receiving supplies and sending back wounded across the Scheldt. Now they were isolated and penned in the last corner of canals with only the floods behind them.

On the 30th the 7th Brigade, advancing westwards along the coast, reached the fortified coastal batteries and spent the next three days reducing them. That night the 8th and 9th Brigades, north of the Sluis, both got across the last canal east of the Leopold. After waiting for a bridge to be built, the 9th advanced again on 1 November, taking a formidable strong point near Knocke and captured General Eberding at Het Zoute nearby. Next day the brigade cleared Knocke, and, at 9.50 on the morning of the 3rd, the 7th Reconnaissance Regiment, entering Zeebrugge from the west, reported that there were no enemy there or between the Bruges Ship Canal and the Leopold floods.

'Op Switchback now complete' said the entry in the operations log at Headquarters 3rd Canadian Infantry Division, and, the official history adds, beside this too somebody wrote 'Thank God'.[15] In the more detailed words of a regimental historian:

The fighting in the Breskens Pocket was marked by the utter misery of the conditions and the great courage required to do the simplest things. Attacks had to go along dykes swept by enemy fire. To go through the polders meant wading, without possibility of concealment, in water that at times came up to the chest. Mortar fire, at which the Germans were masters, crashed into every rallying point. Spandaus sent their whining reverberations across the marshes. Our own artillery was deprived of much of its effectiveness because of the great difficulty in reaching an enemy dug in on the reverse slope of a dyke. Even that most potent weapon, the Wasp, was denied both cover and room to manoeuvre. The conditions for heavier supporting vehicles were so bad that, at first, little use could be made of them. It was peculiarly a rifleman's fight in that there were no great decisive battles, just a steady continuous struggle.[16]

The flame-throwing Crocodiles could only move along the hard tops of the dykes. There was no room for them to turn, and, as their flame-thrower fuel was carried in trailers, they could hardly reverse, so they had simply to go on until they came to a cross dyke. Air support was heavy and effective when weather permitted, but often in that dreary October it did not. In all 1733 fighter sorties were flown in support of the 3rd Division and 308 medium and heavy sorties. A First Canadian Army Intelligence Summary of 7 November called the 64th Division 'the best infantry division we have met.' In defeating it the 3rd Canadian Infantry Division suffered 2,077 casualties, 314 fatal and 231 others missing most of whom were dead, and took 12,707 prisoners.

References

1   2Cdn Inf Div Planning Instruction No 1, 2DS(G)/1-9, 20 Oct 44; Simonds in conversation with the author in November 1969 re doubts about Westkapelle.
2   Stacey *op cit*, p.391.
3   *ibid*, pp.400-2; Ellis *op cit*, p.113.
4   George Blake, *Mountain and Flood: History of the 52nd (Lowland) Division 1939-1946*, Jackson, Glasgow, 1950, Chapters IV-VI.
5   Main Headquarters 2 Cdn Corps 23 Oct 44 copy in 52 (Lowland) Division War Diary.
6   War Diary 157 Infantry Brigade.
7   Brigadier C. N. Barclay, article in *Navy*, April 1970 and correspondence.
8   Barclay as above; *79 Armd Div Hist*, p.149; Captain T. N. Masterman, papers; Captain R. D. Franks, diary and correspondence.
9   Ellis *op cit*, p.112.
10 Blake *op cit*, p.85; R. W. Thompson, *Eighty-Five Days*, Hutchinson, 1957, pp.132-3.
11 Goodspeed *op cit*, p.513.
12 Ellis *op cit*, p.114.
13 Stacey *op cit*, pp.404-6; Ellis *op cit*, p. 114; War Diaries 157 Infantry Brigade and 1st Glasgow Highlanders.
14 Major T. M. Hunter, Article, 'The Capture of North Beveland', *Canadian Armed Forces Journal*, Vol XI, No 2, Ottawa, April 1957.
15 Stacey *op cit*, pp.397-400.
16 Lieut Colonel W. T. Barnard, *The Queen's Own Rifles of Canada 1860-1960*, Ontario Publishing Co., 1960, p.235. It seems possible that he confuses the Crocodile with the Wasp.

10

Inside a Fortress

On 1 November, as the 3rd Canadian Infantry Division thankfully saw its month-long struggle in the polders of the Breskens Pocket draw to a close, Allied forces converged on Walcheren from three directions. At the causeway the 2nd Canadian Infantry Division, after six weeks of hard fighting, made its second attempt to secure a bridgehead before handing over to the 157th Infantry Brigade. At Flushing 4 Commando landed from across the Scheldt to seize a bridgehead for the 155th Infantry Brigade, and at Westkapelle the three Royal Marines commandos of the 4th Special Service Brigade landed from the sea to take the naval batteries on the dunes that commanded the mouth of the Scheldt.

The German navy and army differed in their ideas on the design and siting of coastal batteries. The navy held that they should be sited forward on the coastline in heavily protected casemates of steel and concrete to engage ships at sea by direct fire; the army that they should be further back concealed by the ground in open casemates with wide fields of fire, able to bring indirect fire on the beaches and on landing craft approaching them. During the building of the Atlantic Wall the dispute had several times been referred to Hitler. He had given no decision, but, with his liking for fortifications, had tended to favour the naval system, sacrificing field of fire for protection in closed casemates even for batteries where the instruments required to engage ships moving at speed were not available.[1]

The batteries guarding the mouth of the Scheldt, however, were with one exception naval batteries, sited and equipped to engage ships at sea. The 202nd Naval Artillery Battalion (*Marineartillerie Abteilung*) had started work on the first batteries in Walcheren as early as May 1940, and by September had had three ready for action. Thereafter, from 1941 onwards, heavier batteries were added and others built across the Scheldt near Knocke and Cadzand. By September 1944 there was a powerful force of coastal artillery to cover the escape of the Fifteenth Army from attack from seaward as it crossed the West Scheldt and to guard the minefields blocking the approaches to Antwerp.

Zeebrugge
One battery of two 20.3-cm guns, one of two 15-cm, and one of four 10.5-cm on the mole later moved to the Cadzand area.

Scheldt Fortress South (The Breskens Pocket)
203rd Naval Artillery Battalion

114

One battery of four 9.4-cm guns at Heyst, one of four 28-cm at Knocke, one of four 15-cm at Cadzand, one of four 12-cm at Nieuwe Sluis, one of four 7.62-cm and one of four 10.5-cm at Fort Frederik Hendrik.

702nd Railway Artillery Battalion (Army)
One Battery of three 20.3-cm railway guns south of Knocke.

The naval batteries in the Breskens Pocket took an active part in its defence against attack from landwards, a number of guns being taken out of their casemates to do so, but the railway battery was mistakenly blown up too soon.

Walcheren
202nd Naval Artillery Battalion
(Batteries are given the target numbers allotted by 84 Group RAF and subsequently used by all three British Services: German numbers in brackets.)
W7 (9/202) four 15-cm guns (5.9-inch) immediately west of Flushing
W11 (8/202) four 15-cm guns in the dunes between Flushing and Zoutelande near Dishoek; close defence and flak not known.
W13 (7/202) four 15-cm guns with two 7.5-cm for close defence and three 20-mm flak in the dunes between Zoutelande and Westkapelle.
W15 (6/202) four ex-British 3.7-inch (9.4-cm) anti-aircraft guns captured at Dunkirk and now mounted against shipping with two ex-British 3-inch for close defence, mounted on the sea wall immediately north of Westkapelle.
W17 (5/202) four 22-cm guns (8.7-inch) with one 5-cm gun for close defence, immediately west of Domburg.
W19 (4/202) five ex-British 3.7-inch guns in the rolling dunes at the northern tip of the island near Oostberg.

Schouwen
One battery of four 15-cm guns at the southernmost point of the western extension of the island; one of four 15-cm near Renesse further north.

All the Walcheren naval batteries were sited for direct fire to seaward. Those of W17 were in open casemates and could also fire across the island. The rest, except for the close defence and AA guns, were in thick enclosed concrete casemates. There were radar displays in W11, W13, in the dunes near W19, and immediately south of the Westkapelle dyke.[2]

Guarded by these guns lay the minefields. Between 16 May 1944 and 13 June the Germans laid a total of 1,703 contact and ground mines at the mouth of the Scheldt and its seaward approaches; then between 4 September and 11 October, another 593 in the Deuerloo Channel and in the West Scheldt as far east as the Antwerp docks; and finally in the last days of October, 60 more blocking the approach to Flushing. By mid-October the Wielingen and Deuerloo Channels were extensively mined; there was a line of mines along the southwestern and northwestern coasts of Walcheren and others to seaward; and scattered mines off Flushing, Breskens, Terneuzen,

Lillo and in the Antwerp docks. A flotilla of explosive motor boats was held in Flushing in readiness for attacks on shipping in the Scheldt.[3]

Along the dunes on the southwest and northwest coasts of Walcheren there were twelve smaller, close defence batteries or gun positions. Four more were clustered in the Flushing dock area, two of them on the waterfront. In the low-lying hinterland, concealed by the dunes from observation from seaward, there were seven heavy anti-aircraft batteries manned by the 810th Naval Flak Regiment, and, backing in depth the defences of the southwestern dunes, four surface batteries in concrete casemates. There was a single battery on the northeast coast near Veere, and the field artillery of the 70th Infantry Division was also available for the defence of South Beveland and Walcheren.

The batteries and gun positions along the dunes were defended by infantry trenches, barbed-wire entanglements, anti-personnel minefields and buried flame-throwers, making each a self-contained strongpoint and providing, in conjunction with similarly protected infantry posts, an almost continuous lines of defences along the dunes. Along the beaches obstacles had been erected between the groins. Flushing was defended by concrete bunkers, pillboxes and obstacles in the streets; wire and mines along the seafront; and gun positions and strong points among the buildings. Ferries and harbour craft lay ready to be sunk as blockships at the entrance to the main docks and canal. What would be lacking on the day would be stout-hearted infantry in the numbers needed to man these defences adequately.

The 70th Infantry Division was a defensive division formed from men invalided from Russia and elsewhere with stomach complaints. As its derogatory nicknames, the 'Stomach' or 'White Bread' Division, imply, by concentrating these men in one division with a defensive role in the dairy farmlands of Holland, they could be kept on a special diet and still be usefully employed. To what extent these men were, as some were inclined to suggest, malingerers and shirkers is impossible to say. Under the strain of frequent movement, bombing and floods, the wastage rate was high, but so were those of other divisions at this time. As will be seen, by the time of the assaults at Flushing and Westkapelle, the infantry of the division were very thin on the ground and much disorganised by frequent detachments and redeployment.

During May and June the 70th Division under its sixty-year old commander, Lieutenant General Wilhelm Daser, had taken over from the 165th Division the defence of Walcheren and the Bevelands. Of its three two-battalion infantry regiments, the 1018th and 1019th, together with the 89th Fortress Regiment were in Walcheren with one company in North Beveland, and the 1020th was in South Beveland. In the first days of September, the 1018th and 1020th Infantry and the 89th Fortress Regiments were sent across the Scheldt to join the Fifteenth Army south of Ghent, losing in the fighting there, according to Daser, about a third of their numbers. Ordered back to the islands, they crossed between the 15th and 20th, leaving two companies, a proportion of their heavy weapons and all their vehicles with

116

the 64th Division, and suffering further casualties on the crossing. Then, a the end of September, the 1018th Regiment was ordered away by the Fifteenth Army to the 346th Division on the line of the Albert Canal, taking with it one of the three divisional artillery batteries (12-gun *Abteilung*). Some replacements joined the division, but not enough to make up for the losses.

The breaking of the Westkapelle dyke on 3 October caused few losses to the division; the civilians in Westkapelle suffered much more heavily. To restrain the floods the Germans and civilians working together built a wall nine kilometres long from Zoutelande to Oostkapelle, only to find their work in vain as Bomber Command made new breaches in the dykes. By the end of the month tidal floods had spread over all the low lying interior of the island, flooding out the batteries there.

The flooding of Walcheren and the progress of the Canadian advance northwards from the Albert Canal, in Daser's view, shifted the *Schwerpunkt*, or emphasis, of the division's defence from Walcheren to South Beveland. He therefore gave the 1019th Regiment, which in addition to holding Flushing had on the departure of the 1018th taken over the southwest coast and Westkapelle, a battalion from the Fortress Regiment and made it responsible for the whole of the southwest and northwest coasts. Leaving another battalion of the Fortress Regiment near Veere, Daser transferred the third and regimental headquarters to South Beveland, where he also moved the divisional command post, locating it at 'sHarendskerke, west of Goes. Meanwhile the 1020th Regiment, supported by most of the remaining divisional artillery, prepared to defend the line of the South Beveland Canal, keeping one battalion forward at the isthmus to maintain contact with Battle Group Chill at Woensdrecht and to cover the flooding of the isthmus. By 20 October the new dispositions were complete.

Daser recognised that the loss of Breskens threatened both South Beveland and Walcheren with attack from across the Scheldt. But his division, weakened by the removal of the 1018th Regiment and other detachments, by casualties and by sickness, was overstretched, and he appears to have done little to meet the new danger.

The landing of the 156th and 157th Brigades near Elleswoutsdijke on the 26th, after, Daser claimed, an earlier attempt had been beaten off with heavy loss, brought home the new threat and threatened also to cut off the 1020th Regiment. Daser accordingly brought Colonel Reinhardt, commanding the 1019th Regiment, across from Walcheren with a company each from his own and from the Fortress Regiment. So now the divisional commander and all three remaining regimental commanders were in South Beveland together with more than half the division. As the month ended, the battered units in South Beveland withdrew to a bridgehead covering the causeway, then on the nights of the 29th and 30th made good their escape to Walcheren blowing the causeway behind them. Seeing some of the men returning to Middelburg, Captain Aschmann, Sea Commandant South Holland, commented in his war diary on the poor impression they made,

The men appeared completely apathetic, an undisciplined mob. If this is not set right by energetic leadership, I foresee a black future for the defence of Walcheren.

Daser told him that they had not been equal to the difficult conditions in South Beveland. The enemy artillery fire and armour had been too much for them.[4]

Meanwhile the 1019th Regiment had sent two companies and a detachment of engineers back across the Scheldt to help in the defence of the Breskens Pocket, where the 64th Division still held out, and those naval batteries which could bring their guns to bear had continued to fire across the Scheldt in its support. Daser's command post was now back in Middelburg. The 1019th Regiment continued to hold the northwest and southwest coasts, the 1020th now occupied the northern dunes, and the Fortress Regiment held Veere, the causeway and the dry eastern area, where the divisional artillery was also now deployed.

Ironically the effect of the advance of the 2nd Canadian Infantry Division across South Beveland and the landing of the 156th and 157th Infantry Brigades had been to strengthen the garrison of Walcheren. Having denuded the defences of the island in the vain attempt to hold South Beveland, Daser now found himself back in Middelburg with what remained of his division concentrated in Walcheren.* What mattered now, what had always mattered most in the aim of denying Antwerp to the Allies, was to hold as long as possible the coastal batteries which, with the minefields they guarded, prevented the Allies from using the port.

'It was the flooding which rendered the problem (of defence) ultimately impossible for him', said Reinhardt of Daser at his interrogation.[5] Reinforcement of threatened points and counter-attack are the essence of successful defence, and at the isthmus and along the Leopold Canal it had been the German skill in these that had given the Canadians so much trouble. The flooding of Walcheren would make reinforcement and counter-attack very difficult, perhaps impossible, and had also eliminated the batteries located in depth behind the southwestern dunes which would have made attack on the dune batteries difficult for the lightly equipped forces landed at Westkapelle.

Certainly Daser, who had last held active command in 1941, found no solution to the problem of the floods. Instead he seemed content to leave it

---

*The two periods when the garrison of Walcheren at its weakest were: 5-20 September, when von Zangen had ordered the 1018th and 1019th Infantry Regiments and the 89th Fortress Regiment to the Ghent covering position; and 15-30 October, when Daser had deployed most of his division in South Beveland before being forced to withdraw into Walcheren. The First Canadian Army Planning Section had stipulated, and Simonds seems to have accepted, that the south bank of the Scheldt and South Beveland must be taken before amphibious attack on Walcheren would be practicable. The ability to deploy artillery on the south bank of the Scheldt, was undoubtedly an important advantage, but there was no similar advantage, once the isthmus was cut, in controlling South Beveland, and attack there had the serious disadvantage that it forced the Germans to correct to some extent their mistake in weakening the garrison of Walcheren.

largely to the naval command and the coastal batteries to hold off amphibious attack, while he turned his attention to the more conventional military problem of South Beveland rather than concentrate his division on the solid defence of Walcheren and its vital batteries. In his account, which is mainly concerned with the fighting in South Beveland and self-exculpatory in tone, he says little about the problems of coastal defence and exaggerates the effects of the bombing of the dune batteries, which now with the 1019th Infantry Regiment awaited attack from the sea.

'After overrunning the Scheldt fortifications the English would finally be in a position to land great masses of material in a large and completely sheltered harbour,' said von Zangen in his order of the day of 7 October,

> With this material they might deliver a death-blow at the North German plateau and at Berlin before the onset of winter . . . The enemy knows that he must assault the European fortresses as speedily as possible before its inner lines of resistance are built up and occupied by new divisions. For this reason he needs Antwerp. And for this reason, we must hold the Scheldt fortifications to the end. The German people is watching us. In this hour the fortifications along the Scheldt occupy a role which is decisive for the future of our people. Each additional day you deny the port of Antwerp to the enemy and to the resources that he has at his disposal will be vital.[6]

Except for his use of 'English', neither Eisenhower nor Ramsay would have quarrelled with the summary of the strategic situation which von Zangen expounded to the defenders of Walcheren and the Breskens Pocket. The German command was, indeed, well aware of the value of Antwerp to its enemies. Had it not been, an article in the *Evening Standard*, drawing attention to the tantilising potential of Antwerp, which reached OKW a few days later and was recorded in the war diary, might have given it similar warning.[7] Why then did von Zangen entrust the defence of Walcheren to the 'White Bread' 70th Division and, having done so, weaken that division drastically by repeatedly detaching important parts of it?

In the traumatic days of early September, von Rundstedt, threatened along his front by the Second British and First and Third US Armies, had wanted to shorten his line by withdrawal from southwest Holland, but Hitler, realising the value of Antwerp to the Allies, had overruled him. Since then the Second British Army's drive for Arnhem had further stretched his northern flank, creating the 50-mile deep Nijmegen salient. In early October the greatest danger seemed to von Rundstedt to be a breakthrough in the Antwerp-Tilburg-'s Hertogenbosch sector.[8]

Thus the army ignored the request of the naval Commander-in-Chief North Sea on 21 August to reinforce the defence of Walcheren as well as his later protest at the withdrawal of the 1018th Infantry Regiment. On 30 September, when the naval command again suggested that Walcheren should be reinforced, Lieutenant General Siegfried Westphal, chief-of-staff to von Rundstedt, replied that the Fifteenth Army could spare nothing more for it. He realised well enough that the Allies would attempt to open the Scheldt, but believed that, if the Fifteenth Army were forced back across the Maas, Walcheren and the Breskens Pocket, cut off from supply, would inevitably be lost. Accordingly, although von Rundstedt found a few additional anti-tank and field artillery units for the Fifteenth Army and later another infantry division, none of these found their way to Walcheren or the Pocket. For them, the troops already there together with the coastal batteries and the inundations must suffice.

It may be that Hitler and even von Rundstedt failed to realise the extent to which the 70th Division had been weakened. Von Rundstedt's emphasis on the area north of Antwerp may explain the withdrawal of the 1018th Regiment in mid-September, but throughout von Zangen seemed less concerned with the Scheldt than its importance and the words of his own order demanded. His despatch early in September of three of Daser's four regiments to Ghent and the fact that he used the good 64th Division to hold the Breskens bridgehead, while failing to provide at least an element of fitter more active men for Walcheren, are a measure either of his failure to understand the key role that Walcheren, properly defended, might play, or of his over-confidence in the guns and inundations to protect it against attack. 'The soul of the defence was the naval artillery', said Commander-in-Chief Navy when it was all over. Beset by demands for troops to shore up their strained and breaking western front, it was all too easy for German generals to persuade themselves that the batteries of Walcheren could be left to look after themselves.

Had von Rundstedt and von Zangen really made up their minds to prolong the defence of Walcheren to the utmost, and had they managed to persuade Hitler to permit the withdrawal of the rest of the Fifteenth Army across the Maas with the consequent implication that one day Walcheren, if not relieved, would fall, then Walcheren, properly garrisoned, ammunitioned and supplied, would have been a much harder nut to crack than in the event it turned out to be.

The order to hold out to the last man and last round is not one to be lightly given. Hitler, by scattering garrisons along the Channel coast rather than concentrating on major ports such as Brest and Antwerp, had squandered his resources of manpower. In ordering them all, and the men in the Siegfried Line, to hold out to the last without hope of relief, he squandered too their faith in him and his regime. At Le Havre, Boulogne and Calais younger and more determined generals than Daser had made up their minds not to take their oath literally and, significantly for Walcheren as it was to prove, had decided that, should men without anti-tank guns be attacked by armour, they might without disgrace surrender. Even in the Breskens Pocket the ratio of prisoners taken to killed was high. The logic of von Zangen's order when it was read to them would have been evident enough to the men of the 64th and 70th Divisons, and many no doubt, from pride, patriotism, fear of what might happen to their families or in the hope of some striking turn of events, resolved to give as good account of themselves as seemed reasonable; but the realisation that Germany had lost the war was never far off, and if the higher command were not prepared to support them properly, there would be few who would not take an excuse to survive.

When, two years after releasing Dutch prisoners of war taken in July 1940, the Germans had on account of sabotage recalled them to captivity, many went into hiding, providing recruits for the Resistance. By 1944 there were small groups of reliable men organised in every town and village of Walcheren, mostly of men with naval service. On 6 June they were alerted and were faced with the problem of finding weapons, for air drop was impossible on the small, heavily defended island. The only way was to steal from the Germans, a few at a time as opportunity offered or could by a variety of ingenious means be contrived.

The news that the British had taken Brussels and Antwerp reached Flushing on 5 September, Wild Tuesday, causing great excitement and rumours of further advances and early liberation. The sight of thousands of dispirited German soldiers straggling back from across the Scheldt through Flushing and along the roads leading eastwards under air attack reminded onlookers of Napoleon's retreat from Moscow. Allied bombing of Flushing became more frequent.

The warning leaflets dropped on 2 October started a mass movement of civilians from the island, but the Germans turned them back at the causeway and they went to Middelburg which became badly overcrowded. About one o'clock on the afternoon of the 3rd formation after formation of Lancasters came over to bomb the dyke at Westkapelle. That evening Radio Oranje, announcing that the dyke had gone and that the North Sea was flowing into Walcheren, ended with the Lord's Prayer. Rumour said that nearly 300 people had been killed.* On the 7th the Lancasters came again. The dykes on either side of Flushing 'rolled into the sea like wet bread'. By the 10th the lower part of Flushing was under three feet of water and the Germans were very nervous. Members of the Resistance, warned them that soon the water would be up to the ceilings of their bunkers and when they left for higher ground, helped themselves to weapons and ammunition they had left behind.

The bombing continued, there was artillery fire across the Scheldt and it was clear that the Allies were soon to attack. At 7 o'clock on the evening of the 31st de Heer Poppe, head of the Flushing Resistance, issued his stock of weapons to those of his group who had not been cut off from Flushing by the floods, and, one by one, hiding their weapons, they went to their posts.

---

*198 civilians were killed in the bombing of Westkapelle, almost all by the bombs rather than by drowning and in the island generally there were few casualties by drowning.

major landing craft, beaching either on the broken dyke or on a beach showing at low water produced by the action of the tide in the gap. 'H-Hour should be as soon as after LW as there is sufficient depth of water over the off-lying shoals so as to beach all craft before the water level reaches the bottom of the break in the dyke and commences to rush through the gap in a torrent.'[1]

Two types of major landing craft were available: Landing Craft Tank, Mark III and IV, slow, shallow-draft craft designed to carry armour, which could take Buffaloes and if need be let them swim out short of the beaches; and Landing Craft Infantry (Small), fast craft, much larger despite their name than LCA, taking 96 men each, originally designed for raiding on the Norwegian coast. Both concentrated more men in a single craft than desirable for the first wave of an assault.

Pugsley, who was responsible for the assault until the troops were ashore, felt strongly that they should not be exposed to the fire of the batteries any longer than necessary, and therefore wished to embark the first wave in LCI(S). Of the two types, these were much the faster and more manoeuvrable, but they beached badly, had two shaky plank gangways instead of proper ramps, and plywood hulls which gave no protection against bullets and splinters. In Normandy they had proved death-traps, especially to 48 (Royal Marine) Commando, and the commanding officer protested strongly against putting his men in them again, asking instead that his first wave, as well as those that followed, should go in LCT from which Buffaloes and Weasels swimming out would carry them ashore. After considerable pressure he was allowed to have his way,[2] but the commanding officer of 41 Commando, who had not himself been in the Normandy assault, agreed to put his first wave in LCI(S). In the first wave, also, there would be four LCT landing armoured breaching teams on the sea wall to the north of the gap.

It had to be expected that the Scheldt and its approach channels would be heavily mined. Although the LCT would be vulnerable to ground mines,* there could be little question of sweeping the assault in as had been done in Normandy, and, indeed, as only a small proportion of the ground mines would probably be set to fire at first or second actuation, sweeping for them might increase rather than decrease the risk for the assault passing over them for the first time. On the other hand, if bombarding ships were required to enter a mined area, they would be at risk until it had been swept the full 15 times thought necessary to fire the longest delay.

The mines could, however, be expected to be found for the most part in the navigation channels. The assault would pass well to the north of the Wielingen and Spleet Channels entering the Scheldt from the west, but would have to cross the mouth of the more northerly Deuerloo Channel. A course was therefore plotted beyond what was thought a reasonable limit of a minefield blocking that channel, across the Botkil Bank to Westkapelle.

---

*Types of mine and the problems of sweeping them are described in **Chapter 15**. **The safe** depth for an LCT over a ground mine was about 11 fathoms, the tidal range of Westkapelle on 1 November about 13 feet.

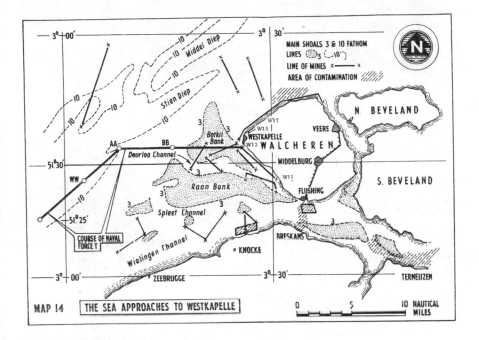

MAP 14 **THE SEA APPROACHES TO WESTKAPELLE**

Motor launches would mark a series of check points along the route from Ostend, the last two being AA, eleven miles from Westkapelle, where the craft would turn on to course for the gap, and BB, in the Deuerloo Channel, where the support craft would deploy to engage the batteries.[3]*

At a fairly early stage in planning it was decided that the Westkapelle assault should be made in daylight. The large number of assault and support craft, the long approach through tidal waters in uncertain weather and the limited navigational facilities would in darkness present high risks of failure in station keeping and in accurate beaching, risks which would in the event have ruled out the decision taken later to assault without preliminary rehearsal. The enemy batteries, although some at least were equipped with radar, would probably be less effective at night, but the massive fire support available to cover the assault would require daylight to be fully effective. It was therefore agreed that a minimum of two hours daylight should be allowed for pre-H-hour bombardment, leaving as much of the remaining hours of daylight as possible for the fighting ashore.[4] This meant that the days suitable for the assault were limited to those when the

---

*Masterman used subsequently to relate that he anchored the *Kingsmill* beyond what he calculated would be the outer limit of the minefields and that all craft mined were those which passed inside her. British and German navigating officers, he claimed, had reached the same conclusions about the placing of mines. Plotting the mine co-ordinates (see Chapter 10 above) on Masterman's chart, however, makes it clear that, while he was in general right, he was a good deal luckier than he realised, are Map 14.

W11 and W13, obstructed by sand thrown up on the 28th, were reported serviceable again in 24 hours. So it was possible that something short of the full weight of bombs calculated as necessary to ensure destruction of the batteries might suffice to get the troops ashore. But undue reliance on the short-term effects of bombing would, in the deteriorating autumn weather, be a gamble on sustained bombing weather coinciding with the tides and weather in the Scheldt needed for the attack on Westkapelle and would rule out any chance of discovering before the assault went in whether the batteries had or had not been silenced. In agreeing at Leigh-Mallory's request to call off the prolonged saturation bombing proposed by Simonds and substituting for it a short intensive bombing programme, Montgomery, consciously or otherwise, had accepted this gamble.

The report of the inter-service committee had also said 'Concentration of bombing effort on a very small number of the larger important batteries in an area will knock out a larger total number of guns as well as ensure that those knocked out are the important guns'. At the level of Naval Force T and the 4th Special Service Brigade, the fire support planners were familiar with the report and determined to secure for Westkapelle at least as high a scale of heavy bombing as has been used in Normandy. Their demands for bombing had to be made through 2 Canadian Corps to First Canadian Army and 84 Group RAF and thence to Bomber Command — Eisenhower's offer of the Eighth Air Force seems never to have been taken up. A detailed target list was prepared and conscientiously, perhaps too conscientiously as it turned out, kept up to date as batteries and strong points were identified or eliminated by flooding. By general agreement all three Services adopted the air force target numbers, an improvement on Normandy where each had used its own system.

But somewhere along the line the need to concentrate the heavy bombers and 15-inch shellfire, the only weapons that could be relied upon to knock out casemated batteries, on the batteries it was most important to knock out was forgotten. On 22 October First Canadian Army sent Bomber Command a list of no fewer than thirty-three targets: W11, W13, W15 and W17, categorised as 'batteries affecting minesweeping and/or deployment of naval bombarding ships'; seven other batteries that could fire on the south bank of the Scheldt; seven anti-aircraft batteries; six other batteries, including two in South Beveland; and nine strong points. The targets were grouped in the order shown, and in the words of the accompanying text:

Request for Air Support

5. It is requested that these targets may be appropriately engaged on a programme of bombing to be completed by 312359A Oct 44   11.59 pm 31 October . In so far as may be practicable it would be desirable for this programme to be compressed in the period 290001A Oct 44 to 312359A. Targets are NOT listed in rigid order of priority but are listed in a general sequence which may be taken as a guide to what is operationally desirable.

Above: Flushing. Men of the KOSB fighting their way through the town./*IWM*.

Below: Flushing. The ship being built in the Schelde Yard and the cranes in some of which the Germans had established snipers' nests. Known at the time only as No 214, the ship was later christened *Willem Ruys* after the manager of the Rotterdamsche Lloyd, shot as a hostage by the Germans in August 1942./IWM.

Above: Men of the 7/9th Royal Scots relax over hot drinks after their wade through the floods and night battle to capture Hotel Britannia early on 3 November.

Left: Colonel Reinhardt, commander of the 1019th Infantry Regiment, after capture./*IWM.*

Top right: 4 Commando, having spearheaded the assault on Flushing, marches off on 4 November to cross the Flushing gap and rejoin the 4th Commando Brigade in the dunes between Flushing and Westkapelle./*IWM.*

Bottom right: Loading at Ostend, 31 October 1944. Divisional sign of the 79th Armoured Division is visible on Buffalo in foreground./*IWM.*

Top: Dawn off the Scheldt 1 November 1944. The leading LCTs with support craft ahead./*IWM.*

Above: The assault goes in. The Support Squadron Eastern Flank ahead of the leading LCT turns to starboard and deploys as it reaches Point BB. The coast of Walcheren is just visible on the skyline with the casemates of Battery W15 on the extreme right of the picture./*IWM.*

Top right: 15-inch shell lands on W15./*IWM.*

Centre right: The last moments of LCG(M) 101 as, riddled along her port side, she sinks after unbeaching. The wounded are brought on deck./*IWM.*

Bottom right: Of six LCG(L), 1, 10 and 11 reported hits and fires; 2 and 17 hits with severe damage; only 9 appears to have escaped scatheless. LCG(L) hit with fire aft./*IWM.*

Top: Transferring wounded from an LCG(L) to what may be an LCT, some of which acted as hospital craft./*IWM.*

Above: First troops ashore. B, P and S Troops, 41 Commando, land from LCI(S), on Red Beach, the remnant of the dyke to the left of the gap./*CC.*

Top right: LCT go in to land the main body of 41 Commando on White Beach inside the gap. Three LCT carrying armoured breaching teams were diverted to White Beach, when Red Beach proved impracticable for them./*CC.*

Bottom right: A shell hits an LCT as Buffaloes and Weasels carrying 41 Commando drive out on White Beach./*CC.*

Top: A Flail Sherman drives out on to White Beach, followed by a second just about to drive down the ramp. Behind these the bridge of an AVRE sticks up from the LCT, a vulnerable shell trap./*IWM*.

Above: More Buffaloes swim ashore to White Beach as the landing continues./*IWM*.

Top right: A Troop, 41 Commando, runs forward across bomb debris to the attack on Westkapelle tower./*IWM*.

Centre right: Later, the prisoners are brought back to the beach area./*IWM*.

Bottom right: Men of 41 Commando in Westkapelle./*IWM*.

Top: During the night of 1 November Green Beach was opened under difficulties east of the gap as the main maintenance beach, but until W11 was captured it was closed in daylight hours by enemy shellfire.

Unloading stores on Green Beach in daylight after W11 had been silenced./*IWM.*

Above: Relics of battle. Drowned remains of the armoured breaching teams left on White Beach.

Top right: British Yard Minesweepers (BYMS) sweeping their way into the Scheldt./*IWM.*

Bottom right: The first minesweeper enters Terneuzen welcomed by Dutch in traditional gala dress./*IWM.*

Above: Minesweepers anchored in Terneuzen. Sweeping continued in all but the worst weather, but occasionally winds rising to gale force made it impossible./*IWM.*

Left: Firing at a mine. Wire sweeps cut the cables of contact mines, which then rose to the surface and could be destroyed by rifle fire./*IWM.*

Top right: Minesweeping operations room in Terneuzen, Captain Hopper (centre) lighting his pipe. "It was in fact one of the most difficult and dangerous minesweeping operations of the war", said Commander-in-Chief, the Nore, in his commendatory signal of 16 December 1944./*IWM.*

Bottom right: The Dutch lay flowers on the graves of the crew of ML 916. The whole ship was blown into the air and then immediately disintegrated. Two survivors were picked up./*IWM.*

Above: The first coaster enters Antwerp docks, 26 November 1944./*IWM*.

Below: The *Fort Cataraqui* leads the first ocean-going convoy into Antwerp docks, 28 November 1944./*IWM*.

Top: Admiral Ramsay, standing beside the Burgomaster of Antwerp, salutes as the national anthems are played at the ceremony which marked the arrival of the first convoy. Captain Hopper still in minesweeping rig, stands in the left foreground./*IWM.*

Above: The docks at work unloading supplies for the Allied armies./*IWM.*

Above: 1 November 1945 — anniversary parade in Erchenswick, Germany. Admiral Burrough, who after Admiral Ramsay's death in an air accident in January 1945 succeeded him in command of the Allied Naval Expeditionary Forces, inspects the naval contingent./*IWM.*

Centre left: Admiral Burrough delivers to officers of the 52nd (Lowland) Division replicas of the Flushing flag presented by the citizens of Flushing./*IWM.*

Bottom left: May 1945 — Field Marshal Montgomery, presented with the freedom of Antwerp, ceremoniously inspects the docks under the White Ensign. By April 1945 the strength of the Allied armies and air forces in Western Europe had risen to 3.4 million men and an estimated 3 million tons of supplies were imported in that month. Of the latter about one million tons would have come through Antwerp./*IWM.*

6. D-day is now set of 1 Nov 44 and therefore it is essential that this programme be effected fully by 312359A. In event of any postponement of D-day, recipients will be informed at once.

This milk-and-water language was intended, no doubt, to humour the susceptibilities, real or imagined, of an independent air command, but it failed to say clearly which were the important batteries and why it was important that they should be eliminated before the landings were attempted. Taken with the excessive number of targets listed and the further emphasis on leaving their destruction to a late moment, it opened the way to failure. Told later of the joint force commanders' uneasiness in the matter, Simonds said that Bomber Harris could be relied upon to do the job in his own way.[8]

On 28 October, 261 heavy bombers attacked W11, W13, W15, W17 and W19 and some batteries in Flushing, dropping 1,189 tons of bombs. On the 29th Bomber Command despatched 338 aircraft against minor batteries and strong points, 327 of which found their targets and dropped 1,527 tons. On the 30th, 89 aircraft dropped 555 tons on miscellaneous targets in Walcheren. Of these attacks, only 167 sorties were against the naval batteries, only 95 against W11, W13 and W15.

For the 31st Bomber Command planned no attacks against the naval batteries, and the attacks by a total of 100 Lancasters planned against batteries around Flushing had to be cancelled owing to bad weather over Holland. Despite the proviso to complete its attacks by midnight on the 31st, Bomber Command, apparently with the acceptance of the First Canadian Army, intended to carry out pre-assault bombing on the 1st, when it planned to bomb W11, W13 and W17, leaving at the request of the joint force commanders, W15 and the radar station south of the Westkapelle gap to fighter bombers to avoid further cratering of the beaches.[9] Meanwhile in the three days 28-30 October, the 2nd Tactical Air Force made a total of 646 sorties against targets, mainly in the Flushing area.

The heavy bombing programme for 1 November had also to be cancelled owing to weather, this time fog over airfields in England, and the effect of bad weather and dispersion of effort can be seen in the report of the army operational research group, which examined the batteries after their capture, and also in German war diaries. The research group estimated that the effect of air attack on W11, W13, W15 and W17 was to put two guns out of action and to destroy one radar station, one command post and one empty casemate.[10] The Germans recorded that on the 28th all batteries of the 202nd and 810th Regiments were under attack by Lancasters and fighter-bombers. No guns were destroyed that day in the coastal batteries, but one in W11 and one in W13 were made temporarily unserviceable, the former by sand thrown up. Three ammunition bunkers were hit: one in W15, with the loss of small calibre ammunition; one in W17, in which 600 rounds of 22-cm blew up; and one in W19 with the loss of 1,347 rounds of 3.7-inch. The Wurzburg radar in W13 was destroyed by blast, and a personnel bunker in W19 hit with the loss of one man missing and 29 wounded. On the 28th and 29th, three anti-aircraft batteries in the Flushing area were hit, with the loss of some guns and men, and on 29th there was minor damage in W15, W17 and W19. At 2 pm on the 29th, however, W13 reported all guns ready for action, and on 1 November, except for W7 which still had only one gun serviceable, the main armament of all the main coastal batteries appears to have been ready for action.[11]

> Had the heavy bombing plan been concentrated for effect on W13 and W15 only, and had the weather remained good enough for bombing until D-day, then it would reasonably have been expected to knock out 9 or 10 of the 12 guns in these two batteries with the accuracy achieved. This would have left a more possible chance for the 15-inch naval guns,

concluded the research group. From 17 September, including the breaking of the sea dykes, Bomber Command made 2,219 sorties against Walcheren, dropped 10,219 tons of bombs and lost few aircraft doing so.[12]

Naval gunfire with air spotting might be expected to be a good deal more accurate than bombing,* but it was also more restricted in the weight of fire that could be delivered. The danger of mines precluded the employment of bombarding ships within the ten fathom line, that is within about 20,000 yards of the nearest point on the Walcheren coast. At that range only battleships, monitors and modern cruisers could engage the batteries. Only three were available: the old battleship *Warspite* and the 15-inch monitors *Roberts* and *Erebus*. Once these had expended their ammunition outfits, the monitors would have to return to Chatham to re-ammuniton, taking three days, while the *Warspite*, whose guns were nearly worn out, would have to have them replaced, a considerably longer process.

The ships were under the command of C-in-C Nore, and it was not until 26 October that Pugsley's gunnery officer, Commander Hugh Mullinieux, was sent to Chatham. There he found himself confronted with a large meeting with the Commander-in-Chief in the chair and himself the only representative from the far shore. 'Apparently nobody, including the C-in-C, knew what was going on', he says. By then it was too late for the monitors to make a preliminary bombardment and re-ammunition in time to bombard again on 1 November.[13]

Each monitor had two 15-inch guns and the *Warspite* four serviceable, her after turrets being out of action. A normal outfit was 100 rounds per 15-inch gun, which could in theory all be fired in the two hours daylight stipulated as the minimum before assault. If all three ships were to fire their outfits at one battery, they would be almost certain to destroy every gun in it. Distributed between the three most dangerous batteries, this weight of fire would still stand a very good chance of silencing them. At a

---

*In Normandy 2.9 per cent of shells fired by ships fell in the acre around the target, compared with 0.1 per cent of bombs dropped. It would therefore have required over 500 shells to obtain a 90 per cent chance of hitting all the casements of a battery. [6]

range of 20,000 yards, however such calculations depended on air spotting being available. Fighters trained and equipped for the task were available on airfields in southeast England, not too far away for high performance aircraft, but good weather over the Scheldt estuary might not necessarily coincide with good flying weather over southeast England. So here again early success came to depend on the unpredictable weather; and here, too, there was in the event a failure to concentrate available effort.

On 1 November a turret failure in the *Erebus* silenced her turret for the first hour and a half, and she fired only 53 shells in the course of the day. In the absence of air spotting, the *Roberts* fired only a few more that day, 58, but most of them were in the vital two hours before touch down. Instead of concentrating on W15 or W13, however, both monitors distributed their fire among minor batteries and strong points as well, between them firing only a total of 32 at W15 and 6 at W13. Against all the odds, one 15-inch shell hit a gun in W15, and either a bomb or a shell hit another; both guns were destroyed and of their crews many killed and wounded. Meanwhile the *Warspite* engaged in a duel with W17, firing over 300 shells at it and a few more at a strong point.[14] None of W17's guns were hit.

Had the monitors started to bombard at the end of September when Montgomery cancelled Simonds's proposed saturation bombing, they could have continued until the dangerous naval batteries were destroyed, returning to Chatham to re-ammunition as necessary. Judging by Normandy experience, it is possible that under cover of this bombardment some progress might have been made with the minesweeping. If that had seemed to repeat the mistake of the Dardanelles, so much the better, for it might have disguised from the Germans the intention to assault later. But it is easy to be wise after the event. Mullinieux, who collapsed with pneumonia shortly after the Chatham conference and cannot be held responsible for the distribution of the ships' fire, felt that Ramsay had been reluctant to use ships for bombardment. Had he been present, Mullinieux, writes, he would have advised Pugsley against going ahead with the attack in the absence of heavy bombing and spotter aircraft, but it does not follow that Pugsley would have accepted the advice or have been right to do so.

As the Breskens area was cleared of the enemy, a great force of artillery was deployed there, amounting by 31 October to four field regiments, seven medium, the equivalent of three heavy regiments, one super-heavy regiment, and two heavy anti-aircraft regiments firing in the surface role, a total of 314 guns.*[15] From the Breskens area most of these could be brought to bear both on Flushing and on Westkapelle, but only the 155-mm guns of the

*Divisional artillery of the 2nd Canadian Infantry Division less 5th Regiment RCA, with 61st and 110th Regiments RA under command
2nd Army Group Royal Canadian Artillery — 3rd and 4th Medium Regiments RCA, 15th Medium Regiment RA. 1st Heavy Regiment RA less two 155-mm batteries, 3rd Superheavy Regiment RA
9th Army Group Royal Artillery — 9th, 10th, 11th and 107th Medium Regiments RA, 51st Heavy Regiment RA, 59th (Newfoundland) Heavy Regiment RA less one 155-mm battery
76th Anti-Aircraft Brigade RA — 112th and 113th Heavy AA Regiments RA.

heavy regiments and the two 8-inch guns and four 240-mm howitzers of the super-heavy regiment could fire on the batteries to the northeast of Westkapelle, while for the 25-pounders of the field regiments the area around Westkapelle was out of range. Even the super-heavies were considerably smaller than the 15-inch guns of the main armament of a battleship and therefore unlikely to be effective against casemated batteries, but everything from the medium regiments upwards would be effective against batteries in open emplacements, while the field regiments would be the most effective for the close support of infantry assault.

The Germans were not completely cleared from the Breskens area until 29 October, and the last regiments to arrive were not in position until the night of the 31st. Earlier arrivals carried out counter-battery and registration shoots in preparation for the attacks on the 1st and passed the registration data to late arrivals.

Except for the two LCG(M), the craft of the Support Squadron Eastern Flank were not designed to deal with heavy concrete defences. They were intended to give close support against strong points and similar beach defences, or, in the case of the LCT(R), to drench a beach with high explosive and so eliminate unlocated infantry defences.* Nor were they armoured against shellfire. Nevertheless Sellar determined to engage the batteries closely. If they had not been silenced by the time the squadron came within range, then it would be essential to draw their fire away from the troop-laden landing craft, and from his Normandy experience he was confident that the batteries would, if he engaged them, fire back at the support craft rather than at the landing craft. In the naval tradition of convoy, the support craft must, in Sellar's phrase, be willing to sacrifice themselves to protect the 'trade' they escorted. So it was that at heavy loss to itself the Support Squadron Eastern Flank came to redeem the gamble on coincidence of tide and weather in the Scheldt with good flying weather over SE England and the failure to concentrate limited resources on essentials.

A relic either of Simonds's earlier plan for saturation bombing, or possibly of Normandy technique not entirely relevant to the present problem,† appeared in the attempts by Keepforce to reconnoitre at Westkapelle, code-named Tarbrush. That these attempts were made after the breaking of the dyke but before any real effort had been made to silence the naval batteries or beach defences seems to indicate that they were primarily intended to discover the practicability of whatever beach had appeared after the dyke had gone. The first attempt was made on the night of 15 October. The night was calm and there was no moon. Motor Torpedo Boat 621, carrying the dory and its eight-man crew from Ostend, stopped 1,200 yards

*Pugsley would have preferred to have given up the use of the LCT(R) when it was decided to make the attack without rehearsal, believing them to be a potentially double-edged weapon, but at the request of the military he agreed to their retention.

†The Normandy beach reconnaissances were primarily intended to take beach samples so that the practicability of the beaches for large numbers of vehicles could be estimated.

from the gap and lowered the dory, but was then challenged by a light flashing from the shore. Hoisting the dory clear of the water, the MTB withdrew at half speed. Four searchlights opened and caught her in their beams, and, as she made smoke to cover her withdrawal, a single shell and a few rounds of tracer were fired at her. A few nights later they tried again in deteriorating weather. This time the dory was lowered undetected, but in pitch darkness and breaking surf the men in the rubber dinghy failed to find the gap, and later the dory lost contact with the MTB.* At 2.15, in in rising wind and sea, Captain Steven in command decided to make the 35-mile run back to Ostend in the dory. After nearly hitting the Zeebrugge pier, they reached Ostend at 9.30 that morning to be welcomed by MTB 621, which, after waiting until 6.30, had herself had a dangerous run back.

Three nights later they tried once more, this time on a hazy night with strong phosphorescence. When the dory was opposite the gap, perhaps a hundred yards from the shore, and the reconnaissance party preparing to enter the rubber dinghy, a Verey light went up from the beach. Others followed it, and soon the whole area was illuminated. It was impossible to land undetected, so, after hoisting the dory and waiting to make tidal observations, the MTB withdrew. As she left the searchlights came on again illuminating the gap.[16]

Interesting though all this was to the commandos and the landing craft crews who were to make the assault, there was nothing to be done about it. Estimation of the practicability of a beach for landing craft calls for lines of accurately located soundings, quite impossible to obtain under these circumstances. Better insurance against failure was the fact that, even should the LCT be unable to beach, the Buffaloes would be able to swim out of them to reach the shore.

Two beaches were designated for the assault, Red Beach on the sea wall to the left of the gap and close to W15, and White Beach across the gap itself; a third, Green Beach, opposite the dunes to the right of the gap, would be opened later for supply.

The advance of the commandos once they were ashore would for most of the way be restricted by the floods to the narrow line of the dunes, offering them little choice of direction from which to attack the succession of strong points, and not much chance of using their own flanking fire to cover assault. Medium artillery could support the advance south of the gap, which would eventually come within range of the field artillery, but north of the

*The method of operation was as follows. An MTB took the dory, hoisted on stern davits, to within a mile of the shore. The dory with eight men on board then towed a rubber dinghy until about 100 yards from the beach, and five men paddled the dinghy ashore. The dinghy was attached to the dory by a floating line with a telephone cable core, and the dory homed on the MTB by 'S Phone'. On the second night the dinghy, swept away by the tide, had still not sighted the gap when 500 yards of line had been run out. On return to the dory, the men in the dinghy were told that the dory's kedge rope had been strumming like a piano wire. By the time that further attempts had been made to find the gap, it was turning into a really dirty night, raining and blowing hard. It was then that they found in the dory that they had lost contact with the MTB.

gap the advance would take the attacking troops away from the Breskens artillery positions, and, while they remained within range, the slow rate of fire, large shell and wide spread of the heavy and super-heavy guns would be far from ideal for close support.

The LCT could carry tanks, but they might have difficulty in landing them on the sides of the gap, and, once landed, the tanks might find the dunes difficult or impossible going. The commanding officer of the 1st Lothians and Border Yeomanry, although pressed, refused to land armour south of the gap where the dunes were steeper, but agreed to provide armoured breaching teams as used in Normandy for the northern side: two gun- or command-Shermans, ten Crabs or Flail-Shermans from the Lothians; eight AVRE's from 87 Squadron, 5th Assault Regiment RE, four with fascines and four with tank assault bridges; four armoured bulldozers from the 149th Assault Park Squadron RE; the whole making four teams each in an LCT. Beyond that it was hoped that the Support Squadron Eastern Flank, once the commandos were ashore, might be able to support their advance with fire from their seaward flank.

Two commandos would lead the assault at Westkapelle landing astride the gap; 48 Commando in Buffaloes of 82 Assault Squadron, 6th ARRE, on the right, 41 Commando and two troops of 10 (IA) Commando with Buffaloes of 26 Assault Squadron on the left. They would be followed by 47 Commando with 80 Assault Squadron in reserve, and by Brigade Head-quarters and administrative units in 77 Assault Squadron. Once ashore, 48 Commando would advance southeastwards to take W13 and Zoutelande, after which 47 would pass through to take W11 and make contact with Flushing. North of the gap, 41 Commando was to take W15 and West-kapelle, then with the Belgian and Norwegian troops of 10 (IA) Commando secure a firm flank until, when the batteries firing across the Scheldt had been taken, they would be released to resume their advance on W17 and Domburg. Leicester, as military force commander, would embark with Pugsley, the naval force commander, in the headquarters ship *Kingsmill* and, when the leading commandos were ashore, land to take charge of the battle there.[17]

For the first fortnight after its arrival from England 4 Commando had planned and trained to land as part of the 4th Special Service Brigade at Westkapelle. Then on 21 October, when all the plans had been made out to load Buffaloes and Weasels, the news came that the commando was to make an assault across the Scheldt on Flushing in LCA, and a day or two later that the 155th Infantry Brigade from the 52nd (Lowland) Division would follow across into the beachhead thus secured.

The 1019th Infantry Regiment and its predecessors had fortified the waterfront and main streets of Flushing with concrete gun emplacements and pillboxes, barbed wire, mines and beach obstacles. The critical problems for 4 Commando were, therefore, first to find a landing place which was at all practicable, and then to reach a beachhead position covering the landing place and establish itself there before a German counter-attack could forestall the build up of the 155th Brigade.

Along the town waterfront there ran a sea wall, 20 to 30 feet high at low water and on its seaward side vertical and unscaleable for most of its length. On top of it there was an esplanade or boulevard, now heavily defended and obstructed, and a number of defended barracks. Beyond it to the west, leading to the gap in the dyke broken by bombing, there was a sandy beach, but that was guarded by pillboxes, beach obstacles, wire and mines, overlooked by the fortified Hotel Britannia and now backed by tidal floods. To the east, a half-mile spit of dockland between the Scheldt and the main docks led to the entrance to the canal and docks; beyond that the floods began again. The waterfront was, however, broken in two places by the entrances of small harbours, each protected by a pair of breakwaters jutting into the Scheldt: Western Harbour, comprising Fishers' and Merchants' Docks, and the Eastern or Dock Harbour.

Western Harbour, one large and one small quayside dock, offered no practicable landing place, but Dock Harbour, two hundred yards of dilapidated, inclined masonry, although mined and obstructed and a mudflat at low water, would if cleared be usable by minor landing craft. Between the two harbours was the Oranje Mill, a large brick-built windmill, the most prominent object on the waterfront, to the east of which the slope of the main sea wall eased from the vertical as it continued around a triangular promontory to Dock Harbour and on along the spit to the main harbour entrance. There seemed a good chance that the inclined sea wall would be scaleable. If so, 4 Commando, landing on the promontory, should be able to take the waterfront defences in the vicinity, after which a naval landing craft obstructions clearance unit (LCOCU) and army engineers would be able to open up Dock Harbour, now christened Uncle Beach, for the 155th Infantry Brigade.

But was the sea wall scaleable? Air photographs, both vertical and oblique, all seemed taken from just the wrong angle to decide the point, and Lieutenant Kenneth Wright, the commando intelligence officer, interviewing over twenty Dutch pilots and others familiar with the area, found opinion sharply divided. So until the first landing craft touched down at H-hour, 4 Commando would not be certain where it would get ashore.

Movement to and from the Old Town and Uncle Beach, was restricted by the main docks to the north, then by a high dockyard wall and the 500-yard long dock of the Scheldt Yard, and finally, to the west, by an artificial lake, the Spuikom. A landing force advancing inland, or Germans moving into the Old Town to counter-attack Uncle Beach, would have to pass through one of two bottlenecks, both guarded by concrete bunkers: between the dockyard gates and the eastern corner of the Spuikom, or along the waterfront between the southern corner of the Spuikom and the Scheldt. To reach this natural beachhead position, 4 Commando would have to advance about three-quarters of a mile through the streets of the Old Town, passing around the northern end of Western Harbour. Studying the problem,

Lieutenant Colonel R. W. P. Dawson, commanding 4 Commando, concluded that, after the first troops ashore had dealt with the immediate defences in the Oranje Mill area, the main effort of his commando should be directed to reaching the two bottlenecks, avoiding as far as possible other German positions on the way there. Then, when the perimeter was secure and the Old Town isolated, any Germans still holding out could be dealt with.

Darkness, as well as being very nearly essential for the tricky business of landing under the Oranje Mill, would, Dawson believed, favour these tactics. An attacker who moved fast and avoided contact could exploit bad visibility to reach his objective, but, should he attempt to attack previously unlocated defences in darkness, then the defender would have the advantage. Pugsley agreed to a night landing, and H-hour was set for 5.45 am on a falling tide, which would help the clearance of beach obstacles.

The artillery massed on the southern bank of the Scheldt could be relied upon to cover the approach of the landing craft, although perhaps at the expense of surprise, by an intensive concentration of fire along the water-front, but neither artillery nor heavy bombers would be able to pick out or, except by chance, destroy small well-protected defence posts in a closely built-up area. Instead, as experience elsewhere during the war had shown, indiscriminate destruction of a built-up area, blocking streets and concealing defences under rubble, would be likely to defeat its own object. The barrage was nevertheless arranged, by whom it is not clear, and the men in the commando were told that the town would be laid in ruins before they landed and the garrison buried alive.*[18] The failure in objective analysis which had characterised the bombing programme for the dune batteries seemed fated to be repeated in the opposite sense at Flushing with dire results for the population and quite possibly for the success of the assault.

Brigadier J. F. S. McLaren, commanding the 155th Infantry Brigade, disembarked with his reconnaissance party at Ostend on 22 October. Visiting Headquarters 4th Special Service Brigade at Bruges that morning, his Brigade Major and Intelligence Officer learnt for the first time of the proposed attack on Walcheren. It had originally been intended, they were told, that the 6th Canadian Infantry Brigade should follow 4 Commando ashore at Flushing. No decision had yet been made that the 155th should take its place, but that afternoon the decision came through by telephone,[19] and in the following days the brigade's plans took shape. As soon as Uncle Beach could take landing craft, the 4th King's Own Scottish Borderers would cross in LCA to push out into the New Town. They would be followed by the 5th KOSB for the advance on Middelburg, by McLaren and his tactical headquarters, and finally by the 7/9th Royal Scots in reserve. Until McLaren landed, Dawson would be in command in Flushing.

Leicester and Pugsley had until now been responsible for the Flushing assault as well as for that at Westkapelle, and both had backed Dawson's

*Very similar briefing had been given to the assaulting infantry and commandos before the Normandy landings. One had only to walk or drive along the sea front afterwards to see that very few houses had in fact been hit by heavy bombs or shells or indeed damaged at all.

136

proposal for night assault. Leicester now handed over command of 4 Commando and responsibility for the Flushing assault to McLaren, and Pugsley brought in Captain Colin Maude, RN, an old friend, who had been a beach master in Normandy and whom he chanced to meet in Antwerp, as his deputy for Flushing. Maude had no staff, so Pugsley continued to plan and issue naval orders for Flushing as well as for Westkapelle. The 155th Brigade remained under command 52nd Division, as did the 156th and 157th in South Beveland.* The 4th Special Service Brigade remained under 2 Canadian Corps, but once firmly ashore at Westkapelle, it would pass under command of 52nd Division. 4 Commando would revert to it as soon as it could be spared from Flushing.[20]

Four more flotillas of LCA and a number of LCP(L), two of them fitted as navigational leaders were brought to Terneuzen by the same route as the earlier LCA, ready to slip down to meet 4 Commando and the Scottish Borderers at Breskens. Twenty Buffaloes of A Squadron, 11th Royal Tank Regiment, would join in subsequent lifts across the Scheldt, bringing Weasels, light vehicles and supplies. 4 Commando and the 4th KOSB would move to Breskens on the 31st to embark.

It remained to take the final decisions and fix the date of the two amphibious assaults. On 20 October Foulkes had held a conference at Headquarters 2 Canadian Corps. The assaults at Flushing and Westkapelle, he said, were to be regarded as alternatives intended to exploit any opportunity offered by the collapse of German resistance under air bombardment, that on Flushing being the more probable. He planned that 48 hours of intensive bombing should be followed by a 48-hour pause, during which reconnaissance parties should inspect the state of the defences at Flushing and Westkapelle. On their reports a decision would be made whether and where it was practicable to land, but no landing would be made until it was established that the defences were 'adequately softened.'

Moreover, although until now it had been expected that the assault on Westkapelle would be made on the favourable tidal period commencing 1 November, Foulkes said that the Buffaloes for it could not be made serviceable again after the South Beveland operation in time to reach Ostend before 29 October. To allow them to train and rehearse with the commandos, and to allow also for the artillery to make good certain deficiencies in ammunition, the Westkapelle assault would have to be postponed until the next favourable tidal period, beginning of 14 November.[21]

The provision of three fresh infantry brigades and a more adequate command system were valuable contributions to the plans for the attack on Walcheren, but the proposals Foulkes now made threatened to take thrust and urgency out of both amphibious assaults, especially that at Westkapelle. In September Simonds had suggested waiting for near surrender under

---

*The naval command thus ran Ramsay-Pugsley-Maude; the army, Simonds-Foulkes-Hakewill Smith-MacLaren-Dawson. Above that Ramsay, as naval commander-in-chief under Eisenhower, was on Montgomery's level.

prolonged saturation bombing. To apply now that idea to the new four-day programme still to begin invited delay and sacrificed any shock effect that might be hoped for from the intensive programme. As far as Westkapelle was concerned, however, delay had already been accepted by the employment of the amphibians with 156th and 157th Brigades.*

Exacting demands for suitable tidal conditions, favourable weather, heavy fire support, and finally for a rehearsal which would increase the time during which amphibious shipping would interfere with the logistic traffic through Ostend, contrasted unfavourably with the alacrity, almost insouciance, with which the operations across the Scheldt were undertaken and executed and sapped Simonds's confidence in the Westkapelle assault, which in September he had sponsored.[22] Yet to stake the early opening of the Scheldt, now when Montgomery was at last entirely committed to it, on an attack through South Beveland was hardly an attractive proposition. To open the Scheldt, as well as seize a bridgehead across the causeway where conditions closely resembled those Simonds had forecast at the isthmus, the attackers would have to find means of crossing the floods to reach the dune batteries. Simonds had expected the Germans would saturate the island, and had forestalled them by bombing the dykes, thus in the event causing the floods which now guarded Middleburg and the batteries from the east.

On 22 October Ramsay, hearing from Pugsley of the outcome of Foulkes's conference, signalled Simonds. After outlining what he had heard of Foulkes's decisions, he continued:

> 2. Considerable naval effort has already been diverted to training and preparation for the operation partly at the expense of the Army's build-up. It is absolutely vital to open the Scheldt at the earliest possible date, and I should like your assurance that the above date does really represent the earliest practicable for Plan B [Westkapelle] which in my view may still be necessary despite the very encouraging reports of flooding recently.[23]

But already a more enterprising proposal for Westkapelle had started on its way up from a lower level, which would meet Ramsay's protest on its way down.

The day after Foulkes's conference a report came in that the floods on Walcheren, which until then had been disappointing, had spread almost over the whole island. That morning, the 21st, Trafalgar Day, Pugsley invited Leicester and Lieutenant Colonel M. W. Hope, who had been lent to the commandos as chief staff officer and artillery adviser, to join him in his hotel at noon to drink to Nelson's memory. This they did, and the talk turned to Walcheren and the unwelcome delay in opening the Schedlt. At that Hope suggested that, if it could be shown from air photographs that Westkapelle had been isolated by the floods and some other conditions

*Had the urgency of the Westkapelle operation been thought to merit it, it seems possible that a higher proportion of LCAs could have been used for the 156th and 157th Brigade, freeing enough Buffaloes for perhaps the two leading commandos at Westkapelle to rehearse with.

fulfilled, the risk should be taken of attacking on the 1st without rehearsal with the Buffaloes.[24]

The offer, made to 2 Canadian Corps, was duly passed to Simonds, so that he was now able to reply to Ramsay giving the 1st as the day of assault, and concluding:

> I have ordered 2 Cdn Corps to work to the above timings and, though you will appreciate weather conditions may cause variations of two or three days in target dates, I intend to take Walcheren and Zuid Beveland by 1 Nov.[25]

Ramsay's reply was short and to the point, 'Red hot, Best of luck.'

So the steam was now back in the amphibious assaults, and when a day or two later new air photographs arrived showing the almost complete flooding of the island, the die was cast. Ostensibly to finalise fire support, but possibly, as the subject matter appears to indicate, to ensure that all was going forward as he intended, Simonds on the 26th held a conference lasting three and a half hours at Headquarters, First Canadian Army. The attack on Walcheren, he said, would now be made under much more favourable conditions than originally expected. Flooding had been successful. The German garrison was depleted and now comprised not more than 1,700 men who no longer had freedom of movement,* and the number of batteries in action had been reduced by air action. Weather, however, remained a vital factor affecting pre-D-Day and D-Day bombing. Pre-D-Day bombing should be compressed into the shortest period possible, but it was for the RAF to decide when to begin to ensure completion of the programme. And, if the weather threatened to make bombing impossible on D-Day, it might be necessary to attack certain D-Day targets earlier.

There would be no reconnaissance patrols to test the state of the defences. The attack on Flushing, Simonds ruled, would be mounted on 1 November, regardless of the availability of air support that day, and regardless of postponement of the attack on Westkapelle. The attack on Westkapelle would also be mounted on 1 November, weather permitting, regardless of the availability of air support, but he would decide later on the latest intelligence information whether the operation would be mounted as planned if it were impossible to complete the bombing programme. Later elaborate written instructions were issued for the method of confirmation or postponement of each operation.

The two brigade commanders then outlined their plans, and bombing programmes were agreed. At Westkapelle, where the pre-D-Day bombing programme had already been settled, fighter bombers were to attack enemy defences between H minus 40 minutes and H minus 20 with instantaneous-

---

*Some 9,000 prisoners were in the event taken in Walcheren. On 25 October, however, the 1020th Infantry Regiment, all except one battalion of the 89th Fortress Regiment and Headquarters 70th Division were in South Beveland, and only the weakened 1019th Infantry Regiment in Walcheren. The estimate of 1,700 might have even been on the high side for the 1019th Regiment, but it greatly underestimated the number of coast and anti-aircraft artillery, naval and administrative personnel. (see p.118 above).

fuse 500-lb bombs in order to kill men and keep survivors' heads down without risking cratering of the landing places. Thereafter a fighter cab-rank of rocket-firing Typhoons would be maintained overhead to attack on call.

At Flushing Bomber Command would bomb four areas, two in the docks east of Uncle Beach, two in the town at the beachhead bottlenecks, and the waterfront joining them, 'to destroy defences, disrupt communications, and demoralise the enemy' — this despite the fact that Simonds had ruled that the assault was to be mounted regardless of the availability of bombing. The last bomb should fall not later than 5.45 am on D-Day, but the task might be undertaken earlier if weather necessitated.[26]

The requirement reached SHAEF in time for Tedder's morning conference on the 29th, attended that day by Portal, and was described as a proposal by the army 'that Bomber Command should launch a heavy attack on the town of Flushing in preparation for amphibious assault', which indeed, intentionally or unintentionally, it was.[*] Tedder ruled that on military grounds heavy bombers should not be used for this purpose, while Air Chief Marshal Sir Arthur Harris, when the proposal reached him at Bomber Command, opposed the attack on humanitarian grounds and took the matter up personally with Churchill. Churchill told the British Chiefs of Staff that the bombing of Flushing should be vetoed. Eisenhower agreed to do so, but on the 31st told the Combined Chiefs of Staff that he proposed to use fighter bombers against Flushing. Churchill then reluctantly agreed that the final decision must rest with the Supreme Commander, and, in the event, the air attack took the shape of 35 Mosquitos from No 2 Group, each of which dropped one 500-lb bomb and fired an average of 70 rounds of 20-mm at Flushing.[27] In view of the very proper reluctance in high places to sanction the use of heavy bombers against an Allied town, and indeed of the fact that in the event Bomber Command sent no aircraft to Walcheren during the 36 hours preceding the assault, the escape was not perhaps as narrow as it seems, but this time the army had cause to be grateful to the air marshals for stopping what can only be judged as an ill-considered demand for heavy bombing.

In the confused and unhappy story of misapplication of heavy bombing and fire-power generally at Walcheren, a chain of cause and effect can be traced. In September Simonds suggested the idea of bombing the Germans into near-surrender. When, after the first attacks had been made, it became apparent that the amphibious assault would not be made for some time, the air force protested against diversion of bomber effort from Germany. Confusion between attack on fortifications and that on field defences then led to the agreement that bombing should be concentrated in the last four

---

[*]Ellis *op cit*, pp.116-7, draws a distinction between the First Canadian Army's request that Bomber Command '*should attack four pin-point targets*' (Ellis italics) and a request for area bombing. The targets were in fact four six-figure grid references (100 metre squares) plus 1,600 yards of waterfront. Even if the very high standard of accuracy achieved at Westkapelle in daylight had been repeated at Flushing in darkness, the effect must have been that of area bombing, which was implied in the stated object.

days before the assault. Later, when the landing at Flushing was added, a bombing programme which might have had some effect on the dune batteries was applied to a built-up area and the idea of waiting for near-surrender re-appeared. Finally Pugsley's and Leicester's Trafalgar Day proposal led to the abandonment of any thought of waiting for near-surrender. To put the blame exclusively either on the army or on the air force would be unfair; the factor common to both was over-estimation of the effect of air attack applied as a panacea.

As during October these problems were thrashed out and decisions taken for better or worse, detailed plans took final shape. Bomber Command broke the dykes, and the spread of floods was anxiously watched in air photographs. Timed programmes for bombing, naval bombardment and artillery fire across the Scheldt were worked out. Forward observation officers and forward bombardment officers with wireless sets and operators to call for fire and close air support after the assaulting troops were ashore joined the commandos and battalions. Together with naval beach commandos, signals and clearance units, army engineers, pioneers and medical units, the Buffaloes and armoured breaching teams from the 79th Armoured Division, they were fitted into landing tables for the two assaults.

The training in the dunes along the Belgian coast and the final planning discussions at various levels drew to a close. The 155th Infantry Brigade prepared itself for its first battle in terrain very different from the mountains in which it had trained, and the 4th Special Service Brigade made ready for its second attack on the Atlantic Wall, which, if no easier than the first, promised to offer more scope for individual decision that the massed assault in Normandy. Reports of the fighting in the Breskens Pocket, at the isthmus and in South Beveland, filtering through, added a feeling of urgency to play a worthy part in the hard struggle in which others were so bitterly engaged.

There was a large hall, possibly a moulding loft, in the Ostend dock area, which had been taken over for support and landing craft officers to work on their plans and orders for the Westkapelle assault. One day about the 29th or 30th, as they and a few commando officers grouped around trestle tables examined air photographs and made final plans, the trim figure of Ramsay appeared without warning on the dais at one end of the hall. He explained to the assembled officers the importance of Antwerp and the effect that the prolonged inability to use it was having on Allied plans. 'I told the Field Marshal before Arnhem that he ought first to open Antwerp, but he would not do so. Now he realises that I was right, and that we must open Antwerp before we can advance into Germany'. Then, had they known it, echoing Eisenhower's words to Montgomery, 'The battle you are about to engage in is at this moment the most important operation in the war.' Such disclosures of a disagreement in high places is highly unorthodox, but, whatever the sticklers for military etiquette may think, it certainly had no ill effect on the morale of those about to assault at Westkapelle.[26]

References

1 Chalmers *op cit*, pp.252-3) COS First Cdn Army Memorandum of 3 October 1944; the late Captain T. N. Masterman, note of 4 October 1944, including Appendix A, *Weather*, which quotes Lieutenant G. Ruitenschildt of the Dutch Naval Hydrographic Service and the British Intelligence Report. Also Masterman, *Operation Infatuate, Appreciation of the Plans for the Operation*, unnumbered and undated, but from its position in his file and contents prepared 2-4 October. First Cdn Army Intelligence Report No 2, Supplement No 2 of 22 Sep 44; Minutes of Conference held at HQ 4th SS Brigade, 1100 hrs, 7 October (copy in Directorate of History, Dept of National Defence, Ottawa); *Operation Infatuate — Combined Plan* 0035/0/NCTF of 11 October 1944. A plan to drive through the gap in amphibians was discarded early in the training period.

2 Major General J. L. Moulton, *Haste to the Battle*, Cassell, 1963, p.140 gives a fuller account of the incident.

3 Masterman Papers, O.I.N. Two, Appendix B, amendment of 26 October, and chart marked with tracks of assault forces.

4 Masterman Papers, Operation Infatuate, Appreciation etc quoted above; Pugsley, correspondence.

5 *The Report of the Inter-Service Committee on Fire Support of Seaborne Landings agaomst a Heavily Defended Coast* COS (43) 770/0 referred to by Stacey as the Graham Report after the name of its chairman, Air Vice Marshal R. Graham.

6 Captain J. C. Dorward RA, Army Operational Research Group Report No 299, *The Westkapelle Assault on Walcheren*, October 1945, pp.64-67.

7 First Cdn Army/84 Group RAF, *Operation Infatuate, Pre-planned Air Targets Prior to D-Day*, 17/1/9 Ops (First Cdn Army, 84/TS 76/3/Ops (84 Group RAF), dated 22/10/44.

8 Brigadier M. W. Hope, conversation.

9 Main First Canadian Army 17-2-3/Ops of 29 October 1944, *Minutes of Conference held on 26 Oct 44*.

10 Stacey, *op cit*, pp.410-11; Dorward, *op cit*, pp.25, 58-60; Ellis, *op cit*, II, pp.115-6.

11 Aschmann, War Diary entries for 28 and 29 October.

12 Ellis, *op cit*, II pp.115, 116: seven aircraft lost to anti-aircraft fire over Flushing 1-23 October; 'virtually no losses in breaking dykes. Stacey, *op cit*, p.411: six aircraft lost in all attacks during October.

13 Commander Hugh Mullinieux, correspondence. Commander Mullinieux formed the opinion that Ramsay was for some reason at first opposed to naval bombardment.

14 AORG Report, logs of HMS Warspite, *Roberts and Erebus*.

15 Stacey, *op cit*, pp.407-8.

16 Captains C. R. Steven and J. M. Barry, correspondence. Barry was a sergeant instructor from the Commando Mountain Warfare Training Establishment attached to Keepforce.

17 Combined Operations Headquarters Bulletin Y/47, *Combined Operations against Walcheren Island*, Appendix D1, 4 SS Bde Gp Landing Table; *The Story of the 79th Armoured Division*, pp.148-51.

18 Lieutenant Colonel R. P. W. Dawson, correspondence and discussion; Lieutenant K. G. Wright (Intelligence Officer, 4 Commando) typescript narrative prepared shortly after the operation, later used in the first part of *Current Reports from Overseas No 80*, War Office, 1945; COHQ Bulletin Y/47, Appendix C, 4 Commando Landing Table.

19 155th Infantry Brigade, War Diary; 4 SS Brigade War Diary for October is missing from the PRO pack.

20 Pugsley, *op cit*, p.182 and correspondence; Stacey, *op cit*, pp.412-3.

21 Stacey, *op cit*, p.412.

22 Simonds in conversation with the author in 1969 and previously.

23 ANCXF (Main) Serial No 127; Stacey *op cit*, p.413.

24 Hope correspondence, Pugsley and Leicester confirm.

25 GOC-in-C First Canadian Army GS 120; Stacey, *op cit*, p.413.

26 Minutes of conference see Note 9 above; 155th Infantry Brigade War Diary.

27 Ellis, *op cit*, pp.116-7.

28 Author was present.

12

Flushing

4 Commando reached Breskens during the afternoon of the 31st and was installed in the ruined houses of the town. Breskens had been shattered by bombing during the escape of the Fifteenth Army and later by the fighting during 21 October. As the Germans left they had further damaged and obstructed the harbour, much of which was still mined and boobytrapped, but a long, wooden jetty was clear, and alongside it lay the LCA waiting to take the commando across the Scheldt. Flushing was clearly visible, but it was a miserable, grey day, and it was not possible to make out many of the landmarks. The forest of cranes in the shipyard, however, stood out clearly against the skyline, one huge one in particular dominating the rest. Everything over there was silent and from a distance Flushing seemed a town of the dead.

Towards the evening LCP(L) laid a smoke screen to cover the Buffaloes for the follow-up swimming down from Terneuzen, and a battery in Flushing, either catching sight of them or guessing from the smoke screen that trouble was brewing, started to shell the harbour. Its fire was accurate and while it lasted fairly heavy. There were a few naval casualties, but fortunately the commando, which had just completed a practice embarkation, had left the jetty, and the landing craft, which were quickly dispersed, were undamaged.

The commando was formed up and ready to move down to the harbour by 3.15 next morning. It was cold and very wet with a steady drizzle limiting visibility and heavy low cloud overhead. It was known by now that the heavy bombers were not coming and that the artillery bombardment would instead begin a full hour before the assault instead of quarter of an hour. As the commando marched down to the harbour, the last of the Mosquitos could be heard diving repeatedly to attack Flushing.

At 4.45, as nearly 300 guns opened fire on Flushing, the first landing craft cast off and left the harbour escorted by spare craft on the look-out for floating mines, German frogmen and small battle units. From the landing craft, cruising in the river waiting for H-Hour, the southern coast of the Scheldt could be seen silhouetted by the muzzle flashes of the British and Canadian guns, while on the northern side sudden bright pinpoints showed where the shells were exploding, with occasional showers of sparks when they hit a beach obstacle. A fire gradually took hold in Flushing, and suddenly the unmistakable silhouette of the Oranje Mill appeared, thrown into relief against the glare.

At 5.40 the artillery lifted to flank targets, and the first landing craft, two LCP and a single LCA, went in to land a reconnaissance party. The first LCP went too far left, and the second, over-correcting on her order, nearly hit the eastern breakwater of Uncle Beach, but the LCA touched down at the tip of the promentory just outside the western breakwater.* Under Captain Rewcastle a section of No 1 Troop quickly cut a way through the wire and took prisoner 26 Germans in their dugouts without a shot being fired. Lieutenant Hargreaves, in command of the LCOCU, called in the four LCA with the covering party under Major Boucher Myers, and they beached two at a time at the same place. A 20-mm Oerlikon at Merchants' Dock opened fire, but at first the tracer went well overhead.

The reconnaissance party had already secured the promontory, and now Numbers 1 and 2 Troops started out left and right, No 1 to work westwards clearing the waterfront defences as far as the Arsenal Barracks on the eastern side of Western Harbour, No 2 to eliminate the gun positions covering Uncle Beach, then to work on eastwards along the spit of dockland and establish a blocking position on it. Meanwhile Dawson set up his command post near the windmill and called in the main body of the commando under Capitaine de Corvette Philippe Keiffer, his senior French officer, now charged to secure the main beachhead.

Number 3 Troop came first, its two landing craft touching down at 6.40. Landing without difficulty, the troop set off as fast as possible for its first objective, Bellamy Park, a town square 200 yards long just inland of Western Harbour. On the way it saw a number of Germans in the streets and came under fire several times from pillboxes and gun positions. By-passing them, it reached Bellamy Park about 7 o'clock just as it got light, took a nearby pillbox and cleared the area, having lost so far two killed, then moved on towards its next objective, the naval barracks on the waterfront some 400 yards beyond Western Harbour. German machine guns were firing down the streets, so the troop took to back gardens, by means of which it reached the barracks. It cleared about half the buildings there, then, having insufficient means to take the rest, secured what it had, firing on enemy who showed themselves.

The heavy weapons troop, Number 4, was the next to land. By now two machine guns had joined in with the Oerlikon at Merchants' Dock, firing at each pair of landing craft as they came in. In the dawn twilight their aim

*The Tarbrush party's dory was wrecked in the bombardment of the harbour the previous evening, and it was in consequence embarked in the two LCP(Sy). Captain Barry was the sergeant climber and crossed in the second LCP(Sy). 'The Royal Navy took us to the wrong breakwater, and by the time we had righted the error, another boat had beaten us. I rushed up an incline a grandmother would have scorned to be greeted by a horrible army commando who scornfully told me "We've been here for ten minutes." He exaggerated, but I was shamed.' The Tarbrush party returned to Breskens in an LCA which was shot up by a German machine gun near the landing place. A Tarbrush officer was killed and the disabled LCA drifted helplessly with its ramp down, the bow slowly swinging towards the gun, which was beating a tattoo on the armoured sides. But Corporal Johns, the dory mechanic, dashed through the engine room door, dragged the dead naval mechanic from the engine and restarted it, saving the craft.

144

had improved, and, although No 4 Troop returned their fire, the coxswain in one craft was hit, and the craft, holed on a beach obstacle, sank before reaching the sea wall. One man was killed, but the rest waded ashore with one mortar, and then the troop commander, the mortar sergeant and others set about salvaging the second. Within half an hour they had both in action.

The landing craft with the first French troop to land, Number 5, were also hit as they came in. Several men were wounded and others had to wade ashore through deep water. Then, setting off in the same direction as No 3, the Frenchmen reached Bellamy Park and turned off right heading for the southern corner of the Spuikom lake. By 7.30 they were in the Groote Markt area, heavily involved in street fighting with Germans in and around the bomb-proof barracks on the waterfront beyond the naval barracks. Half an hour later D Company, the 4th KOSB, came up and took over the attack on the barracks, and No 5 Troop again made for the Spuikom, to be held up finally a block short of the waterfront strong point beside the lake.

The second French troop, Number 6, lost only two men wounded in landing. With Captain van Nahuis, formerly an inspector on the Flushing Police, now a member of the Resistance, showing them the way, the Frenchmen took their first objective, the post office at the northern end of Wilhelmina Straat, with some 50 prisoners. Then on along Wal Straat 500 yards to the big crossroads at the dockyard gates, Betje Wolf Plein. Reaching it, they came under close range fire from Germans in a school in Goosje Busken Straat to their left and rear, but Captaine Vouc'h, the troop commander, got his men into three of the corner houses in time to disperse a German company which at that moment appeared marching down Badhuis Straat along the northeastern side of the Spuikom. Joined by the machine-guns from No 4 Troop and later by B Company, 4th KOSB, in the next two hours they stopped a succession of attempts by German troops to get into the Old Town. '. . . it was always a pleasure to see the French in action' Dawson recollects, 'they showed endless resource and contrivance and were masters of individual action.'[1]

On the far side of Betje Wolf Plein, unknown to them, Poppe's Resistance group held another house and was sniping at the Germans. But the Germans were on three sides of them with machine guns firing down the streets, and it was impossible to cross. At about 10 o'clock Poppe's group was forced to disperse having held out for three hours. Poppe himself went to his home nearby. His story continues:

My wife called to me, "Willem, look outside" and in our street, Scheldestraat, I saw a German officer approaching. I put my rifle and ammunition in a corner and crossed the street very calm. My command post was just across the street from my house, and I advised the officer to take shelter there. "Is that allowed?" he asked, and I said "Oh yes, its my house." Inside we took him prisoner. It was Kapitänleutnant Blissinger, second in command of the harbour . . . Later we heard that

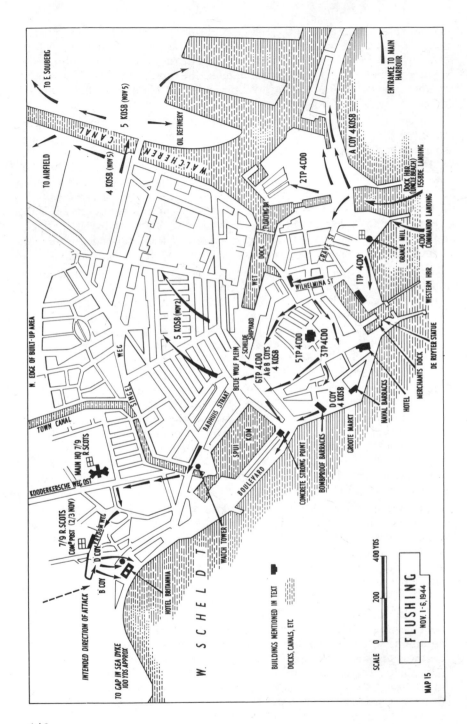

FLUSHING
NOV. 1-6, 1944

SCALE
0   200   400 YDS

BUILDINGS MENTIONED IN TEXT
DOCKS, CANALS, ETC

MAP 15

he had in his pocket an order from General Daser to blow up the cranes and docks of the shipyard.'

Blissinger was lightly wounded and they packed him off to a local hospital. During the day they took other prisoners and searched for snipers, but they were still in the German-held part of the town and out of contact with the British and spent a strained night wondering what would happen.

In the Old Town, in contrast, the Dutch people were out in the streets. They were most friendly and wanted to be helpful, but Dawson found them something of a problem as they would get into areas where fighting was going on. Two sergeants from the Dutch troop of 10 (IA) Commando acted as interpreters to get the Dutch police and members of the Resistance to move civilians away from the danger areas and to arrange for the evacuation of sick and wounded across the Scheldt.[2]

By 7.30, Uncle Beach, although not fully cleared, was able to accept landing craft, and the 4th KOSB began to land. Although it was by now full daylight, the first companies landed without meeting much shellfire either on the way across or on the beach, but by the time the later companies arrived, the Germans had seen what was happening, and both the crossing and the beach were under heavy fire from waterfront batteries still in action and from mortars outside the beachhead. Several landing craft were hit, but the losses were not crippling, and by 8 o'clock the last companies were across and clear of the beach. A Company went through No 2 Troop and pushed on to clear the dockland spit. B and C Companies, turning the other way with the intention of advancing into the New Town, reinforced the French troops at the dockyard gates and on the waterfront, but were unable to make progress beyond. D Company in reserve, at Kieffer's request to the colonel, took over the fighting in the area around the bomb-proof barracks.[3]

Thus by 9 o'clock, 4 Commando supported by the 4th KOSB had established an effective blocking position at the entrance to the Old Town, although on the esplanade short of what had been intended. Inside it the enemy held a number of positions, the most important of which were at the entrance to the Merchants' Harbour and in the two waterfront barracks beyond, but these were isolated and cut off from support. Dawson from his headquarters near the Oranje Mill was in radio communication across the Scheldt calling down artillery concentrations on Germans attempting to reach the Old Town past the dockyard gates, and rocket-firing Typhoons as well on batteries firing on the Scheldt. On one occasion, indeed, when fire from the large hotel near the entrance to Merchants' Dock became particularly troublesome, a motley collection of FOO's signallers, LCOCU and the commando intelligence section turned a captured 75-mm gun on the enemy, and eventually scored a hit, but the artillery was unflagging and the control organisation, tested by incessant calls, did not once fail, although sometimes the salvoes falling short into the Scheldt seemed to endanger landing craft.[4]

For the rest of the day fighting continued in the Old Town, and during the afternoon an attempt was made to mount an attack westwards along the esplanade with intensive artillery support, but it was called off before troops were committed and the beachhead perimeter remained where it was for the night. At Uncle Beach stores and reinforcements continued to arrive, sometimes under sharp shellfire and usually under machine gun fire. Stores had to be manhandled across the mud and treacherous surface below high water mark, the prisoners providing much of the manpower.

The 5th KOSB made its first attempt to cross about noon. '. . . we ran into such a curtain of fire that the leader turned back, and I was not sorry', Franks, who had gone in one of the landing craft for the ride, wrote in his diary, 'We also put up a mine about 50 yards away, which shook us up a bit, and it was good to get back to land, though the harbour [at Breskens] was then shelled and it was very nasty.' Supply and reinforcement had to be suspended, and the battalion was disembarked to take shelter in the Breskens bunkers. A new attempt was made during the afternoon after Typhoons had attacked the batteries with rockets. It was still daylight and the Scheldt and Uncle Beach were under fire, but the LCA, beaching five at a time, landed the companies, and they hurried ashore into the town. They were followed after dark by Brigadier McLaren, who then took control of the fighting in the town, and by the 7/9th Royal Scots.

That first night in Flushing a member of the Resistance reached McLaren's headquarters, claiming that, if a lull in the British shellfire could be arranged and certain other precautions taken, he could bring a large number of civilians from the German-held part of the town by a floating bridge across the mouth of the wet dock below the building slip into the comparative safety of the British lines. The arrangements were made, and under cover of a white flag several hundred women, children and old people were got out.[5] By then there were about 3,000 civilians in the Old Town, and arrangements were made to ferry as many as possible across the Scheldt out of danger.

Early on the 2nd under a heavy barrage fired across the Scheldt A and C Companies of the 5th KSOB began to advance northwards from the dockyard gate area into the newer part of the town. At midday, when they had reached their objectives some 600 yards away at the edge of the floods, B and D Companies followed them, swinging eastwards to reach the Middelburg Canal north of the dockyard. They were met by sporadic mortar and machine gun fire and by sniping. Inside the dockyard a new liner was being built on the slipway. The gantries of the tall building cranes on either side of her overlooked both the Old Town and the area to the north. In the cabins of three of them the Germans had placed snipers' nests. Now the 452nd Mountain Battery, which had rafted across its 3.7-inch howitzers to Uncle Beach, dismantled the howitzers and took them up to first floor rooms. Laying direct through the bore at close range, they fired into the crane cabins, which on being hit disappeared in smoke. By evening all four companies were on their objectives, but the dock area across the canal to the east remained in German hands. Meanwhile No 1 Troop, 4 Commando, had cleared the waterfront barracks, and the Frenchmen of No 5 Troop had gained control of Goosje Busken Straat. From houses at its southern end they were able to dominate the boulevard strong point, which, after an attack by rocket-firing Typhoons in the afternoon, surrendered to them.[6]

Two tasks, or possibly three, now confronted McLaren. One was to reach Middelburg and, either there or to eastwards, make contact with the 157th Infantry Brigade at that time still stalled at the causeway. That night Resistance couriers from Middelburg reached him and Leicester in Zoutelande asking for the shelling of the town to be stopped. Middelburg was crowded with refugees and the morale of the Germans there was low. Daser, the couriers said, would surrender if he were given the excuse of an armoured attack. The shelling seems to have been coming from South Beveland, but there were certainly no tanks in Flushing or at Zoutelande, nor any means of getting them across the floods to Middelburg had there been any, so for the moment it had to be left at that.

The second task was to take the Hotel Britannia, unknown to the British, the headquarters of the 1019th Infantry Regiment, which had been turned into the final keep for the defence of Flushing. The third, and as it was to prove impracticable and unnecessary, task was to cross the gap in the dyke immediately west of Flushing and advance along the dunes to meet the 4th Special Service Brigade. That brigade had landed successfully at Westkapelle and taken three of the four main naval batteries able to fire on the Scheldt. But its progress eastwards along the dunes, although perhaps not unreasonable in view of the difficult conditions and the fact that it had at first to be made entirely without transport for ammunition, signals or supplies, appears to have been slower than Foulkes expected. Its leading troops were still short of Zoutelande on the night of the 1st, and W11 remained in action preventing daylight use of the Westkapelle beaches, but advance on the 2nd had been rapid, and, when McLaren gave orders for crossing the gap, an attack on W11 was in progress. Meanwhile at the Flushing end of the dunes the smaller batteries, W3 and W4, were firing on landing craft approaching Uncle Beach, although not preventing its use.

Either for these reasons or because he thought German resistance was crumbling, McLaren on the evening of the 2nd ordered 4 Commando to attack Batteries W3 and W4 that night, going through the gap in Buffaloes to do so. A rapid tidal current flowed through the gap, which was partly choked with battered beach obstacles and great slabs of concrete from the broken dyke. No air photographs were available in Flushing. All that the commando and Buffalo crews knew was that the gap was there and that at high tide there might be enough water for the Buffaloes to swim through and land troops beyond. By the time orders had gone out for the troops to withdraw from the fighting in Flushing it was dark. The men were tired and hungry after 40 hours fighting, and there was little time to redistribute ammunition and check weapons. A plan for artillery support was hurriedly made out and radioed across the Scheldt, and the troops had assembled and were about to embark in the Buffaloes drawn up in Grave Straat, when it was learnt that the artillery would be unable to put the fire plan into effect in time. At this, and on Dawson's previous representations, what seems to have been an impracticable operation was postponed 24 hours and eventually cancelled.[7]

The third task, the attack on Hotel Britannia by the 7/9th Royal Scots, had it not succeeded, might also have been judged impracticable. The battalion reached Arsenal Barracks just before dawn on 2 November. During the day A and B Companies were employed in the area east of Uncle Beach and in the dockyard, while the rest of the battalion waited to be ordered into action. Shells occasionally fell on the barracks, one killing a young officer. Then in the evening the commanding officer, Lieutenant Colonel M. E. Melvill, was called to brigade headquarters and ordered by McLaren to attack Hotel Britannia in the early hours of the 3rd.

Little opposition was expected either from the hotel, thought to be held by about fifty Germans, or on the way there, and at first it was thought that two companies would be enough for the job; only later was a third, B Company, added. But to reach the hotel meant wading through floods, at least half a mile, more if an indirect route should be chosen. The depth of the floods, some of which were known to be tidal, could not be forecast, but was not expected to exceed eighteen inches. Melvill planned to pass well behind the hotel and attack it from the north. B and D Companies would make the assault from a start line on Vrydom Weg 250 yards from the far side of the hotel; D Company and part of the carrier platoon, dismounted and carrying additional Brens and PIATs, would provide fire support from the flanks. The advance would begin at 1.45. H-Hour for the assault would be 3.15. Two medium artillery regiments would fire on the hotel from across the Scheldt from 1.45 to 2.10, four field regiments from 2.45 to 3.15.

Moving along Badhuis Straat the long line of men in single file passed through the forward positions of the 4th KOSB and entered the floods. There was a burst of Spandau fire from the water tower at the bridge across the town canal and a few men fell wounded, then the German post was silenced by a party from the leading company. Overs from the medium artillery across the Scheldt began to fall close, and there was a long pause while a 22 Set was put together to call on the guns to cease fire or shorten their range. Then the column moved on again, across the bridge, turning right up Koudekersche Weg Oost, then left along Vrydom Straat.

But instead of being eighteen inches deep the water was three foot deep on the paved roadway and five feet deep on either side. It was a bright moonlight night, but in that depth of water it was hard to recognise the line of the streets and all too easy to step or slip into deeper water. Holding wireless sets and weapons above their heads to keep them dry, the men struggled on through the endless water. They wore no more equipment than needed, but, weighed down with weapons and ammunition, must have been

150

glad of the inflated Mae West lifebelts they wore beneath their mountaineers' windproof smocks.* There were a good many casualties, but luckily three Weasels and a few assault boats accompanied the battalion with ammunition, and they rescued the wounded; later two more Weasels were sent to help.

When at last the carrier platoon and B Company reached the start line a couple of hundred yards beyond the Vredehof Laan crossroads, they found the water between them and the hotel five foot deep and running strongly. Melvill ordered B Company commander, Major Rose, to take the lead and find some way to reach the hotel. With the men holding to each other to avoid being swept away, the column turned back to the crossroads, then made for the hotel, approaching it from the northeast rather than the north, with D Company, Major Chater, coming up on the left of B.

This brought D Company within about 75 yards of a pillbox under the sandy rise on which the hotel stood. The Germans in it seemed to be asleep for they did not open fire, and at 4.15, 16 Platoon, covered by Bren and PIAT fire from the two companies rushed it with shouts of 'Up the Royals', taking 35 prisoners. At that the garrison came to life, revealing an elaborate defence system of trenches and bunkers on the higher ground around the hotel, backed by a four-barrelled 20-mm and machine-guns on the hotel roof. Rose and Chater quickly moved their companies forward to the cover of the embankment, but the ground above it was under constant fire and there seemed no way around. The only chance was to rush the open space above and get into the hotel, and this, covered by the fire of every available weapon in the two companies, 17 and 18 Platoons led by Lieutenant George were ordered to do. The plan succeeded and they got into the hotel, clearing a large part of the ground floor, but subsequent attempts to reinforce them were repulsed by fire from the trenches outside and from the roof, and no one outside knew what was happening in the hotel.

Casualties were mounting. Major Thompson, commanding C Company, was killed, but then Lieutenant Beveridge, one of his platoon commanders, managed to get his men into the hotel and up the main staircase to the top floor. This he found unoccupied and the 20-mm he had orders to silence no longer firing overhead. A little after 6.30 however Chater, trying to get across to the hotel to take charge there, was shot dead.

By 7.30 the hotel was burning. There was still no news of what was happening inside it, while outside, as it grew light, the German machine gun fire and sniping increased. The Scots and Germans were far too inter-mingled for artillery fire to be called for, and the batteries of the radio sets were fading. Melvill sent his intelligence and signals officers back to rear headquarters near the canal bridge with orders to report the situation to

*For those familiar with modern protective clothing, it may be of interest that other infantry had nothing beyond their battledress over which a gas-proof cape might, contrary to regulations, be worn in wet weather. The commandos were issued with parachutists' denim smocks for the attack on Walcheren, and took good care to keep them for the rest of the war. During the summer in Normandy, however, usual frontline wear had been shirts and denim fatigue trousers.

brigade and come back with ammunition, then started from his command post on Vrydom Weg for the forward companies. Before he could reach them he was hit and badly wounded and his signaller killed.

Inside the burning hotel the three subalterns decided that they would have to get their men into some bunkers they saw close by, and about 10 o'clock shot a German sentry, then rushed the bunkers, breaking down the door. Inside they found the bunkers packed with Germans, among them Colonel Rheinhardt. The Germans surrendered and outside, as the Scots gained control, the heart went out of the defence.[8]

By noon it was all over. Six hundred Germans were prisoners and fifty more dead. Of the Royal Scots, twenty were dead and forty wounded. Dawson and others of 4 Commando who saw something of this fine feat of arms, greatly admired the courage and determination with which the Scots had carried it through, but, perhaps with some thought of the operation to which they had nearly been committed that night, wondered if more could not have been done to take advantage of tidal conditions.

There followed a pause during which it was hoped that some gesture of surrender might come from Middelburg. Then early on the 5th, under cover of artillery firing across the Scheldt and rocket-firing Typhoons, the 5th KOSB crossed the canal into the eastern dock area. It found the Germans still holding out, firing on the bridge with machine-guns in pillboxes, but cleared the area taking a hundred prisoners. Turning north, one of its companies advanced up the railway to the village of Oost-Souburg, where the railway joins the canal, only the raised banks of which now stood out from the floods. Advancing from Flushing along these, the 4th KOSB made good progress until nearly half way to Middelburg, but was then delayed by Schumines and later held up by pillboxes sunk into the canal banks. Although its casualties had been light and mainly wounded, the battalion had by now spent four days waist deep in water and was getting very tired.[9]

References
1 Dawson, correspondence and discussion; Wright, narrative; COHQ Bulletin Y/47, Appendix C.
2 Dawson as above; Poppe narrative.
3 Blake *op cit*, pp.102-4; Lieut Colonel E. D. Jackson, *The 4th Battalion The King's Own Scottish Borderers*, War History Committee KOSB, Galashiels, 1945, pp.81-3.
4 Wright, narrative;
5 Lieut Colonel G. C. M. Batchelor, *From Flushing to Bremen, The Fifth Battalion, The King's Own Scottish Borderers*, Minden, 1945, p.9. Blake *op cit*, pp.104-5; Poppe narrative; Franks, diary.
6 Batchelor *op cit*, p.9; Wright narrative.
7 Wright narrative.
8 Lieut Colonel M. E. Melvill, correspondence; *Current Reports from Overseas, No 80*, pp.11 to end (narrative here is based on Melvill's account written from hospital); Angus Muir, *The First of Foot, The History of the Royal Scots in World War 2*, Blackwood for the Royal Scots Historical Committee, Edinburgh, 1956, pp.342-355; *The Thistle*, April 1946, article 'Flushing. Extract from the Semi-official History of the 7/9th Royal Scots'.
9 Jackson, *op cit*, pp.83-4; Batchelor, *op cit*, p.10.

13

Westkapelle

Despite the enthusiastic reception by Ramsay and Simonds of the Trafalgar Day proposal to attack on 1 November, two uncertainties still hung over the Westkapelle assault. First, as at Flushing, assault must depend on there being practicable beaching points, on or near the battered shoulders of the gap in the dyke. Something about that could be learnt from the excellent air photographs, which, as the day drew near, began to reach the assault forces. Poring over the stereo pairs, landing craft captains and commando officers familiarised themselves with the jagged outlines of the gap, made their final plans and briefed their men. In the photographs they could see what seemed to be practicable beaching points among the bomb craters and debris, which the tides, swirling through the gap to fill and empty the saucer-like interior of the island, had begun to cover with sand and mud. Close to the tidelines on each side they could identify concrete blockhouses, which, if resolutely held, would dominate the landing places, and now they knew that the Germans, if not resolute, were at least alert. There was nothing to do now but put the issue to the test.

The other uncertainty was the weather. Fog and low cloud might prevent the intensive bombing in the last few days, which had been substituted for the more methodical destruction of the German gun positions; rough seas could make it impossible to beach landing craft successfully. The First Canadian Army instruction of the 30th said that Simonds and Ramsay with the advice of the Air Officer Commanding 84 Group would decide on embarkation and sailing from Ostend or postponement, but thereafter the final decision to assault would rest with Pugsley and Leicester in the *Kingsmill*, who were authorised to bring the assault force back to harbour should beaching be impracticable.

On 27 and 28 October, as Bomber Command began its intensive attack, the naval assault force assembled at Ostend. On the morning of the 31st, despite rough seas, high winds and overcast which had closed down the preparatory bombing a day early, Simonds and Ramsay ordered embarkation. In the late forenoon, as the troops marched down to the wreck-strewn harbour and settled down in the landing craft which thronged it, Ramsay, Simonds, Foulkes, Pugsley and Leicester met in the *Kingsmill* to decide whether the force should sail.

Knowing that Ramsay would ask his opinion, Pugsley has sent Masterman in an MTB halfway along the coast towards Westkapelle to report conditions. Masterman, signalling back 'Weather improving' and confirmed Pugsley's own view. Pugsley, therefore, now said that in his opinion the force could reach Westkapelle, but whether the landing craft would then be able to beach and land troops would remain uncertain until daybreak on the 1st. At that the RAF liaison officer present pointed out that fog was forming over southern England and might prevent bombers and spotting aircraft for the bombarding ships from taking off. He proposed that the assault should be postponed 24 hours. But the improvement in the weather seemed likely to be short-lived, and by the 2nd it might be too rough to land. In this dilemma Ramsay and Simonds decided to amend their instructions to Pugsley and Leicester and to empower them 'to postpone the assault and return to port if in their opinion on all available information (with particular reference to the probabilities of air support, air smoke and spotting aircraft for bombardment ships) at the time of taking such a decision it is unlikely to succeed.' Finally at 10 o'clock that evening, having discussed the question again by telephone, Ramsay and Simonds reaffirmed the discretion they had given the joint force commanders and ordered the force to sail.[1]

Shortly after midnight the darkened landing craft, packed with troops sleeping uncomfortably where they could among the Buffaloes, Weasels and tanks, began to cast off securing lines and get under way, forming up as they cleared the harbour into long lines for the passage to Westkapelle. Outside the harbour the Support Squadron Eastern Flank, which had sailed earlier and anchored, weighed at 3.25 am to lead the force to Westkapelle past the motor launches marking the approach route. In all 182 craft of various types and sizes were to take part in the attack.

During the night the weather continued to improve. On board the *Kingsmill* Pugsley at 5.45 next morning heard the opening roar of the bombardment preparing the way for the Flushing assault, and later a success signal told him that 4 Commando was ashore there. On the bridge of LCH 269 Sellar, having spent the night up as his squadron led the way towards Westkapelle, was in night watchkeeping rig and sea boots, when his recently appointed marine servant, a heavy goods driver in civil life, appeared to ask him in the true Jeeves tradition, 'Shall we be changing our boots before or after the battle, sir?'

At six o'clock that morning Brigadier Church Mann at Headquarters First Canadian Army made an emergency signal.

Pass following to Admiral Ramsay for transmission by him to Force T in clear. Quote extremely unlikely any air support air spotting or air smoke possible due to airfield conditions and forecast. Unquote.

Despite the wide discretion given them, Pugsley and Leicester had agreed that, should the weather permit beaching, the assault should go ahead. But the final word rested with Pugsley, who bore the responsibility for the whole force during approach and beaching, and the moment for it was fast arriving.

The sea was calm, and, although the sky was overcast, it promised to improve. At first the German batteries, except for W17 which was firing

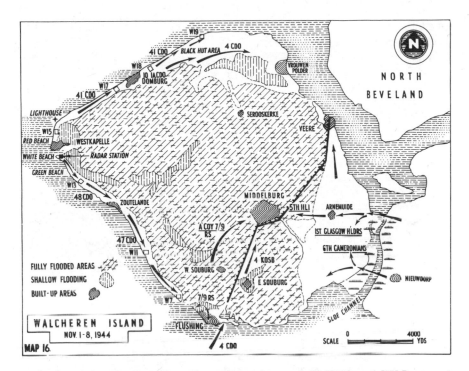

across the island at Breskens, were silent, but at 8.09 W13 and W15 opened fire on ML 902 marking Point BB, the deployment point. At 8.20 the *Warspite* and *Roberts* opened fire on preplanned targets, and a little later the *Roberts* shifted target to W15, which the *Erebus*, silenced for an hour and a half by a turret failure, should have engaged. About 8.30 Pugsley saw 15-inch shells strike the battery and for the moment silence it. About the same time twelve Typhoons of 183 Squadron, 84 Group, appeared overhead. Pugsley ordered the assault to go in and made to Ramsay the signal code-word 'Nelson' telling him of the decision. At 8.45 the guns across the Scheldt opened on their targets along the dunes.[2]

At 8.46, as the Support Squadron approached Point BB,* it came under fire from W13 and almost simultaneously began to deploy to engage the batteries north and south of the gap. By 9 o'clock the support craft were under fire from batteries along the coast from W11 in the south to W17 in the north. The southern group of support craft under direct command of Sellar, and the northern, under Lieutenant Commander Leefe, both in LCH, each comprised three LCG(L), three LCF, three LCS(L) and one LCG(M) with three LCT(R) in the northern group and two in the southern. Before reaching Point BB the six LCG(L) had on Sellar's order engaged W15 with their 4.7-inch guns. Now with the LCF and the LCS(L) they were to distribute their fire along the batteries and strong points from W15 to

* See Map, page 125.

155

W288 beyond Zoutelande to the south to cover the LCG(M) and the landing craft they would lead in to beach.

The LCG(M), which it was planned should arrive just ahead of the first landing craft, were to beach themselves on the shoulders of the gap, flood special ballast tanks to provide a firm gun platform, then blast two concrete emplacements there with the two 17-pounder anti-tank guns each of them carried, firing solid, armour-piercing shot. Specially designed for this hazardous task and more heavily armoured than other support landing craft, they were a new type which had never been in action before. Firing accurately from a steady platform at very short range, they would, it was hoped, find weak spots in the concrete even if they could not penetrate its full thickness. To make sure that they did not broach to in the strong tidal current and block the beaches for the landing craft, they were ordered to drop kedges as they beached.

The smaller, manoeuvrable LCS(L) would go in closest in support of the LCG(M), further out would be the more cumbersome LCF with their Oerlikons and pom-poms, and beyond them again the LCG(L) with their 4.7s. Their guns would not penetrate thick concrete, but it was hoped that by hitting the batteries with a large number of light projectiles they might keep down their fire or failing that draw it upon themselves. To their fire the LCT(R) would add rocket salvos, producing a sudden and awesome cascade of high explosive which could only be repeated after a long loading interval. Like the fire of the other support craft, this might with luck knock out delicate instruments and daze men, but it could not be expected to penetrate the concrete.

Against the low grey clouds and black smoke rising from Westkapelle, the flashes from the German guns were clearly visible from seaward. Hope, who had been working for weeks on the fire plan and knew exactly where to look, counted from the bridge of the *Kingsmill* fourteen out of the sixteen guns in the vital naval batteries in action.[3] At 9.20 they scored their first hit; LCF 37, the leading LCF of the southern group, still 3,500 to 4,000 yards from the shore, well beyond the range of her Oerlikons and pom-poms, was hit aft on the waterline by W15. Her crew shored up the side and plugged the hole, but, as she continued to close the range, she was repeatedly hit until, 25 minutes later when 1,500 yards from the shore, a shell from W13 exploded in her main magazine. A sheet of flame enveloped the ship; everyone forward of the bridge was killed and the ship left a burning wreck aground on a shoal. A returning LCI(S) rescued nine wounded and 29 unwounded survivors from her crew of 65.[4]

The orders for the LCT(R) were to proceed as requisite to engage their targets at H-10 mintues, remaining as long as possible behind the radar counter-measures screen provided by the LCG(L). Observing the LCT to be late in passing Point BB, however, they appear to have assumed that they were free to fire later by observation if not within range at H-10. At 9.37 one LCT(R) of the southern group fired her rockets and saw them fall on the radar station and dunes south of the gap. The other, hit by two shells as she was about to fire, discharged one bank of 42 rockets unintentionally, which fell close to support craft of the northern group, then recovered and at 9.48 fired the rest on target. Of the three LCT(R) of the northern group, one, realising that the radar image of the shore line she was getting was false, held her fire. The other two, after firing ranging rockets, fired at 9.42 when their radar appeared to indicate they were within range, apparently confusing radar echoes from craft ahead with those of the shore line. The pattern of their rockets fell among support craft, 50 yards short of the LCI(S) now going in to beach and about 200 yards ahead of the LCT carrying the armour. Three support craft already under shellfire were hit by splinters, mercifully with no more than a few casualties. The water was covered with bursting high explosive, and in the landing craft going in to beach there were some minutes of dismay and indecision. From a short distance it looked as if disaster had overtaken the assault, and in the *Kingsmill* Leicester called on Pugsley to stop further rocket fire. Pugsley's signal was, however, not received by the LCT(R), and at 9.48 the remaining one of the three, seeing the range clear, fired her rockets which fell on target. As soon as they fell, the air controller called down the Typhoons who placed their rockets accurately on W15.[5]

While all this was happening the two LCG(M) had beached accurately and on time. LCG(M) 101, coming under fire from W15, opened fire at 2,000 yards and was hit just before she beached at 9.45 on the northern shoulder of the gap, 40 yards from the concrete gun emplacement she had been ordered to engage. Once beached, she was partly sheltered from W15, but came under heavy machine gun fire, while W15 continued to hit her aft. Machine gun bullets pierced the recuperator of the starboard gun, so that it had to be pushed out by hand after each recoil, and wounded the layer and loader of the port gun, wrecking the sights. The LCG(M) fired some fifty rounds at the emplacement. Three Germans ran out and were shot down, but from her position on the beach the loopholes were defiladed by concrete, and, although the armour-piercing shot were later found to have dug their way about six feet into the ten-foot thick walls, none penetrated. Fifteen minutes after beaching, with both guns firing very slowly and the crews exhausted, the captain gave the order to unbeach. Going aft to work the kedge, Sub-lieutenant Damen and AB Deverall were killed and a leading stoker wounded, but a shell splinter had almost severed the wire, which, as the ship came off the beach, broke and enabled her to get clear. Wounded were brought up on deck, for the ship was riddled all along her port side. Half a mile from the beach she suddenly turned over and sank, but, except for the two dead, all her crew were picked up by a passing LCI(S).

LCG(M) 102 was hit near the bridge just before beaching on the southern shoulder at 9.43. She, too, fired at a concrete emplacement, but could not penetrate it. At 10.02 she was seen to be on fire, and was later reported broached-to and in flames. There were no survivors from her crew of 41 and only one from the crews of the three LCS(L) supporting her.[6]

Between 10 and 10.20, as the first landing craft came in to beach and the two groups strove valiantly to cover them and the LCG(M), the support squadron suffered its worst casualties. Closing to pointblank range to support LCG(M) 102, all three LCS(L) of the southern group were hit, and were last seen beached or broached-to and burning. Of the three in the northern group, one was hit and caught fire, but was towed out of action and saved. Drawing the fire of the batteries at slightly longer range, all three LCG(L) of the northern group and one of the southern were hit; one sank, but the other two resumed action after putting out fires and stopping leaks. A second LCF was hit, caught fire and had to be abandoned. Sailors and marines worked together to keep the flimsy, mass-produced hulls afloat, to get petrol and ammunition fires under control, to keep engines running and guns firing.

The seven LCI(S) led by Commander Jonas, Deputy Senior Officer Assault Group, in LCH 187 reached the deployment point at 8.52 and a little later passed the leading LCT. Estimating that these would be five to ten minutes late in beaching and that the LCT(R) would not be in position to fire at the planned time, Jonas reduced speed to six knots. Nevertheless at 9.40 the LCI(S) were 2,000 yards from the beach and could therefore still reach it nearly on time; the LCT(R) of the southern group had just fired their rockets, but those of the northern were still 2,000 yards away from their firing position. Reckoning that they would not now fire, Jonas released the three LCI(S) with the assaulting troops of 41 Commando for the beach. A minute later two of the northern LCT(R) fired. The LCI(S) swerved away from the bursting rockets and signalled to Jonas for instructions. Jonas replied 'Go in now', and the LCI(S) turned back on course. Shortly afterwards the leader was hit twice by shells or rockets and turned away again, but at 9.58, or shortly afterwards, they beached on the sea wall.* Astern of them the LCT with 41 and 48 Commandos, acting as they had been trained to do for the Normandy assault, adjusted speed to beach at the planned time interval after the LCI(S), and the first wave touched down astride the gap at 10.05. The Buffaloes and Weasels drove out and the LCT retracted.[7]

The LCT of the first wave had little trouble, but by the time the second arrived, both ends of White Beach were under heavy shell and mortar fire. After unloading LCT 839 saw 979 in difficulties and passed lines to swing her clear. Then at 10.50, in company with 979 and 1132, turned to seaward

---

*The consensus of the naval reports is that the leading waves of landing craft beached at the following times:

LCI(S)	— two rifle troops and heavy weapon troop of 41 Commando	9.58
Group I (g)	— two troops 41 Commando	10.05
LCT	three troops 48 Commando	
Group I (h)	— one troop 41 Commando	first LCT at 1015
LCT	two troops 10 IA Commando	last at 1030
	two troops 48 Commando	

41 Commando War Diary in putting the LCI(S) at 1012 and Group I (g) at 1018 is in a minority of one, but has been followed by AORG Report No 299.

and increased to emergency full ahead. At 10.54 two shells hit 839. Two minutes later she was hit on the funnel, then on the hull and in the port engine room. She began to drop astern and by 1105, after being hit four more times, she was dead in the water and sinking, drifting down the coast in company with LCG(L) 1 and LCF 37 three miles west of the Westkapelle lighthouse. At about 11.30 she got through to the *Kingsmill* on an emergency wireless set and an LCP(L) came with orders to lay smoke around the support craft and sink the LCT. As she came alongside, the Germans opened fire again, and, with the quarter deck awash, wounded and un-wounded survivors were taken off and later transferred to an LCI(S) for Ostend. Several other LCT reaching the collecting area were sunk by mines. But the landing went on, and at 12.30, when it was clear that the commandos were firmly established ashore, Pugsley ordered what was left of the support squadron out of action.

Of its 27 craft, nine were sunk or sinking, seven others were damaged and out of action, four damaged but capable of further action, seven fit for action. Of its officers and men, 172 had been killed, 125 wounded. Their sacrifice, by drawing the fire of the batteries, had achieved its purpose for casualties among the landing craft and the commandos in them had been light.

At about 10.17 guns in W13, having fired 200 rounds per gun at the support group to their front, ran out of ammunition. This says the operation research group, which learnt of it later from prisoners of war, was 'probably the most important single event of the operation'. An entry of 8.30 pm 30 October in Aschmann's war diary records 7/202 (W13) as having 1565 rounds of 15-cm with another 190 on the way to it. W11 had 1751 with 360 on the way. Both batteries had previously been in action against the Canadians across the Scheldt, and early on the 31st were in action across the Scheldt again. Later all batteries except W17 and W19 fired when the smoke screen off Breskens was seen. So it is possible that by the morning of 1 November, W13 had only 200 rounds per gun left, but there is no record of Aschmann or anyone else showing concern on the afternoon of the 31st at what would have been an easily recognisable danger of ammunition shortage in face of seaborne attack, nor of the shortage occurring on the 1st. Another possibility is that there was a check while ammunition was brought to the guns from the battery administrative area on the inland side of the dunes, and that before this could be done the battery was under infantry attack.[8]

Be that as it may, the research group's dramatic assessment could be valid only if it is assumed that in the last ten minutes before the reserve troops of the assaulting commandos landed, the battery commander would belatedly have seen the need to switch the fire of his guns from the support craft to the troop-carrying landing craft, by then drawing away to his flank, and have succeeded in doing so effectively. A more genuine turning point, because it came earlier when there was still time for the guns to sink the assault waves, was when the 15-inch shells of the *Roberts* struck W15 followed by the fighter-bomber attack. Knocking out between them two guns, killing and wounding their crews and inevitably disorganising the battery, these blows must have substantially reduced the fire power of W15, potentially the most dangerous of the batteries. To the extent that it influenced Pugsley to order in the assault, this was indeed a turning point, but the truly decisive moment for the success of the attack was when, as Pugsley and Sellar had calculated, W13 and W15 returned the fire of the support craft, leaving the landing craft unmolested.

The delay of the landing craft of the assault waves in running in to beach unnecessarily increased the time during which both they and the support craft were exposed to enemy fire and left the two LCG(M), which had beached punctually, unsupported by assaulting troops. Both the LCI(S) and the LCT claimed afterwards that they could have beached on time, but the LCI(S) held back thinking the LCT late, and the LCT timed their approach by the LCI(S). The LCI(S) might have beached only a few minutes late, but the LCT(R), seeing the assault waves apparently astern of station, felt free to fire late, and two owing to the radar error, fired into the LCI(S). Tidal conditions were difficult and the complex assault was made without rehearsal, but, as the Deputy Senior Officer Assault Group said in his report, 'The operation stressed once more the absolute necessity of every craft to press on with its allotted task with dash and determination without question and without hesitation.'

'If things happen according to form, you'll be dead within twenty minutes.' At Salerno and again on the Normandy beaches the second-in-command of 41 Commando had been killed almost as the landing craft touched down, and now as the LCI(S) came in to beach, a troop sergeant major stepped into the break of the bridge to make this encouraging remark to Major Peter Wood, the present second-in-command. And indeed the odds could not have seemed favourable at that moment. To Wood, the six-knot approach of the landing craft seemed intolerably slow and the two turns away as the shells and rockets burst around arrant folly. At each he had angrily insisted on return to the original course. Then at last they beached and found they were no longer under shellfire, for the guns of W15 could not be depressed enought to fire on the LCI(S), although a machine gun continued to fire on them.

Under Wood's command, B, P and S Troops were to cover the landing of the rest of 41 Commando, clearing any opposition on the dyke and in the western edge of Westkapelle village. In spite of everything, they had not lost more than a dozen men on the run in. As the shaky LCI(S) ramps went out, they scrambled ashore on the sea wall, meeting scattered fire as they appeared over the top. B Troop moved in on Westkapelle, and P Troop with the medium machine guns of S, turning left, found a position from which to bring W15 under small arms fire. The LCI(S), taking advantage of the cessation of shellfire, made the wounded as comfortable as possible before unbeaching to run the gauntlet again as they withdrew. But now the

German fire was less accurate, and they got away without further damage, although the leading craft later blew up as the result of the earlier hits.

At 10.05 the two LCT carrying commando headquarters, A and X troops under Lieutenant Colonel E. C. E. Palmer, the commanding officer, beached unscathed on White Beach, not far from the LCI(S), at the point where the broken edge of the dyke disappeared into the sand and mud of the northern shoulder of the gap, and the Buffaloes and Weasels drove out into the water towards Westkapelle.[9]

Captain Stevens, commanding A Troop, had the task of taking Westkapelle tower, standing square, tall and solidly built in brick, at the far end of the main street. Coming under fire, he ordered his troop out of the Buffaloes, and the men waded knee-deep into the shattered village. Shots were coming from the top of the tower, and, when a demolition party reached its foot to fix charges on the door, grenades were dropped on it. S Troop's machine guns and a single Sherman from the breaching teams opened fire on the top of the tower, but the problem remained of how to ascend the narrow internal stairway. Bluff seemed the best answer, so Stevens with a German speaker from 10 (IA) Commando walked out into the street and shouted to the Germans to surrender, Stevens imitating the German words. After a little two men came down offering to surrender the tower. Taking one of them with him to guard against booby traps, Stevens went up the stairs and took the surrender of what turned out to be a German artillery observation post.[10]

Meanwhile B and X Troops had cleared the rest of the village and Y Troop and the Norwegian and Belgian Troops of 10 (IA) Commando had landed. Taking Hayden, commanding Y Troop, with him, Palmer went forward about 11.15 to reconnoitre for the attack on W15 and discovered a possible way to assault around the right of P Troop. At 12 o'clock Y troop attacked supported by the fire of P and by 12.30 had taken the battery with 120 prisoners. A quarter of an hour later, the two troops reached the lighthouse, where the coast turns northeast and only a narrow neck of sand dunes separated the sea from the floods. Here the brigade commander had ordered 41 Commando to stop until it was clear that all was well south of the gap, where W13 and W11 still guarded the Scheldt and the approach to the Westkapelle beaches.

The armoured breaching teams of the Lothians and of the Royal Engineers of the 79th Armoured Division in their four LCT were intended to land at Red Beach, the sea wall left of the gap, at H-Hour, but, as we have seen, the assault was late. The first pair carrying breaching teams approached the beach between 10 o'clock and 10.05. As she came in LCT 513, the flotilla leader, was hit six times by 3-inch shells from W15. Holed and temporarily out of control, she swung away from the beach, then as control was recovered withdrew with most of her tanks damaged and the fascine AVRE on fire. The other, LCT 650, hit in the engine room, followed her out without beaching, her captain judging that if he persisted all her tanks would be destroyed. The squadron commander in ML 903 ordered the second pair, LCT 937 and 1005, to beach further south and LCT 650 to join them there. With only two tanks capable of landing and one of those damaged, 513 was later ordered to return to Ostend without beaching.

The three LCT beached at White Beach, where the Buffaloes and Weasels which had landed 41 and 10 (IA) Commandos milled around looking for exits and two Buffaloes loaded with ammunition burnt fiercely. Unlike Red Beach, where the landing was on the masonry of the sea wall, the shoulder of the gap at White Beach was soft clay and sand strewn with large blocks of masonry from the broken dyke. When the first AVRE drove out, it bellied, and, although the three LCT rebeached repeatedly in the attempt to find better going, few vehicles managed to reach firm ground without assistance. In the course of the afternoon, working under shell and mortar fire, the devoted Light Aid Detachment under AQMS Evans REME and the tank and bulldozer crews got a total of eight vehicles — two command Shermans, three Flails, two AVREs and a bulldozer — through the clay, soft sand and scattered masonry into Westkapelle, nine others had to be abandoned to the rising tide, and seven went back to Ostend, six in LCT 513 and one jammed in 650. During the night the tide drowned the three Flails in Westkapelle.[11]

Between tactical air strikes and counter-battery bombardment from the *Warspite*, W17 near Domburg continued to shell Westkapelle and the beaches. At 3 pm, satisfied that things were going reasonably well south of the gap, Leicester freed 41 Commando to advance to Domburg and take the battery. As the commando advanced, there were flurries of shooting, but most of the Germans emerged from their trenches and dug-outs fairly quickly, and there was a steady trickle of prisoners in parties of about 20 or 30 at a time.

It was growing dark as 41 Commando, now with P Troop leading and X Troop out in the dunes to its left, approached Domburg. W17 surrendered without much fight, and P Troop followed by B and Y entered the town by the light of burning houses set on fire by the *Warspite*'s shells. Meeting little opposition but here and there breaking up a German drinking party which threw a few grenades from a house before surrendering, they advanced into the town. By 7 o'clock they had secured the central crossroads and the road running southwards to the woods and the floods. Half an hour later a report came in that X Troop was in trouble in the dunes and B was sent to help.

Advancing in the fading light, the leading section of X Troop had suddenly found itself right under a steep dune on top of which was a strong point, manned, in the words of Lieutenant John Jewers, commanding the section, by fanatics or drunks. The section seemed to be in a defile, and as it moved forward the Germans yelling defiance opened up with everything they had, lobbing stick grenades on the British below. Crawling forward to see what was happening, Captain Brind Sheridan, the troop commander, and his orderly were hit by a burst of fire and killed, and later Jewers withdrew the section to a fire position further back. B Troop arrived in the early hours next morning and after daylight the Germans withdrew into the dunes beyond.[12]

B, X and Y Troops of 48 Commando under their commanding officer, Lieutenant Colonel J. L. Moulton, landed on the southern shoulder of the gap at 10.05 am. Apart from the alarm when the rockets had seemed to hit 41 Commando, they had had an uneventful run it; none of the LCT chugging steadily towards the beach had been hit, and only a few shells had fallen near them. Driving ashore from the beached LCT in Buffaloes and Weasels as the Oerlikons of the LCT and the Polsen guns of the Buffaloes hosed the dunes with fire, everyone had landed dryshod. B Troop had found the large concrete blockhouse on the shoulder of the gap deserted, and X Troop, racing up the dunes under shellfire for the radar station which if properly held could have dominated both shoulders of the gap, had found there only a few Germans who had promptly surrendered.

Reaching the radar station a few minutes later, Moulton ordered Mackenzie, commanding X Troop, to go right on, and the troop quickly took the next strong point, W285, with about a dozen prisoners. Y Troop then went through, took W286, and made contact with W13, but then, attempting to mount a quick attack unsupported, Major Derek de Stacpoole, commanding the troop, was killed and the advance faded out. It would clearly need a co-ordinated effort to restart it.

Meanwhile A and Z Troops and the machine guns, in reserve under the second-in-command, Major Sanders, had landed at 10.25 coming under considerably heavier fire which had damaged and caused casualties in one of the LCT, preventing her from beaching properly. The Buffalo with the machine guns had been wrecked, and other Buffaloes, reaching the beach, had been hit trying to get around the inshore side of the dunes. But before long the two troops, coming forward on foot, reached the rest of the commando now preparing to attack W13.

In the hard-hit support craft the sense of passage of time was, according to the research groups report, lost. 'As when the sun stood still for Joshua and the Israelites, the action appeared to those engaged to last much longer than the clock recorded.' In the dunes it was just the opposite. Every time one looked at one's watch more time had passed than seemed possible. The Weasels with the more powerful wireless sets were back at the beach unable to climb the dunes, and the ligher manpack sets were frequently blanketed. Most of the time control had to be by personal contact and for that or to get a look a hundred yards or so ahead, one had to plod up and down through steep, loose sand. Resupply of ammunition had to come by manpack along those same dunes. Weapons had repeatedly to be cleaned of clinging sand and salt to keep them firing. Worst of all, the only links surviving by which fire support could be arranged were one to the *Roberts*, whose 15-inch guns would be a doubtful help for close support, and one to the support squadron, which was by now in no case to give further help.

A brigade set had, however, turned up a few hundred yards back working to the *Kingsmill*. After giving preliminary orders for the attack, Moulton walked back to it with the Canadian Forward Observation Officer, Captain Skelton, used it to ask for timed programmes by the Canadian artillery across the Scheldt and by tactical air strike, waited for it to be agreed, then walked back to the commando to give his final orders. It is possible that it would have been better to have gone on with the attack quickly without waiting to arrange supporting fire, for while the commanding officer was away, the three foremost troops of the commano were heavily mortared. Z Troop, forming up for the assault, was badly hit, and everyone in it above the rank of corporal killed or wounded. Mackenzie of X Troop was mortally wounded. Davies, the Forward Officer, Bombardment, working the *Roberts*, and his orderly were first wounded, then, as David Winser, the commando doctor, and his orderly dressed their wounds, all four were killed. There were other losses, too, but it was too late to alter the fire plan and Moulton ordered B Troop to take Z's place as assault troop. At 3.45 the fire programme began with ten minutes artillery fire across the Scheldt at normal rate to be followed by five minutes at intense. As it ended Typhoons appeared overhead, diving on the battery a couple of hundred yards ahead of the commando, firing their cannon and dropping 500-pound bombs which could be seen leaving their racks to pass over the commando and fall accurately on target.

As the last aircraft completed its dive, B Troop, covered by 2-inch mortar smoke and by A Troop in a fire position where the narrow dunes luckily broadened slightly to allow some degree of flanking fire, went forward over the dunes, crossed a minefield, which like others crossed earlier had been made ineffective by drifting sand, and entered the battery position. X and Y Troops followed B, and soon the battery control position and three of the four casemates were in the hands of the commando. Later patrols reached the fourth casemate, and, searching the administrative buildings below the dunes, brought in about seventy prisoners. By then it was dark, and a single Oerlikon still firing at the far end of the position was left until morning. Through the cold, moonlit night the men of the commando cleaned weapons, carried up ammunition, patrolled, ate the scanty rations they had in their pockets, slept or shivered, and made ready to advance when it grew light.[13]

The four LCT carrying 47 Commando under Lieutenant Colonel C. F. Phillips had reached their waiting position, some six miles from the gap, at 9.45 that morning. What could be seen of the battle from there was hardly reassuring for the men of the commando as they waited their turn to enter it. They saw, as did everyone else to seaward that morning, the bright flashes which showed that the bombing had failed to silence the German batteries. They passed LCG(M) 101 floating bottom up and saw another support craft explode. To the north LCT 513 drew away from the beach with a fire on board, and someone said that other LCTs astern had struck mines. At some time probably shortly before noon the order came to land, and the LCTs went ahead to beach. In the last few hundred yards shells hit three of the four.

It was the brigade commander's intention that 47 Commando should land south of the gap. This was fully understood within the brigade, and in the brigade operation order is clear from the task given to the commando. But in the landing table 47 Commando is shown as landing on White Beach, described as 'the gap in the dyke 380 yards in width'. Either because of this ambiguity or in the confusion caused by shell damage, instead of beaching just clear of the gap to the south as had 48 Commando's LCTs, 47 Commando's lowered their ramps in the gap for the amphibians to swim out. The leading LCT did so close to the southern shoulder, but two others, instead of coming up on her starboard side, went in close to the northern shoulder, where a huddle of other LCTs had bunched close to the beach.

Weasels could not swim the gap, but Buffaloes could, and a number did so, unfortunately some in the wrong direction. As a result, X and Y Troops and about half of A and S landed in Westkapelle. In the course of the afternoon they either crossed to the southern side in their own Buffaloes or managed to get lifts, but it was 7 o'clock and nearly dark before 47 Commando had assembled in the southern dunes 600 yards from the gap. B Troop had lost about half its men when the leading LCT was hit, S Troop had only one mortar and one machine gun left, and many of the men in A, B and X Troops were soaked either having had to swim ashore or from wading about in Westkapelle trying to find a way across the gap. Most of the Weasels had sunk or had been abandoned in Westkapelle, and a fair amount of equipment had been lost. And the commando had not yet been in action.[14]

Thus when darkness fell on 1 November, some six miles of the dunes were in the hands of the 4th Special Service Brigade. All three commandos and the two troops of 10 (IA) Commando were ashore. 41 and 48 had had losses, but would be ready for action next day; 47 had suffered disorganisation and losses in landing but had largely recovered. Most of the specialised armoured breaching teams had been lost on landing, and, except for the single Sherman which had fired on Westkapelle tower, had not so far managed to get into action.

Fifteen of the Buffaloes had been destroyed or were unserviceable, but the rest, except for their vulnerability to mines, had shown themselves well able to cope with the difficulties of the beaches and to cross the gap as required. They could not climb the dunes south of the gap, but the engineers were clearing a track for them along the inland side of the dunes. The Weasels, on the other hand, had been almost a dead loss, and reliance on them to get forward the more powerful wireless sets had slowed down the advance.

Beach maintenance was in trouble. It had been planned to establish Green Beach for supplies south of the gap. For the clearance of the beach area, four LCTs were to bring in six armoured bulldozers, four of them towing sledges with engineer stores. What happened is called in one report 'a great sapper tragedy'. Three of the four LCTs beached on the wrong side of the gap, and four of the bulldozers drove straight into a clay patch below high water mark to be drowned with their sledges by the incoming tide. The single bulldozer that landed on the right side of the gap, wading through shallow water on a firm sandy beach, fell into a bomb crater and was drowned. Of five Buffaloes allotted to the engineers, two struck mines, one sank, and one was taken back to Ostend in a damaged LCT. Practically all the officers and men of 509 and 510 Field Companies and 144 Pioneer Company detailed for work on the beach*landed safely, but they had very little equipment to work with. Under shellfire and with Buffaloes exploding mines around them, they cleared the area under the radar station and began work on the track forward, but until the last remaining bulldozer could get across the gap, work on filling in craters and removing beach obstacles would be terribly slow and laborious.[15]

The first three LCT to beach on Green Beach were due to arrive on the afternoon ebb tide with more stores. One hit a mine and sank, and at 2.30, as the remaining two came in to beach, one was hit by a shell in and consequence both were ordered away to wait for a quieter time. At 7 pm one LCT beached undetected in the dusk and was allowed to dry out on the falling tide while stores were unloaded. At 3 next morning she unbeached and took 150 wounded and many prisoners of war back to Ostend. An hour later W11 fired star shell and began a two hour bombardment of the beach and later fired on an LCT beaching which had in consequence to withdraw hurriedly. Wounded and prisoners of war had to wait with very little shelter from shellfire or weather until the early hours of the 3rd, when two more LCT arrived and were allowed to dry out. But for the forward troops the main difficulty was to get ammunition up from the beach along the dunes. Rations were a lesser problem, for plentiful supplies of tinned food were to be had for the looking in the German positions.[16]

At first light on the 2nd A Troop (48 Commando) with a fire controller for the single surviving 3-inch mortar, started towards Zoutelande, intended as the advanced guard for the rest of the commando, but shortly afterwards Leicester arrived with Phillips to say that 47 should go through as soon as possible. After a short encounter A Troop took the next strong point, W287, with twenty prisoners, and, after meeting only isolated resistance on the way, entered Zoutelande at 11 o'clock. There was a short fire fight in the village and then 150 Germans surrendered. Captain Dan Flunder, the troop commander, was explaining to the burgomaster that the village was now safe from damage, when a 15-shell from the *Roberts* crashed through the roof of the church.

47 Commando started forward from its overnight assembly area at 9

*Some sappers of the two field companies were attached to the commandos for the advance through the dunes minefields, of whom some, finding no sapper work to do, fought as infantry.

o'clock, a long line of men plodding in single file through the dunes, loaded with weapons and ammunition, chilled and bleary after a comfortless night. About 12.30 the two leading troops reached Zoutelande, where the red, white and blue of the national colours and the royal orange were beginning to appear, and climbed the dunes to the south. W288, the first strong point beyond Zoutelande, surrendered without serious resistance; after that, as the dunes narrowed, they advanced on a single-troop front, Q Troop leading followed by X. They met more Germans surrendering, and may have become over-confident, although in any case it was impossible to take full tactical precautions while advancing through surrendering enemy. After they had gone some way, a German shot and killed the sergeant of the leading section and wounded the subaltern with him.

Q Troop quickly dealt with this resistance, but a little later came under fire from what was probably W238. The troop began a flank attack, but shortly afterwards when close to the battery barracks set into the dunes, was heavily mortared. Q Troop commander and X Troop commander, who had come forward to contact him, were both wounded and there were other losses. With both troop commanders out of action, the attack came to a halt, and Q Troop fell back behind X. Y Troop went through, but was also held up.

At 3.30 Phillips gave his orders for a commando attack, hoping to take W11, rather more than a thousand yards away, after first taking two intermediate objectives, an anti-tank ditch and a searchlight platform beyond it. The German mortars had been quicker against Q and X Troops, than they had been the previous day against 48 Commando, and now 47 suffered from the same difficulty and delay as had 48 in arranging support. Phillips had to fix H-Hour at 5 o'clock and even then had to do without air support. At 4.55 three regiments of artillery from across the Scheldt opened fire lifting southwards at one minute intervals, and at 5 o'clock Y Troop went forward followed by A.

Y Troop reached the first objective and took prisoners, but was then held up. A Troop went through, made ground despite galling fire from the left, inland, flank, lost men, took prisoners and was then in its turn held up. Finally, advancing together in the gathering dusk, the two troops, now badly short of men, got into W11. B Troop followed them into the battery. They passed inland of the first casemate and nearly reached the dominating control tower, but, despite attempts to get round the seaward flank, they could get no further. The moon had not yet risen, and soon it was pitch dark. All three troop commanders had been wounded, and the three troops were by now considerably dispersed and disorganised. In the end the subalterns and sergeants collected the men and withdrew 400 yards to the searchlight platform, where the second-in-command, Major Patrick Donnell and the adjutant, Captain Paul Spencer, took charge and organised defence for the night. Shortly afterwards someone in the darkness opened fire on them and threw grenades. Challenged, it turned out to be a German patrol, which called on the British to surrender. It was driven off, and later either this patrol or another appeared near commando headquarters and caused some casualites.

About one o'clock next morning Leicester arrived at Phillips's command post bringing Moulton with him. The brigadier urged Phillips to continue the advance now that the moon had risen, but Phillips, probably rightly, believed it impossible to collect and re-organise his troops before daylight.[17]

At 11 o'clock on the morning of the 2nd, Leicester, reminded by 2 Canadian Corps of the urgency of making progress southwards towards Flushing and silencing the remaining batteries commanding the Scheldt, had ordered 41 Commando to hand over in Domburg to 10 (IA) leaving two of its troops with it, and return to Westkapelle. By 8 o'clock 41 had reached Westkapelle, passing on the way the remaining four tanks of the breaching teams going up to Domburg.

Sometime after dark Leicester visited 48 Commando in the dunes and warned Moulton to have two troops ready to go to 47 Commando. Moulton pressed him to allow the whole of 48 to go and take over the advance from 47, but Leicester refused, and, after a cup of hot German cocoa with 48, accompanied by Moulton, walked on in the moonlight through Zoutelande, and then along the dunes to Phillips's command post. On the way they passed a number of men from 47 apparently in some degree of disorganisation.

Leicester now had a difficult problem. It would be unrealistic to pretend that 47 Commando had not had a jolt to its confidence. There had been that bad first day in reserve with nothing to show for its losses, and now the attack on its main objective had ended in failure and confusion. In contrast, 48, although one troop short, had its tail well up. Moulton's confidence that it could now take W11 may or may not have been justified, but it was shared by his troop commanders and their men. Something similar was true of 41. If the problem had been set in a promotion examination or staff college exercise, there could have only been one answer, one or both of the fresh units should have been used next day to go through 47 and renew the attack. Any student suggesting that 47 should be required to do so would have been in trouble.

But Leicester had to think of the future. Had the battle ended, as it might quite well have done, with 41 and 48 Commandos going through 47 and pushing on to the Flushing gap, it would not have been quickly forgotten in the brigade, nor would 47 have soon recovered its confidence. It was a risk, but despite Phillips's refusal to resume the attack that night, Leicester left it to 47 to take W11 and told Moulton he need send only one troop to help.

As soon as it was light next morning, the 3rd, troop subalterns and sergeants — all five fighting troop commanders and two troop sergeants major had become casualites — began to collect and organise their troops, while Phillips had a look at the German position and made a new plan. The dunes were wider here, about half a mile between sea and floods, and the previous evening fire from the inland flank had greatly added to the difficulties of the attackers. Phillips now planned that, under Donnell, Y Troop and the much depleted Q should cover that flank and support the attack by fire, while A Troop, passing through B on an intermediate objective and, supported by X, made the assault. H-Hour was fixed either for 8.30 or 9 o'clock, the record is not clear.

Flunder with A Troop, 48 Commando, arriving at Phillips's command post before dawn, met a chilly reception and was ordered to find a way forward on the inland flank beyond Donnell, get level with the battery and support the assault with fire. Feeling very much on his own, Flunder was surprised to meet Leicester out in front of Phillips's command post. Questioned by the brigadier, Flunder, who had been refused covering fire, professed himself satisfied with his task and began to advance across some 500 yards of hummocky dunes making for a pumping station and some cottages about level with the battery. When the troop was halfway there the Germans spotted it and opened fire. Using what cover there was and covering its movement with its own fire, the troop reached the pumping station, which to Flunder's relief the Germans had failed to occupy, and after a burst of rapid fire continued harassing fire until the attack should develop.[18]

Donnell with Q and Y Troops, 47 Commando, began to advance about 8 o'clock and almost at once ran into Germans who quickly surrendered. The two troops continued to clear defences and administrative buildings, then took up fire positions to support the assault of the battery.

Of the assaulting troops, B came under fire as it reached the intermediate objective, and A, passing through it, came under heavier and more accurate fire as it drew close to the battery but was able to get forward below the crest of the dunes on the seaward side until it was underneath the first casemate. Germans lobbed grenades at the British below, but B Troop, came forward with Captain Linzell and a dozen Dutch from 10 Commando, and together the two troops got into the casemate. By then Phillips had ordered X Troop to get forward along the beach. Spencer, who came with it, now organised an assault by A and X uphill into the centre of the battery. Under fire from B Troop at the first casemate and from the three troops inland and now attacked from seaward, the Germans began to surrender. From the pumping station Flunder could see Donnell's party and beyond it, as it reached the higher ground in the battery, Spencer's assault. Loosing off everything it had to cover the assault, Flunder's troop only ceased fire as it saw the Germans coming out of their defences to surrender.

Leaving the rest of the commando to mop up W11, Phillips now took A and B Troops on south towards the last battery, W4. After a brief fire fight in which one of 47 Commando was killed, a German officer came forward with a white flag asking for a truce to collect wounded. Phillips refused, telling the German through his interpreter that his own and another commando were about to attack with overwhelming naval and air support, and, after further discussion, the German agreed to surrender. Germans appeared in large numbers from their defences, and there was a moment of suspense as both sides realised that the British on the spot were heavily outnumbered. Then the Germans began to lay down their arms.[19]

That day back at Westkapelle the beaches were closed by a gale and supplies were dropped by air. On the 4th 41 Commando, which had crossed the gap southwards early on the 3rd, recrossed northwards, reaching Domburg during the afternoon. 4 Commando arrived across the Flushing gap, reverted to the 4th Special Service Brigade and reached Zoutelande. Looking down from the dunes the commandos could see the minesweepers at work in the Scheldt.

References

1 Puglsey *op cit*, p.188; Stacey *op cit*, pp.413-4; *Memorandum Concerning First Canadian Army Instruction No 41 dated 30 October 44 in so far as it related to Operation Infatuate II*, GS Plans, HQ First Canadian Army, 2330, 31 Oct 44.

2 Stacey *op cit*, p.414; Pugsley, correspondence.

3 Hope, correspondence.

4 AORG Report No 299, p.32; Captain P. G. Cowper RM, letter.

5 Naval Commander Force 'T', HMS *Squid*, Southampton, No 82/1/255, *Operation Infatuate II. Report to Allied Naval Commander Expeditionary Force*, 17 November 1944, which includes as appendices reports of Deputy Senior Officer Assault Group, Commander, Support Squadron Eastern Flank, flotilla officers, support and landing craft commanders, and is used throughout the narrative which follows. (Hereafter Force T Report). One of the latter is illustrated by a diagrammatic representation of the radar image.

6 Force T Report, Appendix F, Commander Support Squadron Eastern Flank, including Enclosure 8 CO LCG(M) 101 Report. Paul Lund and Harry Ludlam, *The War of the Landing Craft*, Foulsham, 1976, pp.203-206, gives a number of other personal accounts by members of the Support Squadron Eastern Flank.

7 Force T Report, Appendices D, DSOAG Report, and F, Commander, SSEF Report including LCT(R) Flotilla and individual craft reports.

8 AORG Report 299, pp.33-5, but see footnote re timings at p.10 above. The author saw what he took to be two dead German officers in W13, which may indicate that the prisoners interrogated were guns crew. The forward troops of 48 Commando, having landed at 10.05 and advanced very rapidly, were probably in contact with W13 by 10.30. Aschmann war diary for dates and times indicated.

9 41 Commando Operation Order No 3 of 28 October 1944 and War Diary; P. N. Wood, narrative and correspondence, the story of the TSM's remark quickly spread through the commando brigade.

10 Colonel T. M. P. Stevens, conversation.

11 Force T Report, Appendix F, Commander 'N' LCT Squadron's Report; *79 Armd Div History*, pp. 155-8 and illustrations. AORG Report 299, pp.35-7. The two latter use LCT code names not always identifiable by LCT numbers in the naval reports.

12 41 Commando War Diary; Wood narrative; Major J. W. Jewers conversation.

13 Moulton *op cit*, pp.147-59 circulated and checked by troop commanders etc in typescript before publication, also *48 Royal Marine Commando* anon. (not by present author) privately published 1946, based on the war diary and notes by participants.

14 The late Major General Sir Farndale Phillips and others in 47 Commando, typescript narrative prepared shortly after the battle, kindly made available by Lieut Colonel P. M. Donnell, and correspondence with Donnell.

15 COHQ Bulletin Y/47, pp.24-9.

16 Commander Naval Force T Report, Appendix H, Report of Principal Beach Master.

17 Phillips typescript.

18 Captain D. J. Flunder, narrative prepared in 1962 for Moulton *op cit*.

19 Phillips typescript.

14

Surrender

With responsibility for the 155th Brigade's attack on Flushing and for the 4th Special Service Brigade, if and when it landed at Westkapelle, as well as for the 156th and 157th Brigades in South Beveland. Major General E. Hakewill Smith, commanding the 52nd (Lowland) Division, had had to remain in the Breskens area rather than go to South Beveland to take charge there. On 30 October, after it had finally been confirmed that the 52nd Division would be responsible for land operations in Walcheren, he instructed Brigadier L. B. D. Burns, his CRA, to take command in South Beveland, where now the 156th and 157th Brigades supported by the bulk of the divisional artillery waited for the 2nd Canadian Infantry Division to secure a bridgehead in Walcheren. Headquarters Burnforce was to open at noon on the 31st, said Hakewill Smith's instructions to Burns, if the 5th Canadian Infantry Brigade had crossed the causeway, Burnforce was to relieve it and prepare to advance either on Flushing or Westkapelle; if not, it was to look for another way to cross the Sloe channel and work out a plan to use that instead of the causeway. As we have seen the third and last attempt of the Canadians to force the causeway ended during 2 November with the 1st Glasgow Highlanders and Le Regiment de Maisonneuve back at the eastern end of the causeway.[1]

During the morning of 1 November, Foulkes called on Hakewill Smith at his headquarters, which had just moved into Breskens, to insist that the 156th and 157th Brigades should attack along the causeway. Hakewill Smith protested strongly. An attack down the causeway, 1,700 yards long, dead straight, wide enough for the deployment at most of a single infantry section, raked by machine guns and under heavy shellfire, was not in his view a practicable operation of war. 'Of course, I will obey your orders, but I must have them in writing', he told Foulkes, adding that he would protest to Headquarters 21 Army Group that his division was being put into an attack which would lead to very serious casualties and achieve nothing. 'What are you going to do then?' Foulkes angrily demanded. Hakewill Smith replied that he would find another way across, but that it would take time to do so. In the end Foulkes gave way, but made it plain that, if Burnforce was not in Walcheren within 48 hours, he would see that the 52nd Division got a new commander. He left, and Hakewill Smith radioed to Burns to come across the Scheldt to meet him at Terneuzen.[2]

At high water the Sloe channel was 300 yards wide, but at low only about 40 yards, although still too deep to wade. Beyond the channel on the

Walcheren side there were some 1,000 yards of saltings with tidal runnels of soft mud in which a heavily loaded man would sink out of sight in minutes. In 1940, it was rumoured, the Germans had lost a large number of men trying to cross. As his instructions to Burns indicate, Hakewill Smith when he sent him there was already thinking of finding some other way than the causeway of crossing. On the 31st his CRE, Brigadier F. W. Houghton, had gone round to South Beveland with his headquarters, and after meeting Burns that evening he had set his staff to work investigating the load bearing capability of the saltings and ordering up stores. Hakewill Smith had ordered large blow-ups of air photographs of the channel and the saltings, but he had not seen them at the time of Foulkes's visit. 'With memories of the ice, snow, bogs and marshes behind us in Scotland, I felt certain that, if we could find a way, the Jocks would get across.' Now he called for the air photographs and took them with him to Terneuzen, where, after explaining the situation to Burns, he gave them to him.

When Burns got back to South Beveland and Houghton and his engineers took the photographs from their envelope and laid them out, 'the only pathway lay before us crystal clear.' His staff waited for Houghton to speak, but he was sure that the line across was as clear to them as to him. Two miles south of the causeway, near the village of Nieuwdorp, they could see that the tidal runnels leading to the main channel divided as from a watershed leaving clear a strip of saltings across to the Walcheren dyke. Houghton told Burns that he would arrange for a reconnaissance that night by the 202nd Field Company. Shortly afterwards Lieutenant F. Turner, who had on the 31st been sent to look for a crossing lower down, and Sergeant Humphrey reported for briefing.

Pointing out the watershed, Houghton gave Turner and Humphrey two bearings and distances, carefully measured by his staff, which would lead them from the far side of the channel to a cairn, which should show up against the flat skyline even at night. After that a third bearing would take them clear of the marshes on the Walcheren side, but they must not risk going too far or leaving traces which the Germans might discover in daylight. In the early hours of the 2nd, Turner and Humphrey returned. They had got across, found the cairn and pushed on until they heard Germans talking, then returned without being discovered. Houghton crawled up to the sea dyke on the South Beveland side to take a look for himself, but forbade any other movement in the area during daylight. Then after dark the infantry and the engineers with their assault boats and other equipment came forward together.[3]

That night, the 2nd, while the field company worked to improve the route from Nieuwdorp to the channel and clear Schumines, Turner crossed again with three sappers and taped the route on the far side. When, three hours later he got back at 3.30 on the morning of the 3rd, the leading troops of the 6th Cameronians were waiting to cross in assault boats.

Shortly after midday on the 2nd, the commanding officer of the 6th Cameronians, warned his company commanders that the battalion, temporarily under command of the 157th Brigade, would cross the Sloe that night. The companies marched up to Nieuwdorp after dark, and A Company, the first to cross, had been waiting an hour at the channel when Turner at last appeared out of the darkness from the far side. Ten minutes vigorous paddling took the men across the channel, but after that they had to struggle through mud, knee-deep and often waist-deep, to reach their objective, the sea dyke on the far side three-quarters of a mile from the channel. It took them a full hour to do so, but when they got there, they rushed a German post, taking 25 prisoners at the cost of two wounded. Meanwhile the next company, B, had crossed to come up on the left taking a farm on the dyke with 60 prisoners. C and D Companies followed, passing through A and B shortly after daylight. On the right A and C gained ground, as at first did B and D on the left, but about midday the two latter ran into trouble and in the afternoon withdrew to defensive positions close to the sea dyke, having lost 16 killed including D Company commander, and 27 wounded.[4]

The Germans shelled and mortared the crossing point most of the day until towards the evening the British artillery and rocket-firing Typhoons began to get the better of their batteries. In the afternoon, as the tide fell, expanses of mud dried out sown with Schumines. Clearing the mines and laying Kapok assault bridging and chespaling on the mud, the sappers kept the ferry running to get carrying parties with ammunition and supplies forward and wounded and prisoners back. The divisional historian describes the scene:

> The gap cleared through the minefield was no wider than the average suburban street. This passage, marked by two muddied white tapes, had to take all the traffic of infantry eager to get down to the boats, of supply personnel claiming priority for their bulky, awkward cases of food and ammunition, and of sappers desperately anxious to see that the route they had so painfully created might be kept in reasonable order . . . Against this tide came the flow of wounded and still more prisoners from the other side, while forlorn groups of beaten Germans waited disconsolately on the Walcheren shore . . . Over there, too, the rolls of paling were being dumped and laid over the mud between water and saltings. To get down to the mud and the boats on the Beveland side meant an ungainly slither, voluntary or otherwise.

At dusk the first companies of the 5th Highland Light Infantry began to cross, but a rising southwesterly wind had by then raised an unpleasant chop in the channel, and the crossing was very slow.[5]

Next afternoon, the 4th, A Company, the Cameronians, advanced again, while C Company, supported by a heavy barrage, swung left to take in flank the Germans facing B and D. In the evening the 5th HLI relieved D Company and next morning the rest of the Cameronians. Then pushing northwards the HLI linked up with the 1st Glasgow Highlanders, who by then had crossed the causeway and reached the village of Gronenburg on the Walcheren side. By nightfall the brigade held a bridgehead 2,000 yards deep and two miles wide in the dry eastern corner of the island. Next day it advanced through Arnemuiden to the edge of the floods, beyond which only the heavily mined road and railway leading to Middelburg a thousand yards away showed above water, and the Germans blew the bridge across the canal on the far side.

Meanwhile at Flushing a way had been found to reach Middleburg and to reach it with something that might be mistaken for the tanks Daser wanted as an excuse for surrender. On the night of the 4th, Brigadier Watkinson, commanding the 1st Assault Brigade with officers from Headquarters 155th Brigade and the 7/9th Royal Scots took a Buffalo to investigate the possibility of crossing the flooded airfield beyond Souburg to reach Middelburg from the southwest and returned to report that it was possible to do so with care. Next morning all available Buffaloes were mustered, and at 12.30 eleven of the most serviceable from A Squadron, 11th Royal Tank Regiment, under Major Newton-Dunn, with A Company, 7/9th Royal Scots, commanded by Major R. H. B. Johnston, and a machine gun platoon of the 7th Manchesters on board, started out for Middelburg, expecting to be followed by the rest of the battalion when more Buffaloes could be made available.

Guided by a Dutch civilian, the Buffaloes swam out into the floods across the nearby airfield, outflanking the pillboxes which were holding up the 4th KOSB to join the road beyond. One became entangled in the airfield obstructions and had to be left behind, and later another, sent to find a way around a nest of pillboxes near Middelburg, struck a large mine and was completely destroyed with six of the men in it killed and six wounded. A third was sent back with the wounded, but the remaining eight reached Middelburg and climbed out of the floods along the rising streets of the town.

By then the Germans must have been expecting attack from the east, where the 157th Brigade faced them across the floods, for the Buffaloes entered Middelburg unopposed. Threading their way through cheering crowds as Typhoons circled overhead, the Buffaloes, the squeak and clatter of their tracks on the cobbles sounding like so many tanks, reached the central square one by one. There they found a rapidly increasing crowd of German soldiers assembling. They did not šeem hostile, so Johnston, after posting the Buffaloes to command the Square as best they could, went in search of Daser accompanied by a Norwegian officer, known to him only as Johnny, who had come as interpreter. They found the headquarters in a smaller square packed with Germans. The Norwegian went in to find Daser and came back saying that he refused to talk to anyone below the rank of colonel. 'So I forthwith became a colonel and A Company an unspecified but very potent formation of the British Army', Johnston's narrative continues:

As I was wearing a windproof smock with an old scarf around my neck, I looked more like a tramp than a soldier, and I was certain that if General Daser accepted me as an officer at all, he would be just as likely to accept me as a Colonel. We found General Daser pacing his office, surrounded by his staff and in no very affable mood. I informed him that the British Army had arrived, that he must order "Cease Fire" immediately, and I detailed to him the surrender terms given me by the Brigadier.

Threatened with the total destruction of Middelburg by bombing and shellfire, Daser agreed to send a staff officer around the town with Newton-Dunn to order his troops to cease fire. He also agreed to consider himself a prisoner, but asked that any formal surrender of the town should be made in private, as he was afraid of the Dutch population.

Relieving him and his staff of their weapons, Johnston placed a guard on them and set about trying to restore order out of the chaos outside. In the larger square the number of Germans was increasing alarmingly. At one time a battalion marched in complete. They were all armed, and in gathering darkness in the midst of a hostile population of 40,000 it was impossible to disarm them systematically. About this time Newton-Dunn and the German staff officer arrived back. The German, going around the town, had seen that there were very few British troops in Middelburg and no signs of more coming. Johnny, the Norwegian, however, was with Daser when the angry staff officer began to protest that the surrender had been premature. With great presence of mind he interrupted him and hustled him out of the room, where he was put into solitary confinement until more British troops should arrive.

Out in the square Germans began to sing the Horst Wessel song, and Dutch who had been celebrating liberation too enthusiastically in the bars began loosing off discarded weapons. It only needed someone to fire into the mob to start a massacre which the British would be helpless to stop. To Johnston's relief the well organised Dutch Resistance took charge, rounded up and disarmed the drunks, posted guards on the prisoners and even organised civilian bakers to make bread with German assistance for the now hungry prisoners.

About midnight Johnston got through to his own brigade headquarters by radio. It was out of touch with the 157th Brigade and could not promise to send help until daylight. At 2.30 am, however, word came that reinforcements were on the way. An hour later the colonel and intelligence officers of the 5th HLI from the 157th Brigade, finding a way through the crowded Germans, reached Johnston's headquarters. Shortly afterwards the 4th KOSB arrived from Flushing with a company of the 7/9th Royal Scots under command. When a count could be made, it was found that there were over two thousand prisoners. Except for the killed and wounded in the mined Buffalo, Middelburg had fallen without casualties to the British.[5]

In Breskens, Hakewill Smith, as soon as he heard that the amphibians had reached Middelburg, set off with two jeeps for the city via Antwerp and

South Beveland. It was an eerie journey through the night, past floods on both sides of the road, fallen trees, derelict tanks, ruined houses and other relics of battle. He reached the causeway about dawn and half a mile from the canal had to take to his feet along a narrow pathway through the mines. Crossing the canal by assault boat, he reached the city and there in the town hall found the city fathers in conference.

After speeches of welcome, they told him that they were planning the evacuation of the 58,000 people now crammed into Middleburg, for the Germans had cut the water main from Domburg and there was nothing for them to drink. Children were crying for water, and their elders demanding it. The British must provide boats to evacuate the city. Hakewill Smith could not do so — the few assault boats still left were quite inadequate for the purpose. The Dutch must use their own boats, he told them. The Germans had taken them away or destroyed them, they replied, if the British did not provide boats, the children and others would die of thirst. It was clear that 58,000 people could not walk out by the narrow pathway through the mines by which the general had reached Middelburg. Were they sure, Hakewill Smith asked them, that the Germans had blown up the water main? The fresh water had stopped coming into the town, they said, the Germans must have blown the main.

'I said I would try to send an amphibian to the Domburg reservoir', the general's story continues, 'but was there no communication with Domburg? Oh, yes. There was a direct telephone line, but the Germans had destroyed that. I asked them to test it, and after a few minutes the curator in charge at the reservoir said he had turned off the fresh water to Middelburg because he was sure that the Germans had blown up the pipeline. It was under 12 feet of seawater and about 6 to 8 feet underground. He was ordered to open the cocks, and a few minutes later all the taps in Middleburg were running.' That day, the 6th, Veere on the east coast of Walcheren surrendered to the 156th Brigade advancing from the causeway.[7]

At the northern end of the island, however, in the wider strip of partly wooded dunes beyond Domburg, what was left of the 1020th Infantry Regiment together with two coastal batteries, W18 and W19, and a number of Germans from other units who had escaped to join them in the hope of reaching Schouwen, still held out. The fall of Domburg to 41 Commando and the capture of W17 on the night of the 1st had secured the Westkapelle beachhead from the northeast. Since then all that had been required of 10 (IA) Commando and the two troops of 41 left with it was to prevent any counter-attack from that direction, while the rest of the 4th Special Service Brigade got on with its primary task of taking the batteries commanding the West Scheldt. With that done, Leicester could turn his attention to the north, and the bridgehead the Germans still held for escape to Schouwen, the next island eastwards, or, should they be so resilient, for counter-attack from it.

41 Commando crossed the Westapelle gap northwards on the 4th and

176

was back in Domburg by 2 o'clock that afternoon, taking over the seaward flank from 10 (IA). An hour later the two troops of 10 (IA) and B Troop 41 Commando supported by the two surviving gun tanks began to advance through the woods bordering the floods, meeting patchy resistance. B Troop was held up and one section of the Belgian troop was ambushed, but elsewhere the Germans surrendered fairly quickly, and by nightfall, the two troops had gained 800 yards and taken about sixty prisoners.

On the 5th 41 Commando took W18. In the early afternoon, after a long delay while attempts were made to arrange artillery and air support, A and B Troops, supported by the two Shermans, reached an intermediate position among the minefields in the dunes from which to cover the assault by Y Troop, which the mortars of 41 and 48 Commandos would also support. Peter Hayden, commanding Y Troop, had at the age of nineteen won a DSO at Salerno and four days ago had led the assault on W15. Now, as his friend Michael Aldworth of 48 Commando helped him on with his equipment, Hayden, very youthful in appearance and intense, said to him 'This time a VC or bust'. Despite heavy fire, Y Troop got into the battery position, but then Hayden and one of his subalterns were killed, the other subaltern wounded and there were other casualties among the NCOs and marines. Stevens, coming up with A Troop, took charge, and the two troops completed the capture of the battery. Woods came up with P Troop to consolidate, and by the time that darkness fell the battery was secure. Later Palmer joined them with X Troop, and mopping up among the concrete defences continued long into the night. Next morning, Wood, who spoke German, persuaded the battery commander to show him the way back through the minefields, firmly insisting that the German should go first.[8]

On the morning of the 6th, 10 (IA) and 41 Commandos pushed on again, making slow headway through the minefields. During the day Typhoons of 84 Group made rocket attacks on W19 and on the Black Hut area, a commanding feature 2,000 yards beyond W18 and 1,500 short of W19, where a number of German-held concrete emplacements had revealed themselves in the last two days. On the 7th, after further rocket attacks by Typhoons, 41 Commando supported by the two Shermans and the last remaining AVRE, later disabled by a mine, attacked the Black Hut area, which surrendered during the afternoon.

By now 4 and 48 Commandos had reached Domburg, and for the 8th, Leicester planned a brigade attack, 4 Commando advancing on the right just clear of the woods, followed by 48 in reserve ready to go through when ordered. Advancing at 5.30 that morning in darkness on a narrow front between the woods and the dunes against scattered resistance and taking a number of prisoners, 4 Commando got within a mile of Vrouwenpolder, on the west coast of the island where the area of broad dunes ends. As it grew light, Dawson halted his leading troops to look at the ground and issue orders for the advance in daylight. While he made his reconnaissance, his RSM took the battle headquarters into a small copse, and there met four fully armed Germans, who, when challenged, proved to have come from the

German regimental commander at Vrouwenpolder to establish contact and arrange formal surrender. They took the commando intelligence officer to their company headquarters in a dugout close by the command post, whence they telephoned their colonel. Shortly afterwards Dawson arrived in the dugout:

'I availed myself of the field telephone to have a chat with the colonel in Vrouwenpolder, following which he sent a car to take me and Ken Wright, the IO, to his headquarters, where he quickly agreed that further fighting was pointless. The tactics of penetration by night was really the same as we had used at Flushing, but this time the Germans were cornered, isolated and exhausted.

When the German car arrived in Vrouwenpolder, with a British officer sitting on the bonnet, the Dutch wondered at first whether it was advisable to wave and cheer, but the beaming smile on Wright's face did not leave them long in doubt. There was a formal meeting with an elaborate exchange of salutes and speeches, then the German colonel surrendered and the troops were allowed to march out with their weapons and as much of their personal gear as they could carry. The surrender brought the total number of prisoners taken by the brigade to about 4,000.[9]

Unhappily the end of the fighting was marred by a last tragedy. In order to make contact with the 156th Brigade and ensure that the whole of the coast was in British hands, A Troop, 48 Commando, was sent in three Buffaloes through the floods towards Veere. It reached Serooskerke without incident taking a few prisoners on the way. But on leaving the village at a road junction the second Buffalo was shattered by a heavy explosion. One officer and eighteen men were killed and the remaining nine wounded. Later, villagers said they had seen Germans in a boat dropping heavy shells from the naval batteries, which must have been fused as mines.

References

1 52 Division's GO6 of 30 Oct 44 addressed Brigadier Burns, CRA, 52 Division; 52 Div Op Inst No 1 of 28 Oct 44, addressed to Commanders 156 and 157 Brigades, orders 157th Brigade with one battalion of the 156th under command to advance northwestwards on the 29th to the eastern end of the causeway, the brigade commanders arranging details among themselves.

2 Hakewill Smith, correspondence.

3 Brigadier F. W. Houghton, letter; Blake *op cit*, pp. 94-5. Headquarters RE 52nd Division, War Diary.

4 Anon, *The War History of the 6th (Lanarkshire) Battalion, The Cameronians (SR), World War 2*, John Cossar (printer), Glasgow 1945; 6th Cameronians, War Diary.

5 Blake *op cit*, p.96.

6 Major R. H. B. Johnston, article in *The Thistle*, July 1946; *A Short History of the 11th Royal Tank Regiment, Walcheren*; *The Tank*, Vol 32, No 375, September 1950; 155th Infantry Brigade, War Diary. Johnston's article does not mention the story in Blake and others that, in order to represent himself as a colonel he borrowed the stars from a subaltern to add to his major's crown.

7 Hakewill Smith, letter.

8 41 Commando War Diary; Woods, Stevens and Jewers letters or discussion; Baldewyns & Herman-Lemoine, *op cit*, pp.199-201, differs in timings and detail.

9 Dawson and Wright, narratives.

15

Antwerp Opened

With the batteries taken it became possible to sweep the mines which in the sea approaches and the fifty-five miles of estuary and river below Antwerp still closed the port to traffic. There were two main types of mine: moored mines actuated by contact with a ship's hull, and ground mines, resting on the bottom and actuated either by the magnetic field of a ship passing over them or by the noise of her propellers.* Each had to be dealt with by the appropriate method.

To sweep moored mines, minesweepers towed wire sweeps, known as Oropesa sweeps, spread in their wake and controlled in depth by kites and otters, devices developed from fish trawling. The sweeps cut the cables of the mines, allowing them to float to the surface, where they could be destroyed by rifle fire or other means. To sweep magnetic mines, pairs of sweepers towed floating cables between which an electric pulse was passed through the water actuating the firing mechanism of the mines. To deal with acoustic mines, the sweepers were fitted with electrically operated hammers, whose noise would operate the firing mechanism at what was calculated to be a safe distance ahead of the sweeper. Alternatively grenades were sometimes thrown into the sea. The acoustic hammer could be used at the same time as the wire-cutting or the magnetic sweep, but the two types of sweep could not be used simultaneously.

Minesweepers were small, shallow draft craft which could usually hope to pass over moored mines during the hours around high water, and, by taking station within the spread of the sweep of the next ahead, all except the leader could pass through swept water. They were either built of wood or degaussed so that their hulls would not actuate magnetic mines. But mines might be laid with snag lines floating close to the surface to catch them, and others might be laid around wrecks in which their sweeps would become entangled. LCP(L) with special sweeps were used to deal with snag lines, but in the worst cases the mines laid around wrecks had to be neutralised manually by men working from a rubber dinghy. Another and very serious complication was that ground mines did not necessarily detonate at first actuation, but could be fitted with 'clickers' set to fire the mines after a given number of actuations.

---

* A third type of ground mines, the Oyster Mine, which had recently appeared, was actuated by water pressure from ships passing and was virtually unsweepable. None were discovered in the Scheldt.

Ramsay had taken steps before the assault on Walcheren to have mine sweeping forces provided by the Commander-in-Chief, Nore, in readiness to begin sweeping as soon as the batteries were silenced. These comprised:[1]

Minesweeping Force A (Captain H. G. Hopper RN, Captain Minesweeping, Sheerness)

Mostly from Sheerness to sweep the estuary and river
157th, 159th and 165th Flotillas — 120-foot British Yard Minesweepers (BYMS) equippped with both Orpesa sweeps and magnetic sweeps

102nd, 110, 139 and 140th Flotillas — 105-ft motor minesweepers equipped with magnetic sweeps

131st Flotilla — 105-foot MMS equipped with magnetic sweeps for use in fresh water

15th and 19th Flotillas — motor launches equipped with Oropesa sweeps
197th, 198th and 199th Flotillas* — Motor Fishing Vessels (MFV) equipped with magnetic sweeps

704th Flotilla — LCP(L) with snag-line sweeps

HMS *Tudno* — Headquarters Ship

Minesweeping Force B (Captain T. W. Marsh, RN, Captain Minesweepers, Harwich)

From Ostend where it was already at work on the channels as far east as Zeebrugge.

160th Flotilla — BYMS — to sweep the approach channels on into the Scheldt

Two MLs of the 19th Flotilla detached to Ostend from Sheerness, and Five Belgian-manned MMS of the Ostend local forces under Commander S. S. Stammwitz RN, to sail under Marsh's orders for the Scheldt and then go on to Antwerp to sweep the freshwater section between Valsoorden and Antwerp.

On 1 November, on a report that the Canadians had taken the Knocke batteries, Ramsay ordered Force B to make a bid to reach Breskens. Next morning it came under fire, three minesweepers were hit, and in accordance with instructions it returned to Ostend, having swept five mines. Early on the 3rd, leaving Ostend in time to pass the batteries in darkness, it reached Breskens safely, although it came under fire off Flushing.

The two MLs from Sheerness which had joined Stammwitz in Ostend went on the 4th to reach Antwerp, sweeping Oropesa all the way, and

* Probably from Ostend.

were the first Allied ships to arrive there since 1940. They found the port considerably disorganised by the early V1s and V2s sent against it from occupied Holland. Later they were joined by Stammwitz and by the rest of 19th Flotilla. On the 8th as the MLs were sweeping down to Terneuzen ML 916 blew up an accoustic mine. The captain of another ML remembers seeing the whole ship being blown into the air and then immediately disintegrating. Two survivors were picked up.[2]

Meanwhile Force A had sailed from Sheerness on the 2nd, but had been ordered to put back to the Downs when the Ostend minesweepers were fired on. Sailing from the Downs at 3 am on the 3rd, it entered the Scheldt and swept itself up to Terneuzen, anchoring off the port at 6 pm, having swept 74 mines on the way. The LCP(L) had been delayed, and so the minesweepers went ahead without them, taking the risk of snag lines. Winds rose to gale force on the night of the 4th, and the bad weather continued through the 5th, but intensive minesweeping continued between Breskens and Flushing, and Hopper's staff began to organise supply and repair facilities at Terneuzen. In the small Scheldt pilot port, Mr Hook, the chief Scheldt pilot who had escaped to England in 1940 and now accompanied Hopper, met his wife whom he had last seen four years ago, and there were other family reunions among the crews of four minesweepers of the force manned by the Royal Netherlands Navy.

Sweeping continued on the 6th, but that night winds rose to gale force, and on the 7th all sweeping had to be abandoned. Next day sweeping was resumed and 23 mines swept. On the 9th the weather stopped sweeping again in the Terneuzen area, but Stammwitz in the more sheltered waters near Antwerp swept 13 mines. So it went on. Commander Kimmins described it for the BBC:

... what struck me most about them was firstly their persistent delight in getting mines ... and secondly their quite amazing stamina. They were such long, long days; sometimes desperately exciting with a record catch; but always long, always tiring, and always nerve-racking. Never a moment without the constant threat of what might suddenly happen, and then, often just when it was least expected, it did: the sudden jarring impact, sometimes enough to knock you off your feet; the roar of the explosion, and, as the great plume of mud and water subsided, the cheers of all the crew at the thought of another white chevron to be chalked up on the funnel ... Down in the engine room were two men who, with that first violent impact, had instinctively grasped a handrail ... and, being unable to see, could not be sure how close it really was.[3]

In Antwerp itself some mines were dealt with by shore sweeps mounted on lorries, while others, so close to the quayside or lock gates that they could not be detonated without doing unacceptable damage, were defused by skilled divers working in freezing cold and pitch darkness in the mud.

Minesweeping continued until on the 19th, 20th and 21st no mines could be found, and Hopper after consultation declared that, subject to the risk of odd mines still being present, the channel could be used. Then on the 22nd and 23rd nine mines were detonated. It meant that the channel had to be closed again, and the number of times it had to be swept to activate the delay mechanisms increased. Before the sweeping was over it rose to something between fifteen and twenty times.

At last on the 26th Hopper felt it safe to report again that the channel was clear, by then 229 ground mines and 38 moored mines had been detonated or swept. That day three coasters reached Antwerp, and on the 28th the first sea-going convoy. As the Canadian official historian somewhat wryly writes, the Canadian Army was not represented at the small ceremony with which Ramsay welcomed it at Antwerp, but he points out, at least the first ship was the Canadian-built, *Fort Cataraqui*. Hopper, who led the convoy up in a minesweeper, was taken by surprise and appropriately enough attended the ceremony in his minesweeping rig.

In the words of Admiral of the Fleet Sir John Tovey, Commander-in-Chief, Nore:

'It was in fact one of the most difficult and dangerous minesweeping operations of the war and it was only due to the high efficiency and unremitting energy and zeal of the minesweepers working under the inspiring leadership of Captain H. G. Hopper, Royal Navy, that the clearance was effected in twenty-two working days, six days inside the estimate.[4]

The opening of Antwerp 'effected nothing less than a complete revolution' in the supply position of the Allied armies.[5] Until it was opened the build-up and operations of the armies had to be constantly watched and limited to what could be administratively supported, and it was the Americans, with larger forces now deployed and divisions still crossing the Atlantic, who suffered the worse. Once Antwerp was open and working, excess port capacity became available and build-up and operations could continue without restriction on that count. But much had to be done to get Antwerp working, and even when working began, difficulties would remain. As might be expected, the enemy would do what he could to add to them.

SHAEF was taking steps to develop Le Havre, Rouen, Cherbourg and Marseilles to maximum capacity when on 4 September Antwerp fell into the hands of the Allies. Since then, all SHAEF port policy and plans had been based on its use. But as the first optimism about the early use of Antwerp faded, ComZ made a complete survey of the north coast of Belgium and France looking for ports and possible LST landing places. Only four were found to have additional potential value: Boulogne, Dieppe, and Ostend, all three allocated to the British, and Calais, at first allocated to the Americans for LST but later handed back to the British.

Meanwhile work continued at Antwerp. That port presented a very different picture from the desolation of demolitions and obstructions to which British and Americans had become accustomed in other ports taken from the enemy, but there was much to be done before it could handle heavy traffic. Quaysides and roads were obstructed by heavy concrete blocks. Thirty-five miles of railway track and two hundred points and crossings were missing, having been removed by the Germans during the occupation. Shell and mortar fire during September added to the damage. Extensive new railway construction would also be needed for the base.

Then on the morning of 21 September the Germans counter-attacked Kruisschans Lock again. The Canadians drove them off, but that evening a heavy explosion close to the outer lock gate told of the detonation of a floating mine. Examination showed that the gate still retained water, but major repairs would be needed before it could pass shipping to and from the dock complex.

On 19 September Eisenhower, on the grounds that joint Anglo-American port operation had been shown by experience to be unsatisfactory, overruled a proposal that the port should be jointly controlled and decided that instead the port should be operated under British control with a due share of its capacity allocated to the Americans. Meetings were held at Antwerp on 24-26 September and in Brussels on 5 October to establish a system of operation and to plan the development of the port, and on 18 October a formal Memorandum of Agreement was signed by representatives of 21 Army Group and ComZ.

The target date for completion of work needed to open the port was set at 15 November. Defence by land, sea and air would be the responsibility of the British. A British Naval Officer in Charge (NOIC) would control shipping (later taken over by the Port Executive Committee), and a British base sub-area commander would control local administration. The northern and southern sectors of the port, each with its own marshalling yard, were allocated respectively to the Americans and the British. River berths were unassigned, allocation being left to the Port Executive Committee to adjust the daily unloading tonnages from quayside and river to targets finally set at 22,500 for the Americans and 17,500 for the British. Port rehabilitation became a British responsibility with a call on US forces to meet the target date. Storage capacity being insufficient for both British and Americans, it was agreed that, while the British should establish a base in Antwerp, the Americans would clear direct to Liege and Namur, an arrangement that would give trouble and have to be modified. Common user facilities, including the unloading of petrol, oil and lubricants (POL) were agreed. Roads, railways and canals were allocated, the Americans having primary rights over those to Liege and Namur, the British to Brussels. The British sector was worked by the 7th Base Sub-Area, the American by the 13th Major Port arriving from Plymouth and Falmouth and the 5th Major Port arriving from Brittany at the end of November.[6]

A British port construction company arrived on 12 September and set to work with civilian assistance, and later US forces undertook the main work of rehabilitation of the inner docks and quays of the northern sector, of the marshalling yard which served it and of Kruisschans Lock which led directly to it. As the port was repaired and developed and later as unloading started, both Americans and British employed, directly and indirectly through contractors, large numbers of civilians and Belgian special equipment. The numbers employed by the British rose to 17,000; those employed by the Americans to an average of 9,000 with a temporary peak of 13,000.[7]

Despite the target date, work was not finished when on 28 November the first convoy arrived, but of the 242 berths 219 were completely cleared, all of the 600 odd cranes were working, and all the bridges needed to work the docks were repaired.[8] By the end of December the average daily unloadings were 13,700 tons for the Americans, 8,600 for the British, and the port was handling all British supplies except for some special items. But a bottleneck had developed in the onward clearance of American tonnage. Within two weeks of opening a backlog of 55,000 tons had accumulated, and despite an allocation of 50,000 tons of storage space from the British, the Americans were forced to dump stores in the open where they could. In consequence, after reaching a peak of 19,000 tons a day in the second week of December, the American unloadings had declined. During December the bulk petrol installations at Hoboken, developed as a joint project, discharged 160,000 tons.

On the day that the first Allied ship entered the port, the Germans had warned the people of Antwerp, 3,000 German aircraft would appear to attack the city. That was, of course, a boast quite beyond the powers of the Luftwaffe to fulfil. A powerful air defence system was, nevertheless, deployed around Antwerp and the West Scheldt comprising 216 3.7-inch guns, 486 40-mm light anti-aircraft guns, seven searchlight batteries, six smoke companies, a balloon barrage, a local coastguard for mine-watching and a lighted decoy site six miles downstream from the port.[9] In the event the guns and searchlights would find their main employment against V-weapons, which were to prove a far more serious menace to Antwerp than manned aircraft.

The V-weapon bombardment began well before the port was opened. The first V2 ballistic missile hit Antwerp on 12 October, and the first V1 flying bomb on the 23rd. Between then and the end of March, when the bombardment ended, 1,214 V-weapons fell on the 65 square miles of Greater Antwerp.[10] They killed about 3,000 people, the majority civilians, and seriously injured perhaps another 12,000. 150 V1s and 152 V2s fell in the docks. They sank two large ships and 58 smaller ones, damaged Kruisschans Lock, although only enough to slow its working, and twice hit the Hoboken petrol installations, again with only limited damage.

The worst incident occurred on 12 December, when a V2 hit the Rex Cinema killing 242 military and 250 civilians with 500 others seriously injured. The first V2 to hit the Hoboken plant fell on 19 January; it demolished a petrol train and three storage tanks which burnt for 48 hours, but otherwise did surprisingly little damage. The second fell on 14 February and started fires which were quickly extinguished.

184

The anti-aircraft defences were reinforced by 120 British 3.7-inch and 192 American 90-mm guns and about 150 40-mm light anti-aircraft guns. The guns, assisted at night by the searchlights, were fairly effective against V1s, but all that could be done against the V2s was to reinforce passive defence measures. Belgian relief and repair services were built up, and a civil defence regional column was brought over from England to help.

The main effect on the working of the port was to restrict its use for ammunition. When, early in November, SHAEF asked for views on the subject, ComZ recommended that all ammunition should be excluded from Antwerp and routed through Cherbourg, but 21 Army Group and ANCXF recommended that, subject to prompt clearance of ammunition ships and avoidance of dumping, ammunition should be accepted at Antwerp. SHAEF agreed to the latter with some additional precautions, but by mid-January the Port Executive Committee reported that current practices in the handling of ammunition were simply courting disaster. More stringent regulations were introduced and enforced. American ammunition was without difficulty diverted to other ports, and British ammunition clearances through Antwerp reduced to a minimum by the use of Ostend and Ghent.[11]

Air mining of the river and estuary was another threat to the working of the port, for a single large ship sunk in the channel could have closed the port for days. Part of the air defences were sited to cover the river and estuary, light craft patrolled it and a force of minesweepers was held in readiness. On 23 January, in what turned out to be a last attempt to mine the Scheldt, twenty Ju 88 dropped mines, and in the next five days the minesweepers exploded 36 of them.

At sea 50 E-boats based at Den Helder, Ijmuiden and Rotterdam made forays by night seeking to intercept convoys bound for Antwerp. Some 26 Seehund two-man submarines were sent to attack shipping in the sea approaches, and a number of the 140 one-man midgets available tried to reach the estuary with varied success. Sea and air patrols watched for them and attacked them when sighted; Bomber Command and the Eighth US Air Force bombed their bases. There were losses, but the effect on the traffic to Antwerp was slight.[12]

On land, the First Canadian Army took over the line of the Maas and Waal and the Nijmegen salient, while the Second British Army renewed its attack eastwards for the Ruhr. The German Ardennes offensive of mid-December, aimed in Hitler's wild imaginings at the recapture of Brussels and Antwerp, was held short of Liege and Namur. Thereafter, with no serious threat on the Maas, defences were progressively thinned until by the end of March the 4th Commando* Brigade, with three Dutch and one Belgian battalion under command, held 93 miles of waterfront stretching eastwards along the Maas from the tip of Walcheren.

The Ardennes offensive caused an embargo to be placed on American onward clearances from Antwerp to Liege and Namur, while at the American

*The title had been changed from Special Service to avoid the abbreviation 'SS'.

bases transport was retained under load, locking up rolling stock, barges and lorries needed for the clearance of supplies from Antwerp. The resultant congestion further reduced the discharge rate in the American sector, which during the first half of January fell to 10,500 tons a day, while the British rate rose to the same figure. After that, as the threat to Liege and Namur disappeared and new storage depots came into use, the American discharge rate recovered, reaching 18,000 tons a day by the end of the month. By the end of April the Americans were discharging 25,000 tons a day, although still with a large backlog for clearance from the port. [13] A shipping backlog of 232 vessels awaiting discharge in September by the end of February had fallen to less than a hundred, and by the end of March to 57. Spare port capacity allowed ships to be directed to the ports best suited to handle them and to the first beginnings of civilian traffic.

Meanwhile the Allied forces under Eisenhower's command reached their peak in February of 84 divisions and 285 air squadrons. Their numbers, 2.6 million in November, by April had risen to 3.4 million. Added to the supplies needed by them as they fought the final battles of the war in Europe, were those needed to sustain life in the liberated countries and later in occupied Germany, the need to feed and repatriate liberated Allied prisoners of war, and the need to feed and in the not too distant future set to work the vast numbers of German prisoners as their armies surrendered. Total imports into northwest Europe, estimated at 2 million tons a month in November, rose to an estimated 3 million tons in the month of April. [14]

With Antwerp working and excess port capacity available, these needs could be met, and the recovery of Belgium and Western Europe after five years of enemy occupation and destructive warfare could begin.

The task of opening the Scheldt cost the First Canadian Army between 1 October and 8 November 703 officers and 12,170 other ranks killed, wounded and missing, of whom almost exactly half — 355 officers and 6,012 other ranks — were Canadians, the rest among the British, Polish, American and other Allied units under its command. [15] Added to those were the earlier Canadian casualties on the Leopold Canal and south of it, of the 11th Armoured Division in liberating Antwerp, of the Second British Army in October, the losses of the faithfully supporting tactical air forces and Bomber Command, and at sea, most prominent among them those to the Support Squadron Eastern Flank. Not unworthy to be counted among these, too, were the killed and wounded of the Belgian and Dutch Resistance, together with the citizens of Antwerp and the men, military and civilian, working the docks under the V-weapon attacks.

To all of them the words of the Canadian official historian describing the fighting for the Scheldt might be applied 'It had been a hard and bloody business', and of the Canadian regimental historian already quoted 'A hard job had been well and truly done.'

References

1   Particulars of minesweeping forces and their operations from Naval Historical Branch and discussions with Captain H. G. Hopper RN; Captain J. S. Cavie, *Mines, Minelayers and Minelaying*. O.U.P., 1949 for additional particulars of mines and sweeps at end of World War 2.

2   Lieutenant Commander D. Clayton RNVR in letter to Captain Hopper.

3   Commander A. Kimmins RN (retd) 'Clearing the Scheldt', *The Listener*, of 7 December 1944.

4   C-in-C Nore, No 6519/525/36 of 16 December 1944.

5   Ellis *op cit*, p.138.

6   Ruppertal *op cit*, pp.104-110 for Memorandum of Agreement and working of port; *Admin 21 AG*, p.71 for additional particulars of damage. War Diary 4th Canadian Infantry Brigade for damage to Kruischans Lock.

7   For unloading figures and civil employees see Ruppertal p.110, Ellis p.140, Admin 21 AG p.71.

8   Ruppertal p.110 describes arrival of the American *James B. Weaver* on 26 November; Stacey p.422 and Ellis p.127 agree that only three coasters arrived on the 26th and the first convoy of Liberty ships headed by the *Fort Cataraqui* on the 28th.

9   Ellis *op cit*, p.149.

10   Ellis *op cit*, p.149. Ruppertal p.115 (nearly 4,000 V-weapons) and Admin 21 AG (4,248 V1s and 1,712 V2s) differ widely from Ellis. The estimates appear irreconcilable unless Ruppertal and Admin 21 AG refer in some way to the total number of V-weapons falling on the Continent.

11   Ruppertal *op cit*, p.114.

12   Ellis *op cit*, p.230-1.

13   American unloading and back log, Ruppertal pp.113, 395-6.

14   Ellis II, *op cit*, pp 138-140.

15   Stacey *op cit*, p.424.

APPENDIX 1

Ships against Forts — The Dardanelles Experience

The Dardanelles are 40 miles long and for most of that distance four miles across. At the western entrance at Cape Helles, however, they are two miles wide, and at the Narrows, eleven miles up, only 1600 yards. In sharp contrast to the low-lying Dutch coast, the hills of the Gallipoli peninsula on one side and those of the Asiatic mainland on the other dominate the Dardanelles. In February and March in the Eastern Mediterranean the weather is frequently stormy with rain and cloud, but less apt to close right down in sweeping rain and low cloud than in the North Sea in October and November.

When war broke out the Turkish Army, ragged and hungry after its defeats in the Tripolitan and Balkan Wars, was being re-organised re-equipped and retrained by a strong German military mission under General Liman von Sanders, which had arrived in December 1913. At first much underrated by its enemies, it was in Gallipoli to show a fierce determination perhaps not very different from that of the German paratroopers and Waffen SS of 1944 in the aftermath of the summer's holocausts in Russia and Normandy. Until they got used to it, however, its men were reluctant to face naval gunfire.

The British forces engaged, both naval and military, came to the Dardanelles with little battle experience and with nothing approaching the long, systematic training and preparation which preceded the Normandy landings. Except for the availability of steam picket boats able to bring in tows of ships boats, the equipment for amphibious assault hardly differed from that of the Napoleonic Wars, although in England the ageing First Sea Lord, Admiral of the Fleet Lord Fisher, jealously hoarded a small number of unhandy powered landing lighters, which he had had built for landings on the German coast.

The traditional defences of the Dardanelles were the forts: eleven grouped on either side of the Narrows, four others astride the Helles entrance, one fort and a number of light batteries guarding the minefields between. By February 1915 the forts mounted a hundred guns 15-cm or larger, but most of them were obsolete. The most modern were the long (high calibre) Krupps guns bought in 1885: five 35.5-cm (14-inch), fourteen 24-cm (9.4-inch), one 21-cm (8.2-inch) and eight 15-cm (5.9-inch). The rest were older guns of low muzzle velocity and in consequence with short range, poor penetration and difficulty in hitting moving targets. All were hand loaded, the loading interval for the 35.5-cm being about five minutes, and

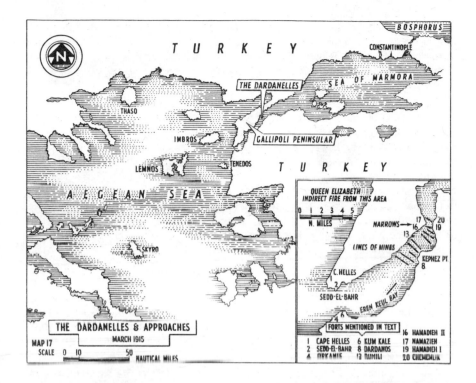

THE DARDANELLES & APPROACHES

MAP 17
SCALE 0   10   50
MARCH 1915
NAUTICAL MILES

QUEEN ELIZABETH
INDIRECT FIRE FROM THIS AREA
0 1 2 3 4 5
N. MILES

NARROWS

LINES OF MINES

KEPHEZ PT
8

C. HELLES

SEDD-EL-BAHR

EREN KEUL BAY

FORTS MENTIONED IN TEXT
1	CAPE HELLES	6	KUM KALE	16	HAMADIEH II
2	SEDD-EL-BAHR	8	DARDANOS	17	NAMAZIEH
4	ORKANIE	12	RUMILI	19	HAMADIEH I
				20	CHEMENLIK

none had fire control systems capable of dealing with ships moving at moderate speed. Some fifty lighter naval guns and army field guns and some seventy howitzers and heavy mortars were also deployed to cover the Straits, most of them in batteries commanding the area between Cape Helles and the Narrows.

At the outbreak of war with Turkey in November 1914, a Franco-British squadron had bombarded the entrance forts for twenty minutes, during which a lucky shot or shots had exploded a magazine in the fort at Cape Helles dismounting its guns. Since then German officers and naval artillery-men had been brought in to re-organise the defences, the howitzers and mortars had been deployed in the broken country below the Narrows to harass ships attempting to bombard the forts at long range, and the minefields extended.

The first mines were laid in September 1914 after the *Goeben* and *Breslau* had evaded the British Mediterranean Fleet to take refuge in Constantinople. By February 1915 there were 377 contact mines moored in ten lines at the Narrows and in the five miles below, reaching just beyond Kephez Point. A small number of floating mines were held in reserve, and one torpedo tube had been mounted at the Narrows.

Thus, as at Walcheren, the naval defences of the Dardanelles were based on minefields and coastal batteries. The mines were much less numerous

189

than those in the Scheldt, more primitive, and in consequence much more easily swept. The guns were of considerably heavier calibre and more numerous, but, as at Walcheren, there was a comparatively small hard core of guns likely to be fully effective against attacking ships, in this case predreadnought battleships.

For the naval attack decided upon by the War Council in January 1915, Vice-Admiral Carden was provided with a fleet of twelve British predreadnoughts, later increased to fourteen, and, under Contre-amiral Guépratte, four French, to which were added the modern battle cruiser *Inflexible* and the just completed superdreadnought *Queen Elizabeth*. The predreadnoughts had mixed armaments, 12-inch and 9.2 or 6-inch. The 12-inch on hydraulic mountings had a loading interval of rather under a minute, but Carden's orders from the Admiralty instructed him to be sparing in the use of ammunition. Dumaresq and range-keeping clocks enabled sighting to be corrected for ships' movement, but really effective range correction called for flank or air observation, the latter at the time very much in its infancy.

To sweep the mines Carden was sent twenty-one small 5-knot North Sea trawlers manned by fishermen under contract retaining, in theory at least, their civilian status, and fourteen French trawlers even slower. Wire sweeps towed between pairs of trawlers would engage mine moorings, but at that speed would not cut them, requiring the trawlers to stop and bring the mine to the surface for destruction.

The naval attack which began on 19 February 1915, the anniversary of the day in 1807 when Admiral Duckworth forced the Straits, would in the event fall into four overlapping phases: an attack on the entrance forts; an attempt to sweep the mines by night while battleships bombarded the intermediate defences by day; a bombardment of the Narrows forts by the *Queen Elizabeth* firing across the Gallipoli peninsula and by the predreadnoughts within the Straits below the mines; and on 18 March a massed attack in an attempt to subdue the forts and intermediate defences while the trawlers swept the fleet to close range and eventually through the Narrows, abandoned after losses of ships on the first day.

The Attack on the Entrance Forts

Eight ships, five British and three French, engaged the entrance forts on 19 February, opening deliberate fire at ranges between 9,000 and 12,000 yards. After they had anchored to increase the accuracy of their fire, they appeared to be hitting the forts. In the afternoon, however, after the ships had closed the range, the forts came to life and returned their fire fairly effectively. After a spirited action at ranges down to 3,000 yards, the ships withdrew for the night confident of success next day. During the night the weather broke, and it was not until the 25th that the bombardment could be resumed. Then, with orders to destroy each gun by a direct hit, the *Vengeance, Cornwallis, Suffren* and *Charlemagne* bombarded the forts at close range supported by the *Inflexible, Queen Elizabeth* and *Irresistible* at longer range. By 3 pm the forts were silent save for occasional shots, and the bombarding ships withdrew for the night, leaving three of their number to cover the trawlers sweeping the entrance to the Straits.

Next day, while the *Albion, Triumph* and *Majestic* entered the Straits to engage the intermediate defences, the *Irresistible* and *Vengeance* landed demolition parties at Sedd-el-Bahr and Kum Kale respectively escorted by their Marine detachments. Under cover of the ships' guns they got ashore without difficulty, and, although their advance inland was opposed, withdrew with only light casualties after destroying guns found undamaged. In the next eight days the *Irresistible*'s Marines and demolition party landed twice more at Sedd-el-Bahr and once at Kum Kale, but on 4 March two companies of the Plymouth Battalion RMLI, which had recently reached the fleet with the Chatham Battalion and Headquarters 3rd (Royal Marine) Brigade, Royal Naval Division, landing at Sedd-el-Bahr and Kum Kale in an attempt to reach the more distant forts at Cape Helles and Orkanie, were held up by stronger Turkish forces, the company at Kum Kale losing 24 killed, 4 missing and 24 wounded.

Despite the close range at which the forts had been engaged, the *Irresistible*'s demolition party on the 26th found four of the six heavy guns at Sedd-el-Bahr undamaged, and on 1 March at Kum Kale eight of nine heavy guns undamaged. These they blew up together with a battery of six heavy mortars and another of six light guns found on other days near Sedd-el-Bahr. Turkish reports were later to say that the undamaged guns at Sedd-el-Bahr and Kum Kale had been temporarily put out of action by falling masonry. One gun at Orkanie had been destroyed by a direct hit and another put out of action, and at Helles both guns were disabled

The Attempt to Sweep the Mines

During the night of the 25th a group of seven trawlers escorted by destroyers entered the Straits and swept a wide channel for four miles up them without finding any mines. Next morning the *Albion, Majestic* and *Triumph* entered to bombard the intermediate fort, Dardanos, and the batteries on either side of the Straits up to Kephez Point. Dardanos, engaged by 12-inch guns at 12,000 yards made no reply, but the howitzer and mortar batteries, now found to be in much greater numbers than indicated in intelligence reports, harassed the ships through the day until at 4 pm they were ordered to withdraw.

The weather was stormy again on the 27th and 28th. On 1 March the same three ships entered the Straits together with the *Ocean* to bombard the intermediate defences, while the *Vengeance* and *Irresistible* completed the destruction of the entrance defences. They were received by intensive howitzer fire and spent some time returning the fire of such batteries as they could locate, but, judging it impossible to engage Dardanos effectively under these circumstances, left without doing so.

That night a section of seven trawlers * covered by four destroyers attempted to sweep off Kephez Point. At 11 pm, when they were just short of the first line of mines, searchlights illuminated them and batteries on both sides of the Straits opened fire. The destroyers did what they could to cover them, making smoke and firing on the searchlights, but after forty minutes the trawlers, unable to make headway with their sweeps down against the current that flows westwards through the Straits, and surrounded by bursting shells, withdrew. Their conduct that night excited the admiration of their naval escorts, but they had not in fact reached the first line of mines, nor had they suffered casualties.

On the 2nd the *Canopus, Swiftsure* and *Cornwallis* entered the Straits, the two former to bombard Dardanos, the latter to engage the harassing batteries. After two hours Dardanos returned their fire suddenly and effectively, hitting the *Canopus* three times and causing the ships to lengthen the range. Half an hour later the fort was silent again, and the ships claimed that they could see one gun out of action, but Turkish reports say that none were damaged. That night the trawlers entered the Straits again, only to be illuminated by searchlights, fired on and forced to withdraw before anything useful could be accomplished.

Eight more attempts were made to sweep the mines by night, by the British on the 3rd, 6th, 9th, 10th, 11th and 13th, and by the French on the 7th and 12th. The French trawlers proved too slow to stem the current, and the British, although on two nights they got above the first lines of mines to sweep down stream, were each night illuminated and except on the last driven off by intense fire. On the night of the 11th it became clear that the trawler skippers would no longer face the fire. On the 13th, with naval officers and petty officers in charge of volunteer crews, the trawlers, assisted by picket boats, although illuminated by searchlights, constantly hit by shells or splinters and drenched by splashes, swept a considerable number of mines at the cost of five killed and four wounded with four trawlers, one picket boat and much gear damaged. In the escorting cruiser *Amethyst* an unlucky hit killed 24 and wounded 36.

After that Carden gave up the attempt to sweep by night. In an exchange of signals with the Admiralty, he agreed that his fleet would have to make a concentrated attack on the forts and batteries, under cover of which the trawlers would sweep a channel for them up to and eventually past the Narrows forts. Until he was ready to do so, the trawlers would best be engaged in checking the area already cleared within the Straits. This on the nights of the 14th to 17th they did.

Meanwhile on the night of 7 March the small Turkish minelayer *Nousret* undetected had laid a line of twenty mines in Eren Keui Bay, on the Asiatic side well below Kephez, where the Turks had seen bombarding ships manoeuvring. Unlike the other lines, this one ran parallel with the coastline.

---

*The trawlers swept in sections of seven or less; the same trawlers did not sweep each night. Commodore Roger Keyes, Chief of Staff to Carden, was later to say that they appeared to accept the risk of being blown up by mines with equanimity, but not that of shellfire.

On the night of the 15th, the trawlers exploded three of these mines in their sweeps, and on the 16th another, but the rest were not swept, nor apparently the danger reported.

The Bombardment of the Narrows Forts

On 5 March the first attempt was made to destroy the Narrows forts. Carden had been forbidden to risk the *Queen Elizabeth* within the Straits, but the range of her 15-inch guns permitted her to bombard the forts across the Gallipoli peninsula at a range of 15,000 yards even with three-quarters charge. Meanwhile the *Canopus*, *Cornwallis* and *Irresistible*, inside the Straits and keeping under weigh to avoid howitzer fire, spotted for her. After firing eighteen rounds at Fort Rumili, she appeared to drop the next ten inside the fort. She then shifted target to Fort Namazieh and a magazine explosion was seen in Fort Hamadieh II between the two targets. The bombardment had started late, and by now the afternoon mirage was seriously interfering with observation, so after firing five shells at Namazieh, the *Queen Elizabeth* ceased fire for the day. An attempt at air observation had failed, one seaplane having crashed and the pilot of a second having been hit by a Turkish bullet.

A second attempt on the 6th was even less successful. The *Queen Elizabeth*, although supported by the *Ocean* and *Agamemnon* endeavouring to keep down howitzer fire from the Gallipoli coast, had twice to shift berth to avoid it with consequent delay. The *Albion* inside the Straits spotting for her, although supported by the *Majestic*, *Prince George*, *Vengeance* and *Suffren*, was effectively harassed by other unseen howitzers, and visibility deteriorated early. By 4 pm the *Queen Elizabeth* had fired only seven rounds and the admiral ordered her to cease fire for the day, leaving the ships inside the Straits to do what they could against the forts and batteries while any light remained.

Deciding that indirect fire was useless without more effective air observations, Carden on the 7th sent in the *Albion* and *Lord Nelson* to bombard the Narrows forts from the swept area, while Guépratte led in the four French ships to deal with the harassing batteries. Steaming back and forth across the Straits to bring their broadsides to bear, the two British ships came under a hail of fire from the batteries and from Rumili and Hamadieh I apparently unaffected by the two previous days' bombardments. The *Albion* was hit aft by a heavy shell, a shell from the *Lord Nelson* was seen to cause a violent explosion in Rumili, and later a magazine blew up in Hamadieh I. The ships bombarded for two and a half hours, then with the Narrows forts silent, but the batteries despite all that the French ships could do still active, they withdrew. Although the *Albion* had been hit eight times by heavy shells and the *Lord Nelson* seven, thanks to their armour their casualties were light and the damage largely superficial.

Carden had already received permission from the Admiralty to take the *Queen Elizabeth* inside the Straits and on the 8th did so with the *Vengeance*, *Cornwallis*, *Canopus* and *Irresistible* to support her against the batteries. That day the visibility closed right down and in the afternoon the bombardment was given up after the *Queen Elizabeth* had fired only eleven rounds.

By now Carden was seriously concerned about his expenditure of ammunition, which, he felt, was largely wasted at long range against the forts, which came to life after each bombardment, and against the mobile batteries, which without air observation it was almost impossible to locate. He therefore called off further bombardment for the time being and for the next nine days prepared to make a concentrated attack in conjunction with the minesweeping.

The naval attack had only been undertaken because Lord Kitchener, in face of competing demands for France and possibly for Salonika, had felt unable to make military forces available. Pressed by Churchill, he had on 20 February shown the first signs of relenting and three days later had ordered Lieutenant General Birdwood, commanding the Australian and New Zealand forces in Egypt, to visit Carden. On 5 March Birdwood reported to Kitchener that he did not believe that the fleet alone could force the Straits, and on the 12th Carden, while professing confidence in a message to the Admiralty that he could do so, suggested that large scale military operations to secure his communications once he had reached the Sea of Marmora should begin at once. In reply the Admiralty told him that General Sir Ian Hamilton, nominated Commander-in-Chief, Mediterranean Expeditionary Force, would reach him on the 16th, that some 60,000 troops would reach Lemnos by the 18th, and that aeroplanes to replace the ineffective seaplanes were on their way to him. On the 16th Carden, who had for some time been unable to eat or sleep properly under the strain of his responsibilities, was invalided, and his place taken by his second-in-command, de Robeck, promoted acting Vice Admiral.

The Massed Attack of 18 March

So it was that with de Robeck flying his flag in the *Queen Elizabeth* the fleet entered the Straits at 10.30 am on 18 March. At 11.25 the *Queen Elizabeth* got a good view *of her targets, Chemenlik and Hamadieh I, and opened deliberate fire at a range of 14,000 yards, followed shortly afterwards by the remaining ships of Line A, the *Agamemnon, Lord Nelson* and *Inflexible*, while the *Triumph* and *Prince George* on either flank engaged the intermediate defences. The forts, except for a few rounds, made no reply, reserving their ammunition for closer ranges, but the fire of the batteries, which had begun as the ships came within range, increased in violence and accuracy. The effect of the ships' fire was difficult to judge, but they seemed to be hitting the forts, and there was a tremendous double explosion in Chemenlik. At 12.5 de Robeck ordered Line B, the French

---

*Keyes says that the light was not favourable for engaging the Narrows forts until late in the forenoon, while other accounts refer to mirage in the latter part of the afternoon on previous days.

194

ships supported on their flanks by the *Swiftsure* and *Majestic*, to pass through as planned to close the range.

Leaving the centre of the Straits clear for the fire of Line A, the *Suffren* and *Bouvet* steamed up the Asiatic coast and the *Charlemagne* and *Gaulois* up the European. As they closed, the Narrows forts, except for Chemenlik, opened fire on them and a violent struggle for mastery developed at ranges down to 9,000 yards. By 1.45 the enemy fire had slackened; the *Inflexible* with her bridge and foretop on fire and other damage, had fallen temporarily out of Line A, the *Gaulois*, repeatedly hit, had been badly holed forward and was in danger of sinking, and the *Bouvet*, with fires in her bridge and steering compartment, had two casemates out of action.

De Robeck now ordered up Line C, the *Venerable, Irresistible, Albion* and *Ocean*, hoping that under its cover mine-sweeping could commence. As the two French ships on the Asiatic side withdrew, two explosions were seen in the *Bouvet*, and within two minutes she had turned over and disappeared, taking with her all except 35 of her crew.

Meanwhile Line C had opened fire at 12,000 yards closing to 10,000. The reply, except from the German-manned Hamadieh I, was no longer formidable. Chemenlik remained silent, as for a time did Namazieh; Hamadieh II, which the *Ocean* hit five times with her first seven shots, ceased fire, and there was a fire burning in Rumili, but Hamadieh I, although the *Vengence* dropped shell after shell in it, continued to fire accurately and effectively. A spotting seaplane * reported that most of the shells, falling into the centre of the fort, did little damage to the guns. It was doubtful if the other forts had been permanently silenced — later the Turks were to say that they had checked fire to clear away debris — but, if the chance were taken, it seemed that some at least of the mines might now be swept.

Two pairs of trawlers had got their sweeps down and swept ahead of Line A, exploding one mine and bringing two others to the surface in Eren Keui Bay. But then, coming under fire, they had turned and steamed out of the Straits, as had the third pair earlier, stultifying the object of the concentrated attack.

At 4.11 the *Inflexible*, which had returned to Line A, struck a mine and began to settle by the bow. In danger of sinking she made for Tenedos to beach. Then at 4.14 the *Irresistible* struck a mine and appeared unable to move. Not realising that these were moored mines laid after the earlier sweeping, de Robeck ordered the *Ocean* to stand by her, and at 6.5, having given up the attempt to tow the *Irresistible*, she too struck a mine. Destroyers took off the crews, and during the night both ships sank in deep water inside the Straits. Meanwhile, seeing the *Irresistible* abandoned, de Robeck called off the attack.

By then the ammunition for the more modern guns at the Narrows was nearly expended, and according to several accounts the Turks expected

---

*Corbett, p.219; Keyes p.232, 'As we . . . had neither aerial nor flank observation, it was necessary to wait (before opening fire) until the forts were clearly distinguishable.' Corbett, p.215, says that the *Ark Royal* was to provide one seaplane every hour.

defeat next morning, when, as seemed to them inevitable, the ships resumed the attack. Keyes, who re-entered the Straits that night in a destroyer looking for the two abandoned ships, writes:

> Except for the searchlights there seemed to be no sign of life, and I had a most indelible impression that we were in the presence of a beaten foe . . . it only remained for us to organise a proper sweeping force and devise some means of dealing with drifting mines to reap the fruits of our efforts.'

It appears that at first de Robeck intended to renew the attack as soon as practicable, and on the 19th the Admiralty informed him that four more old battleships would be sent him to replace those lost and that ample supplies of 15-inch ammunition were available for the *Queen Elizabeth*. That day Keyes arranged for the eight Beagle-class destroyers with de Robeck to be fitted as minelayers to provide a fast, disciplined mine-sweeping force, and requested that others of the same class might be sent from England. But on 22 March, de Robeck, opening a conference with Hamilton and Birdwood, told them that he could not get through the Straits without military assistance, and the decisions were taken which would lead to the long, costly and ultimately unsuccessful Gallipoli campaign.

The transports at Lemnos were found to have been loaded in disorder, and the whole land force had to go back to Alexandria and Port Said to restow for the assault, which could not in consequence take place until 25 April.

By 4 April the eight Beagles were ready, eight more were ready by the 14th and two days later eight fast cross-Channel steamers fitted as fleet sweepers arrived. Trials showed that the Beagles could sweep in formation at speeds between 14 and 20 knots, at which their heavy sweeps parted the mine mooring wires without them having to stop. Between 25 and 28 April they swept to within 8,000 yards of the narrows with only a single battleship in support, suffering only light casualties. Meanwhile Hamilton's infantry shattered itself against the now fully prepared Turkish defences on the beaches and in continuing frontal attacks inland.

The Relevance of the Dardanelles Experience

Critics were quick to claim that the failure of the naval attack on the Dardanelles proved once again the maxim that ships should not attack forts. That ships were in 1915 at a tactical disadvantage against forts and shore batteries is clear enough. Whether their strategic advantage in being able to concentrate a strong force against a chosen objective was enough to balance the tactical disadvantage remains debatable.

The danger of generalised maxims is that they obscure genuine complexities and balances. It was the combination of guns and minefields which stopped the fleet at the Dardanelles, not guns alone, and the inadequate and amateurish means provided to sweep mines. By 1944 mines had become far too sophisticated to be swept under aimed fire, however expert and dedicated the sweeping force. The Dardanelles experience confirms the perhaps rather obvious point that both banks of the West Scheldt had to be securely in friendly hands before the mines could be swept or Antwerp opened to traffic. Bombing the Walcheren batteries into silence would not by itself have been enough.

The howitzers of the Dardanelles go some way, too to support Simonds's decision to flood Walcheren, taken in September for the reasons described in Chapter 6. Had the German batteries inland hidden by the dunes remained in action, they would certainly have made conditions off West-kapelle and in the beachhead worse than they were, and might have turned the scale there. The alternative of taking Walcheren from South Beveland alone might, in view of the weakness of the infantry defence of the two islands, perhaps have succeeded. In September it would have been rash to count upon the failure of the German command to provide anything better than the weakened 70th Infantry Division to defend the islands.

Assuming that the attack on Walcheren had to be made much as it was, under-estimation of the weight of fire needed to suppress well-protected batteries stands out strongly as a factor common to the Scheldt and the Dardanelles. The Graham Committee may have been rather too sweeping and theoretical in saying 'a casemated gun can be neutralised only by its destruction', but in both operations the weight of shells or bombs needed to suppress forts or batteries was much greater than expected or provided for. Had the need been understood at Walcheren, something nearer the necessary weight might have been provided by concentrating on the vital batteries. The failure to do so was due in part at least to over-simplification in Britain between the wars of the lessons of the Dardanelles. In the United States the Marine Corps made a full study of that campaign. Perhaps as a result, whatever other mistakes may have been made in the great Pacific amphibious campaigns of World War II, under-estimation of fire power requirements was not among them. For their part, the German naval batteries at Walcheren, ignoring the ammunition crisis of the Dardanelles forts, expended their limited ammunition firing across the Scheldt in support of the lost battle of the Breskens Pocket. In the days of guided missiles, the arithmetic of the Graham Committee is no longer valid, but the general principle that it is dangerous to trust to widely distributed fire power to hit vital targets remains.

Finally, and most important, there was in both operations a failure of integration of effort between the Services. In reading accounts of the Dardanelles, one senses the almost audible sigh of relief with which de Robeck on the morrow of 18 March handed over to Ian Hamilton the responsibility for silencing the guns and howitzers on Gallipoli. It was followed later by a growing feeling of guilt in the navy after the slaughter on the beaches and in the continuing attacks ashore. But admirals had been trained to think of sea battles as the proper task of the fleet, not bombardment of forts or sweeping mines.

Tedder's cynical reference to the 'part-worn battery at Walcheren' was less excusable, but derived from a comparable dogma, inculcated by Trenchard, that the proper task of air forces was strategic bombing and that any diversion from it must be resisted. It was an irony of history that the price should be paid mainly by a naval force, which in the opening of the Scheldt never spared itself in support of the army.

Sources

In contrast to a number of fine accounts of the fighting ashore on Gallipoli, the naval attack on the Dardanelles has been neglected. Sir Julian Corbett's official naval history (*History of the Great War, Naval Operations*, Volume II, Longmans Green, 1920) is detailed but not very clear and certainly not easy reading. Roger Keyes's memoirs (*The Naval Memoirs of Admiral of the Fleet Sir Roger Keyes*, Volume I, Thornton & Butterworth, 1934) is also detailed and takes a distinctly more robust view of the naval problems. I have relied on these two for my main narrative. Professor Arthur J. Marder, in the Dardanelles chapters of his *From the Dreadnought to Scapa Flow*, Volume II (OUP, 1965) is primarily concerned with policy and events in London, but in his more recent *From the Dardanelles to Oran* (OUP, 1974) he examines in detail the questions of air spotting and mine sweeping, and discusses, too, the resistance likely to have been put up by the Turks had the naval attack been continued. Perhaps as a result, he takes a noticeably more optimsitic view of the chances of British success than in his earlier book. Captain L. A. K. Boswell's article 'The Naval Attack on the Dardanelles' (*RUSI Journal* for May 1965) is important on the minesweeping problem and confirms Keyes both on the inadequacy of the trawlers for the task and the much greater effectiveness of the fast sweeper force provided too late to influence de Robeck.

APPENDIX 2

Landing Craft, Specialised Armour and Amphibians

Combined Operations was the term used in the British forces during World War II for what later, following American practice, became known as amphibious warfare. In June 1940 on Churchill's instructions a Directorate of Combined Operations — renamed in 1941 Combined Operations Headquarters (COHQ) — was set up charged to develop technique and material for the return to the continent of Europe. Its large range of operational, training and technical activities included the development and procurement in conjunction with the Admiralty, War Office and Ministry of Supply of landing ships and craft, specialised armour for the assault on beach defences, and amphibians.

LANDING SHIPS AND CRAFT

Landing ships and craft were classified as: *landing ships*, notably the specially built Landing Ship Tank of about 4,000 tons and the Landing Ship Infantry, converted passenger ships; *major landing craft*, too large to be hoisted by davit or derrick but capable of limited sea voyages; and *minor landing craft*, normally hoisted by LSI or cargo ships for the voyage to the assault area. Support craft were almost all major landing craft.

These ships and craft played an essential part in the series of overseas operations which began with the seizure of Diego Suarez, Madagascar, in May 1942, continued through the great amphibious operations in North Africa in the same year and in Sicily and Italy in 1943, and reached their climax in the Normandy assault of June 1944.

Landing Ships

Only two landing ships were used in the Scheldt operations: a Landing Ship Dock to ferry LCA and LCP(L) to Ostend, when they were taken by rail and canal to the Scheldt at Terneuzen; and a Landing Ship Headquarters (Small), HMS *Kingsmill*, used by Pugsley and Leicester as headquarters ship for the Westkapelle assault.

Landing Ship Dock — LSD

The LSD was a British design built in the USA, displacement about 11,000 tons, speed 14 knots, with a pointed bow and a large dock aft. By flooding ballast tanks the ship could increase her draft, allowing landing craft to enter and leave the flooded dock.

199

Landing Ship Headquarters (Small) LSH(S)

The LSH(S) was, as the name implies, much smaller than the better known LSH(L) used in the Normandy assaust at the level of naval force commander/divisional commander. Sometimes provided at the next lower level, naval assault group commander/brigade commander, the LSH(S) was usually a specially equipped frigate. The *Kingsmill*, a diesel frigate of the 1943 American-built Captain-class (equivalent to US destroyer escorts) displaced 1,085 tons, speed 20 knots, with three 3-inch guns and light AA.

Major Landing and Support Craft

Landing Craft Tank — LCT Marks 3 and 4

A ramped beaching landing craft capable of carrying six Churchill tanks or nine Shermans and also used extensively for soft-skinned vehicles and stores. Marks 3 and 4 were both within a few feet of 190 feet in length, the latter having increased beam and shallower draft to give better beaching characteristics on the flat Normandy beaches. Speeds: Mark 3, 9 knots; Mark 4, 8 knots. Seaworthy in seas up to Force 4. Originally unarmed, later 20-mm Oerlikons added for AA defence. Very limited armour for wheelhouse, etc. The specification called for utmost simplicity to facilitate industrial production. Crew — 12.

Landing Craft Gun (Large) — LCG(L)

After the Dieppe raid of 1942 much greater emphasis was placed on the need for close support for troops landing on a defended beach. A total of 23 LCT 3 and 10 LCT 4 were in consequence decked over to take two 4.7-inch destroyer guns, mounted in gun-shields, and a number of lighter weapons. Their shallow draft enabled them to go close inshore, although they would not normally beach, and gave them a fair degree of immunity from contact mines. Crew, including RM gun crews, 3 officers and 44.

Landing Craft Flak — LCF

Another LCT conversion, intended as the name implies to give close AA cover to craft approaching a beach and landing troops and transport. Armament: eight 2-pdr Bofors and four 20-mm Oerlikons, or alternatively four Bofors and eight Oerlikons. Crew: 2 naval officers and 10 ratings, 2 RM officers and 48 other ranks gun crews.

Landing Craft Tank (Rocket) — LCT(R)

Another LCT conversion intended to increase the weight of fire brought down on a beach immediately before assault. 800 to 1,000 5-inch rocket projectors were mounted on the decked over LCT to be fired electrically dead ahead in a ripple salvo on a radar range of 3,500 yards as the craft closed the beach. A second outfit of rockets was carried, but reloading took a long time. Rockets were normally HE, but smoke rockets could be fired. The idea was viewed with suspicion by the Gunnery Division at the Admiralty, but the first LCT(R), used in the invasion of Sicily, were reported on highly favourably and in Normandy 6-10 LCT(R) were used on the front of each assaulting brigade group.

Landin Craft Gun (Medium) — LCG(M).

A later and experimental design of LCG built as such, not a conversion, and intended to deal with thick concrete or similar defences by firing into loopholes and similar weak points at close range. The craft were armed with two 17-pdr anti-tank guns firing solid shot and were intended to beach and flood ballast tanks to give a steady aiming platform. The only two ever used operationally were both lost at Walcheren. As J. D. Ladd sapiently remarks, they broke the golden rule of combined operations — get off the waterline as quickly as possible either ashore or back to sea.

Landing Craft Support (Large) — LCS(L)

Early LCS were modified versions of minor landing craft (see below). When the demand came for much increased fire power, however, ten LCI(S) (below) were converted to carry one 6-pdr anti-tank gun in a turret forward, a power-operated twin .5-inch Vickers aft and a 4-inch mortar firing smoke. Performance and vulnerability similar to LCI(S). Crew: 2 officers and 23 including RM gun crews.

Landing Craft Infantry (Small) — LCI(S)

Design adapted from coastal forces craft built by Fairmile with reduced scantlings to permit troop spaces between decks. Later some armour added, reducing speed. Landing by gangplanks launched by rollers over the deck. Originally intended for raids, the craft were much too vulnerable for beach assault. Speed: 12 knots (with armour) endurance 700 miles; load, 100 armed men. After their heavy losses in Normandy, which might have been still worse had the enemy used incendiary ammunition against their unarmoured tanks carrying high octane petrol, the wing tanks were filled with sea water for the Westkapelle assault.

Landing Craft Headquarters — LCH

A conversion of the Landing Craft Infantry (Large) to take headquarters at the level of naval assault group/brigade. American-built to an initial British specification, the LCI(L) was a steel craft with properly fitted landing gangways intended for the follow-up rather than the first waves of an assault. Speed 12 knots, load as LCI(L) 200 armed men.

Motor Launches — ML

These were not landing craft but a number of them acted as markers, guides etc for the Westkapelle assault. Nos. 100 to 919 were Fairmile Bs, length 112 feet, speed 18 knots at sea; armament, one 3-pdr or 40-mm AA and four 20-mm Oerlikons. Crew, 18.

Minor Landing Craft

Landing Craft Assault — LCA

Speed — 10 knots claimed, probably less in practice. Load 35 armed men and 5 crew. Endurance 90 miles. Designed by the Inter-Services Training and Development Centre in 1938-9 at 10 tons to be within the capacity of a liner's lifeboat davits and to land infantry in beach assault, a small number of these craft had been built by the outbreak of war and were used at Dunkirk and in Norway. They are said to have been inferior to the comparable American LCV(P) in speed, manoeuvrability and seaworthiness, but to have had the advantage over them in bullet-proof protection, troop-carrying capacity, rapidity of disembarkation on a beach, silence and low silhouette and were in any case a highly successful design used by the British in almost every amphibious assault.

Landing Craft Personnel, Large — LCP(L)
Speed up to 20 knots, weight about ten tons, load 22 fully equipped men. Another highly successful prewar design, built by Higgins of New Orleans. 50 were bought by Britain in 1940 for commando raids and combined operations generally. In the course of the war 900 were allocated to Britain out of a total US production of 4,851, appearing with minor variations as LCP(L); Landing Craft Personnel, Ramped — LCP(R); Landing Craft Personnel, Survey — LCP(Sy); Landing Craft Navigation — LCN; and minesweepers. They had, except for the LCP(R), an unramped, spoon bow over which troops landed by gang-plank, and were basically unarmoured, although some were given light armour of doubtful value.

Landing Craft Personnel, Survey — LCP(Sy)
The same design as above fitted with an additional compass, chart table and a QH2 type radar as navigational leader to other landing craft. A much more elaborate navigational outfit converted the LCP(L) to the LCN, which appeared too late for operational employment. The names are confusing; normally 'Survey' would indicate the more fully equipped craft. The explanation may be that there appears to have been a seldom seen variant of the LCP(L) in which the 'N' stood for nesting i.e. packing one above another.

Note on Royal Marines in Support Landing Craft

In mid-1943 the Chiefs of Staff approved the disbandment of the Royal Marine Division and the two RM Mobile Naval Base Defence Organisations and the transfer of their personnel to commandos and landing craft, except for AA units which, as the 5th RM Anti-Aircraft Brigade, later played a major part in the defence of Antwerp against V1s. A number of marine manned minor landing craft took part in the Normandy assaults, but probably more marines were employed in manning the guns of support landing craft, especially LCG(L) and LCF. A fair estimate of the total strength of the Support Squadron Eastern Flank at Westkapelle might be 600 Royal Navy and 500 Royal Marines.

SPECIALISED ARMOUR

When from 1942 onwards the fortifications of Hitler's Atlantic Wall began to appear along the coasts of France and the Low Countries, COHQ in conjunction with the War Office and Ministry of Supply developed a range of specialised armoured vehicles and other devices to deal with the problem of assault from the sea in face of concrete defences, beach obstacles and minefields. As the armoured vehicles came into production and were issued to units they were concentrated in the 79th Armoured Division, to the command of which Major General P. C. S. (later Sir Percy) Hobart, an early pioneer of armoured warfare, was appointed in March 1943. Specialised armoured vehicles used in the Scheldt operations comprised:—

Duplex Drive Sherman — DD Sherman
The Duplex Drive system invented by Nicholas Straussler comprised a boat-shaped canvas screen secured to the track guards of a waterproofed tank which could be erected around the turret by inflatable rubber tubes and locked into place by metal struts. This gave the tank sufficient buoyancy to float. A propellor driven off the main engine gave it a water speed of 4 knots. On beaching the tracks took over the drive, and as the tank emerged from the water the screen was dropped, revealing the turret and gun ready for immediate action. The system was developed originally for the Valentine tank, and a Sherman version was put into production in the winter of 1943-4 for the Normandy assault.

Crab or Flail-Sherman
The roller and chain system of dealing with land mines was invented in the Middle East for use in the Western Desert as the Scorpion fitted to the Matilda tank. This was driven by a separate engine and the tank gun had to be removed. The idea was adapted as the Flail for the Sherman tank, which when so fitted was called the Crab. Here the roller was driven by the tank engine and the gun retained. Flailing speed was 1¼mph, and the Flail exploded Teller mines down to a depth of 4 or 5 inches. Each mine exploded destroyed a chain, and after 12 or 14 mines the roller had to have chains replaced. A Sherman without a Flail accompanying Crabs was referred to as a command Sherman, that being its function.

Assault Vehicle Royal Engineers — AVRE
A Churchill tank Mark IV fitted in place of a gun with a 12-inch spigot mortar firing a 25-lb, shaped explosive charge up to 80 yards to break down concrete obstacles and defences. An AVRE could in addition carry either a large brushwood fascine, which could be dropped without exposing the crew to fill an anti-tank ditch or crater, or a 20-foot tank assault bridge which could be dropped across a similar obstacle. There is a tendency in naval reports to call all the armoured vehicles of a breaching team AVRE, which until understood is confusing.

Crocodile
A Churchill Mark VII fitted with a hull flame gun in addition to its turret gun and towing a trailer with 400 gallons of flame-thrower fuel and a nitrogen pressure system. To avoid undue loss of gas the Crocodiles did not 'pressure up' (i.e. open the nitrogen bottles) until just before going into action.

Wasp
A Bren carrier fitted with a flame-thrower system similar but smaller and less effective than that of the Crocodile.

AMPHIBIANS
Except for the DUKW, amphibians arrived late in the European theatre. Those used in the Scheldt operations comprised:

Landing Vehicle Tracked — LVT
The Buffalo an American tracked amphibian which reached the 79th Armoured Division in August 1944. Water speed 5 knots, land speed 11mph. Shaped grousers on tracks provided water traction. Limited track mileage ashore; some light armour in front of driving cab. The Mark 2 had no ramp and could take 24 armed men; the Mark 4 had a stern ramp and could take a jeep, bren carrier or 25-pounder field gun. The tracks gave the appearance and sound of a tank, but the LVT were much too vulnerable to be used as such. Maximum speeds: land, 25mph; sea, 5½ knots.

Weasel
A light, unarmoured, tracked snow-mobile with very limited water performance. Its light track pressure gave a degree of immunity against land mines, but it was very slow and unseaworthy in water and should not have been classed as an amphibian. Issued to the 52nd (Lowland) Division for mountain training in Scotland, it was found to have reasonable cross-country ability in skilled hands, but the steep dunes south of Westkapelle were too much for it.

DUKW — initials from maker's code pronounced 'duck'
American six-wheeled load carrying amphibian. Water speed 6 knots, land speed 50mph. Unarmoured but very handy and seaworthy afloat.

Terrapin
British-built eight-wheeled load carrying amphibian, which appeared in the latter part of 1944. Generally considered inferior to the DUKW.

Sources
Landing Ships and Craft: *History of the Combined Operations Organisation 1940-1948*, AWHQ, 1956 downgraded to unclassified 1973: additional detail from *Janes Fighting Ships 1945*; J. D. Ladd, *Assault from the Sea*, David & Charles, 1976; P. Lund & H. Ludlam, *The War of the Landing Craft*, Foulsham, 1976; and from the Royal Marines Museum, Portsmouth. Specialised Armour and Amphibians: *The Story of the 79th Armoured Division October 1942-June 1945*; N. Duncan, *The 79th Armoured Division: Hobo's Funnies*, Profile Publications, 1972; K. Mackesy, *Armoured Crusader*, Hutchinson, 1967.

APPENDIX 3

Code Names of Operations

The use of operational code names has as far as possible been avoided in the text. The following may be useful for reference to orders, messages and reports and to other accounts:

Astonia	capture of Le Havre
Calendar	mine sweeping of West Scheldt
Comet	Second British Army plan for seizure of Waal and Rhine crossings replaced by the Arnhem plan, Market Garden
Infatuate I	amphibious attack on Flushing
Infatuate II	amphibious attack on Westkapelle
Market Garden	the Arnhem offensive
Switchback	clearance of the Breskens Pocket
Undergo	capture of Calais
Vitality	clearance of South Beveland
Wellhit	capture of Boulogne

Index

Aachen 37
Abbeville 50
Albert Canal 18-81 *passim*, 117
Allied Expeditionary Force (SHAEF) 15
  1 Airborne Army 43, 59, 69
  1 & 3 Army 43, 62
  Army Groups: (6) 62; (12) 38, 56, 60, 63, 96; (21) 37, 39,
    43, 49, 56, 59, 62, 68, 71, 95, 98, 171
  Tactical Air Force 129
Amber Beach 91, 106, 108
Amiens 21, 60
Amsterdam 43, 65
Antwerp 8, 10, 19, 22, 29
Ardennes 1, 16, 37, 42, 99, 185
Arnhem 1, 33, 39, 42, 51, 55, 61, 65, 82, 100, 119, 141
Arsenal Bks 144, 150
Aschmann, Capt 117, 159

BBC 19, 22, 181
Bailey bridge 41
Barclay, Brig 77, 106
Bayeux 40, 59, 65
Bedell Smith, Lt-Gen 43, 96
Belgian Forces 134, 161
Bell, Maj 26
Bergen-op-Zoom 12, 69, 86, 99
Berlin 40, 52
Betjewolf Plein 145
Blissinger, Kapt-Lt 147
Bonn 68
Boom 20, 24, 29
Boomse Steenweg 27
Bottomley, AM 75
Boulogne 39, 49, 60, 64, 68, 71, 182
Bradley, Gen 15, 37, 43, 56, 63, 95
Breda 13, 100
Breendonk 23, 29
Bren mg 150
Brereton, Maj-Gen 71
Breskens Pocket 6, 46, 52, 77, 88, 100, 111, 114, 117, 131,
  137, 141, 175, 181 *See also* Scheldt, R
Brest 64
Brigade Blanche Fidelio 18
Britannia Hotel 7
British Forces
  Airborne Divisions: (1) 43, 45; (6) 69, 78
  29 Armoured Bde 21, 28, 53
  34 Armoured Bde 99
  Armoured Divisions: (7) 17, 50, 84, 98; (8) 41; (11) 17, 20,
    33, 40, 52, 186; (79) 69, 77, 111, 141, 161
  2 Army 15, 17, 38-61 *passim*, 82, 94, 119, 185
  Assault RE 67, 77, 91, 134
  6 & 7 Cameronians 106, 172
  Commando Regts: (4) 78, 114, 134, 143, 147, 170, 185;
    (41) 134, 160-77 *passim*; (47) & (48) 134, 164-178 *passim*
  Corps: (1) 20, 54, 60, 81, 84, 100; (8) 20, 33, 61, 98; (12)
    84, 98; (30) 21, 33, 54, 98
  5 Devon Regt 32
  5 Dorset Regt 33
  10 Dragoons 51
  202 Field Coy 172
  509 — 510 Field Coy 166
  2 Fife & Forfar Yeomanry 28
  Guards Armoured Div 17, 29, 33, 40, 52, 98
  Hallamshire Regt 82
  51 Highland Div 68, 78, 84, 100, 106, 173
Infantry Bde: (70) 33; (146) 81, 84, 99; (147) 84; (151) 41;
  (155) 114, 134, 141, 171; (156) 77, 104, 108, 117, 138,
  171, 176; (157) 90, 105, 117, 138, 149, 172, 175; (159)
  21, 30

Infantry Divisions: (15) 99; (43) 21, 52; (49) 60, 68, 81; (50)
  21, 27, 33, 41, 52; (52) 171, 137
Irish Guards 41
4 KOSLI Regt 27, 31, 40, 53
5 KOSB Regt 136, 145, 148, 150, 174
4 Leicester Regt 99
4 Lincoln Regt 81
Lothian & Border Yeomanry 134, 161
52 (Lowland) Div 95, 102, 104
7 Manchester Regt 174
144 Pioneer Coy 166
3 Monmouthshire Regt 22, 29, 33
452 Mountain Battery 148
8 Rifle Brigade 21, 26, 30
Royal Air Force
  Bomber Command 72, 75, 117, 126, 130, 140, 153,
    174, 185
  Groups: (46) 59; (83) 98; (84) 75, 90, 128, 155, 177
Royal Armoured Corps:
  7 Recce Regt 112;
  8 Recce Regt 111;
  3 RTR 21, 24, 27, 30;
  11 RTR 77, 108, 137, 174;
  141 RTR (The Buffs) 77
  4/5 Royal Scots Fusiliers 108
  7/9 Royal Scots Fusiliers 136
    148, 174
  15 (Scottish) Div 41, 98
  4 Special Air Service Bde 68, 78, 114, 128, 136, 141,
    149, 165, 170, 176
  Staffordshire Yeomanry 77, 106
  Welsh Guards 41
  53 (Welsh) Div 33, 68, 80, 98
  49 (West Riding) Div 81, 99
Royal Navy 30, 69, 71:
  19 Flotilla 181;
  Naval Force T & J 75, 128;
  Royal Marine Commando 114;
  46 Commando 78;
  48 Commando 124
Brittany 57, 63
Brooke, FM 37, 44, 51, 94
Bruges Canal 46, 50, 112
Brussels 20, 29, 37, 40, 46, 54, 59, 185
Buffaloes 77, 89, 105, 124, 133, 141, 165, 174, 178
Burns, Brig 171

Cadzand 46, 112
Caemerlinck, Prof 19
Caen 20, 65
Calais 39, 49, 61, 64, 68, 182
Canadian Forces
  Algonquin Regt 50, 86
  Argyle & Sutherland Highlanders of Canada (50)
  2 Armoured Corps 60
  4 Armoured Div 50, 68, 86, 89, 99
  10 Armoured Regt 104
  27 Armoured Regt 82
  1 Army 7, 15, 38-101 *passim*, 128, 139, 153, 185
  Artillery Groups 89
  Black Watch of Canada 80, 86, 104, 110
  Calgary Highlanders 81, 85, 110
  Canadian Scottish Regt 89, 112
  1 Corps 21
  2 Corps 50, 68, 71, 82, 84, 100, 106, 128, 137, 168
  Essex Scottish Regt 80, 87, 104, 109
  16 Field Coy RCE 90
  Fusiliers Mont-Royal 81, 84, 104
  1 Glasgow Highlanders 171, 110
  Highland Light Inf of Canada 91, 111

206